Brown v. Board of Education and the Civil Rights Movement

MICHAEL J. KLARMAN

Abridged Edition of *From Jim Crow to Civil Rights:
The Supreme Court and the Struggle for Racial Equality*

OXFORD
UNIVERSITY PRESS

2007

OXFORD
UNIVERSITY PRESS

Oxford University Press, Inc., publishes works that further
Oxford University's objective of excellence
in research, scholarship, and education.

Oxford   New York
Auckland   Cape Town   Dar es Salaam   Hong Kong   Karachi
Kuala Lumpur   Madrid   Melbourne   Mexico City   Nairobi
New Delhi   Shanghai   Taipei   Toronto

With offices in
Argentina   Austria   Brazil   Chile   Czech Republic   France   Greece
Guatemala   Hungary   Italy   Japan   Poland   Portugal   Singapore
South Korea   Switzerland   Thailand   Turkey   Ukraine   Vietnam

Copyright © 2007 by Oxford University Press, Inc.

Published by Oxford University Press, Inc.
198 Madison Avenue, New York, New York 10016

www.oup.com

Oxford is a registered trademark of Oxford University Press

Library of Congress Cataloging-in-Publication Data
Klarman, Michael J.
Brown v. Board of Education and the civil rights movement: abridged edition of
"From Jim Crow to civil rights: the Supreme Court and the struggle for racial
equality" / by Michael J. Klarman.
p.   cm.
Includes bibliographical references.
ISBN 978-0-19-530746-7;   978-0-19-530763-4 (pbk.)
1. Segregation—Law and legislation—United States—History—20th century.
2. United States—Race relations—History—20th century.
3. United States. Supreme Court.   4. Brown, Oliver, 1918-—Trials, litigation, etc.
5. Topeka (Kan.). Board of Education—Trials, litigation, etc.
I. Title.   II. Title: Brown versus Board of Education and the civil rights movement.
KF4757.K58 2007
344.73'0798—dc22   2006028068

9 8 7 6 5 4 3 2 1

Printed in the United States of America
on acid-free paper

Brown v. Board of Education
and the Civil Rights Movement

To the memory of my parents:

Muriel Klarman (1929–2004)

Herbert Klarman (1916–1999)

CONTENTS

INTRODUCTION

Brown v. Board of Education is one of the most important decisions in the history of the U.S. Supreme Court. The ruling influenced the path of America's racial transformation, shaped our understanding of the Supreme Court's role in American society, and altered our conception of the relationship between law and social reform.

Yet many of the conventional notions regarding this landmark decision are flawed. The unanimity of the justices in *Brown* has given rise to the misconception that the case was easy for them. This is emphatically not so. The justices were initially deeply divided. As we shall see, in 1952–1953, there was no clear majority to invalidate public school segregation.

In addition, *Brown* is typically viewed as a classic example of the Court's safeguarding the rights of a minority group from majoritarian oppression. Yet, paradoxically, opinion polls make clear that a majority of the country endorsed *Brown* from the day it was decided. *Brown* would have better fit the paradigm of the Court as savior of oppressed minorities had it been decided ten or twenty years earlier. But, as we shall see, the justices would not have invalidated racial segregation at that earlier date, both because public opinion would not have supported such a result and because the justices themselves would not then have found the practice to be constitutionally objectionable.

Finally, *Brown* is often portrayed as the origin of the modern civil rights movement. Yet the justices who decided the case repeatedly expressed their astonishment at how much American racial attitudes and practices had *already* changed. Moreover, *Brown*'s most immediate effect in the South was to stymie progressive racial change and bolster the political standing of racial extremists. *Brown* did make important contributions to the 1960s civil rights movement, but they were mostly counterintuitive and, occasionally, almost perverse.

This book seeks to offer a richer, more complex understanding of the Supreme Court's decision in *Brown*. It situates the decision within the social and political context of World War II, which had a transformative impact on American race relations. It goes behind the scenes to examine the justices' internal deliberations in *Brown* and to reconstruct why they found the case so difficult. It seeks to explain the justices' controversial choice after *Brown* to vacate the field of school desegregation for nearly a decade. It explores how and why white southerners were so successful in the short term at defying the Court's mandate to end racial segregation in public education. And it considers the various ways in which *Brown* influenced the subsequent course of American race relations—raising the salience of race issues, convincing blacks that transformative racial change was possible, encouraging blacks to litigate rather than use alternative methods of social protest, impelling white southerners to try to destroy the National Association for the Advancement of Colored People, creating concrete occasions for violent conflict over school desegregation, radicalizing southern politics, and creating a climate ripe for violence once direct-action protest finally erupted in the early 1960s.

Though *Brown v. Board of Education* is the principal focus, this book also aims to shed light on broader questions of legal history: What sorts of factors cause constitutional values—such as racial equality—to change over time? How do judges decide cases? That is, how much are they influenced by legal factors—such as text, original understanding, and precedent—and how much by political considerations, such as the judges' personal values and external political pressure? Finally, what is the relationship between Supreme Court decisions and social change? Specifically, how much do the justices' decisions simply reflect societal values and how much do they shape those values?

This book is a revised and condensed version of *From Jim Crow to Civil Rights: The Supreme Court and the Struggle for Racial Equality* (Oxford University Press, 2004). The purpose of writing this abridged volume was to make the themes and arguments of the original work accessible to a broader audience.

The very considerable debts—both personal and professional—that accrued during the production of the larger volume were acknowledged there and will not be repeated here, though it bears mentioning that everyone who played a role in improving that work deserves some credit for this abridged version as well. I would be remiss, however, not to thank several research assistants—at both Harvard Law School (where I did most of the revisions) and the University of Virginia School of Law— who contributed specifically to the production of this shorter volume: Candice Chiu, Maggie Gardner, Keith Hamilton, Charlie LaPlante, Kelly Phipps, Geoff Weien, and Jennifer Yeh. I also wish to thank Paula Prather for secretarial assistance and Dedi Felman, my editor at Oxford University Press, whose support and encouragement made both versions of this project possible.

Brown v. Board of Education
and the Civil Rights Movement

1

The Jim Crow Era

Extraordinary changes in racial attitudes and practices occurred in the Reconstruction decade following the Civil War. Slavery was abolished. Blacks were granted basic civil rights, such as freedom of contract and property ownership, as well as political rights, such as the rights to vote and to serve on juries. In the South, blacks voted in extraordinary numbers, electing thousands of black officeholders. Black jury service was common; streetcars generally were desegregated; and blacks finally gained access to public education.

The standing of southern blacks worsened with the end of Reconstruction in 1877, but it was not until the last decade of the nineteenth century that conditions of racial oppression calcified. The number of blacks lynched each year in the 1890s averaged more than 100, and in some years it was closer to 200. Southern states adopted poll taxes and literacy tests to suppress any black voting not already nullified by fraud and violence. Newly enacted statutes mandated segregation in railway travel. Blacks seldom sat on juries any longer. Black officeholding waned, then disappeared. Racial disparities in educational funding became enormous. State legislatures adopted new measures for coercing black agricultural labor.

The deterioration in southern race relations grew out of the interplay between regional developments and national ones. Economic hardship among southern farmers fostered powerful protest movements, such as the Farmers' Alliance. The growing political power of poor white farmers, whose precarious economic and social status inclined them to treasure white supremacy, did not bode well for blacks. Higher-status whites, who sometimes displayed paternalistic racial attitudes and supported qualified black rights, were supplanted around the turn of the century by political demagogues, such as "Pitchfork" Ben Tillman and James Vardaman, who preached unrestrained white supremacy. As governor of South Carolina in 1892, Tillman pledged that he would himself "willingly lead a mob in lynching a negro who had committed an assault upon a white woman." The political challenge posed by Populism also impelled conservatives to invoke the threat of "Negro domination" to disrupt potential cross-racial alliances among poor farmers.[1]

The inclination of southern whites to subordinate blacks was a necessary, but not a sufficient, cause of the worsening of race relations in the 1890s. Without northern acquiescence, southern racial practices could not have become so oppressive. Several factors explain the increasing willingness of white northerners to permit white southerners a free hand in ordering southern race relations.

reasons for northern acquiescence

Black migration to the North, which more than doubled in the decades after 1890, heightened the racial anxieties of northern whites, leading to greater discrimination in public accommodations, occasional efforts to segregate public schools, and an increase in the number of northern lynchings. The immigration of millions of southern and eastern Europeans, which began in the 1880s and accelerated around 1900, fed concern among northerners about the dilution of "Anglo-Saxon racial stock" and made them more sympathetic to southern racial policies. The resurgence of American imperialism in the 1890s, with the annexation of Hawaii and then the acquisition of Puerto Rico and the Philippines after the Spanish-American War, also fostered the convergence of northern and southern racial attitudes. Imperialists argued their case partly in the racial terms of Manifest Destiny—the "white man's burden"—and their rejection of full citizenship rights for persons thus incorporated into the United States hindered their ability to criticize the disfranchisement of blacks in the South.

A final factor in the growing northern acquiescence to oppressive southern racial practices was the disintegration of the Republican party's historical commitment to protecting black rights. That commitment had dissipated but not disappeared with the end of Reconstruction in 1877. By the 1890s, however, three decades' worth of Republican efforts to create a viable southern wing of the party had plainly failed. After winning 40–41 percent of the southern presidential vote between 1876 and 1884, the Republicans' total fell to 37 percent in 1888 and 30 percent in 1896. Moreover, a new generation of white voters in the North proved to be less offended by southern suppression of black voting. Finally, after the transitional congressional and presidential elections of the mid-1890s, the Republican party was, for the first time, able to securely maintain control of the national government without southern electoral support, thus removing an important incentive to defend black suffrage in the South.

For these reasons, Republican racial policy changed. In 1896, the party's national platform diluted its usual demand for a "free ballot and a fair count" in the South. In 1898, President William McKinley declined to criticize the election riot of whites in Wilmington, North Carolina, which killed a dozen blacks and destroyed black political power in that city. Republican parties in northern states became less inclined to run black candidates, and black representation at party conventions declined.

That was the extralegal context in which Supreme Court justices decided cases involving race and the Constitution in the *Plessy* era. Had such traditional legal sources as text, original understanding, and precedent plainly resolved the issues, then the background context might have been less important to the justices' rulings. But legal sources did not definitively resolve the issues.

RAILROAD SEGREGATION

Plessy v. Ferguson (1896) involved the constitutionality of a Louisiana statute requiring railroads to provide separate and equal accommodations for black and white passengers. The text of the Fourteenth Amendment provides no definitive answer to that constitutional question. It does not specifically forbid racial classifications, and "equal protection of the laws" does not plainly bar "equal but separate" facilities. Advocates of abolishing all legislative racial classifications proposed suitable language when the Fourteenth Amendment was being debated in 1866, but it was rejected.

Racism remained strong in the North in the years after the Civil War. Most northern states still disfranchised blacks, either excluded them from public education altogether or segregated them, and forbade interracial marriage. Most northern whites supported only *civil* rights for blacks, such as the freedoms of contract, property ownership, and court access. They resisted granting blacks *political* rights, such as voting or jury service, and *social* rights, such as interracial marriage or school integration. When white supremacist Democrats would occasionally argue during legislative debates that the 1866 Civil Rights Act or the Fourteenth Amendment would produce horrible consequences, such as compulsory school integration, Republicans invariably denied such possibilities.

Not only do the text and original understanding of the Fourteenth Amendment not plainly bar state-mandated racial segregation, but judicial precedent in the three decades before *Plessy* strongly supported the practice. Two lines of precedent were especially relevant: cases that sustained railroads' practices of segregation and those that upheld school segregation laws.

Before the enactment of segregation statutes, railroad policies of segregation were subject to three sorts of legal challenge. First, the common law required carriers to afford access to everyone who could pay the fare but did permit reasonable regulations for public convenience. For example, companies were allowed to establish separate "ladies" cars, which excluded unaccompanied males. Beginning in the 1850s, common-law decisions generally sustained railroad segregation as reasonable, opining that "repugnancies" between the races arising from natural differences created friction that segregation could minimize. But, to be reasonable, the separate facilities had to be equal.

Second, federal courts interpreted the provision of the 1875 Civil Rights Act that guaranteed "full and equal enjoyment" of common carriers regardless of race to forbid racial exclusion and inequality, but not segregation. Finally, the Interstate Commerce Commission interpreted its enabling act, which barred "undue or unreasonable prejudice or disadvantage," to permit segregation, provided that facilities were equal.

Thus, courts and agencies interpreting three texts dealing generally with equality and ambiguously with segregation overwhelmingly deemed separate but equal to be permissible. No court construing the Equal Protection Clause of the Fourteenth Amendment would have felt compelled to reach a different conclusion.

Because formal segregation was imposed earlier in public schools than on railroads, many lower courts prior to *Plessy* had confronted the

Fourteenth Amendment issue in education. These decisions almost unanimously concluded that public school segregation was constitutional, thus rejecting the "color-blindness" position embraced by Justice John Marshall Harlan in his *Plessy* dissent. Indeed, in 1883, the Court in *Pace v. Alabama*, with Harlan's acquiescence, had squarely rejected color blindness and unanimously sustained an Alabama statute that imposed heavier penalties on fornication when the participating parties were of different races. *Pace* reasoned that so long as both fornicators were subject to similar penalties, the races were being treated equally. Analytically, *Plessy*'s endorsement of separate but equal was a straightforward application of *Pace*.

Finally, by 1900, the Court's Fourteenth Amendment jurisprudence outside of the race context had established that laws that impinged on property and liberty interests were constitutional if reasonable. For example, *Holden v. Hardy* (1898), which rejected a challenge to a maximum-hour law for miners, stated the constitutional question to be

"reasonable std."

Figure 1.1. John Marshall Harlan, the sole dissenter in *Plessy v. Ferguson* (1896), in 1907. Library of Congress, Prints and Photographs Division, George Grantham Bain Collection.

"whether the legislature has adopted the statute in exercise of a reasonable discretion, or whether its action be a mere excuse for an unjust discrimination, or the oppression, or spoliation of a particular class." Thus, to find racial segregation permissible because it was reasonable would simply align race with the rest of the Court's Fourteenth Amendment jurisprudence. Given dominant public opinion in the mid-1890s, it would be easy to deem racial separation a valid exercise of the state's power to promote health, safety, and morals.[2]

Thus, the traditional sources of constitutional interpretation did not dictate a contrary result in *Plessy*, while the broader racial mores of the time strongly supported the Court's decision. By the 1890s, escalating white-on-black violence in the South, including lynchings, made segregation seem "the embodiment of enlightened public policy"—a progressive solution to growing interracial conflict. Northern whites too had become more accepting of segregation. A black newspaper in Boston, commenting in 1896 on the exclusion of a black bishop from a white hotel, observed that social equality "appears more unthinkable today than ever." The Republican party had grown relatively indifferent toward the rights of blacks.[3]

The justices are usually not oblivious to such large-scale shifts in social attitudes. *Plessy* simply mirrored the preferences of most white Americans. Most northern newspapers gave the decision routine notice or none at all. The *New York Times*, which reported several other decisions that day on its front page, relegated *Plessy* to a page-three column on railway news.

DISFRANCHISEMENT

The Fifteenth Amendment, adopted in 1870, forbade the state and federal governments from denying the right to vote based on race. With their suffrage rights secured, huge numbers of southern blacks voted, overwhelmingly for Republicans. Given large black populations in all southern states, Republicans won resounding victories everywhere. Large numbers of blacks were elected to office—at the local, state, and national levels.

The political power of southern blacks was short-lived, however. Southern whites, even where in the minority, wielded preponderant economic, social, and physical power. Through fraud, intimidation, and often murderous violence, whites eventually succeeded in suppressing black voting, which enabled Democrats to "redeem" the South from Republican rule. The administration of President Ulysses S. Grant sporadically used military intervention in the 1870s to curtail such violence but eventually concluded that doing so alienated too many northern voters, whose support for military coercion quickly waned. Freed from external constraint, southern whites did whatever they deemed necessary to regain political control. *[whites regained political control]*

Black voting in the South, though reduced, did not end with Reconstruction; a majority of blacks still voted in most southern states in 1880. It was not until the 1890s that the political participation of southern blacks declined dramatically, as Democrats, often through fraud and intimidation, seized political control. Democratic legislatures then enacted laws, such as complex voter registration requirements and residency requirements, that further reduced black voting and Republican representation. This facilitated state-level constitutional changes, such as poll taxes and literacy tests. *[black voting]*

As a result of such measures, black political participation in the South had been nearly eliminated by the early 1900s. In Louisiana, black voter registration fell from 95.6 percent before the adoption in 1896 of a new registration law to 1.1 percent in 1904. Alabama's black voter registration plummeted from 180,000 in 1900 to 3,000 in 1903. Registration figures undoubtedly overstated turnout. In Mississippi, black voter turnout was estimated at 29 percent in 1888, 2 percent in 1892, and zero in 1895

Disfranchisement had calamitous consequences for southern blacks. When blacks could not vote, neither could they be elected to office. Sixty-four blacks had sat in the Mississippi legislature in 1873; none sat after 1895. In South Carolina's lower house, which had a black majority during Reconstruction, a single black remained in 1896.

More important, disfranchisement meant that almost no blacks held local offices. In the late nineteenth century, sheriffs, justices of the peace, jurors, county commissioners, and school board members were the most important governmental actors. The preferred method of denying constitutional rights to blacks was to vest discretion over the administration of laws in local officials and trust them to preserve white supremacy. Disfranchisement was essential to this strategy, and it facilitated the exclusion of blacks from juries and the diversion of their share of public school funds. *[blacks excluded from holding office]*

The legal question confronting the justices was whether disfranchisement measures violated the Fifteenth Amendment, which provides that the right of citizens to vote "shall not be denied or abridged by the *[15th A]*

United States or by any State on account of race, color, or previous condition of servitude." Southern whites carefully avoided open contravention of the amendment, which they assumed would prompt federal intervention.

Yet, most white southerners thought the Fifteenth Amendment was illegitimate. A leading Louisiana disfranchiser called it "the greatest crime of the Nineteenth Century"; crazed Republicans bent on partisan gain had imposed ignorant "negro domination" on the South. Deterred from explicitly nullifying the amendment, white southerners generally felt morally justified in evading its purpose, and they were not subtle about their objectives. At the Virginia disfranchisement convention, Carter Glass acknowledged that his mission was "to discriminate to the very extremity of permissible action under the limitations of the Federal Constitution, with a view to the elimination of every negro voter who can be gotten rid of legally."[4]

The original understanding of the Fifteenth Amendment seemed to permit suffrage restrictions that disparately affected blacks. Many Republican congressmen had favored a broader amendment that forbade suffrage qualifications based on property and education. Yet Republicans could not secure consensus in the limited time available to the lame-duck Congress of 1869, and the conference committee adopted the most limited version of the amendment, which seemed plainly to permit property and literacy qualifications. With black illiteracy rates of roughly 50 percent in 1900 and most southern blacks still impecunious tenant farmers and sharecroppers, voting qualifications such as poll taxes and literacy tests, even if fairly administered, disfranchised most blacks.

To be sure, other constitutional grounds for contesting disfranchisement did exist. One might challenge voter qualifications based on the discriminatory motive that animated them. In addition, the procedure for administering literacy tests might be unconstitutional because the task of determining the "good character" of prospective voters or the adequacy of their "understanding" of the law conferred too much discretion on registrars. Finally, one might challenge actual—as opposed to merely potential—discrimination in the administration of voter qualification tests. Around 1900, several suits challenging disfranchisement raised these claims. The law relevant to resolving them was slim.

In *Williams v. Mississippi* (1898), the plaintiff in error challenged the suffrage qualifications in the state's 1890 constitution, arguing both that they had been adopted for a discriminatory purpose and that they conferred unbridled discretion on registrars. The justices rejected both challenges.

[handwritten margin notes: "tools of disenfranchise", "Enforcement options", "legal challenges to disenfranchisement—"]

First, the Court invoked the traditional judicial aversion to examining legislative motive in evaluating a law's constitutionality. In *Fletcher v. Peck* (1810), Chief Justice John Marshall denied that allegations that legislators had been bribed justified rescission of a land grant, as courts could not properly consider legislative motive. More recently, the Court in 1885 had unanimously rejected an equal protection challenge to a San Francisco ordinance imposing a curfew on laundries. The city council's animus toward Chinese, who operated most laundries, was no secret, yet the justices refused to look at the legislature's motive for adopting the law.

Yet the tradition of rejecting motive inquiries was not the only one available to the Court in 1898. Marshall had seemed to contradict his *Fletcher* views in *McCulloch v. Maryland* (1819), where he observed that courts would be duty-bound to invalidate laws that Congress enacted "under the *pretext* of executing its [enumerated] powers"—apparently a motive inquiry. Similarly, in post–Civil War decisions, the Court invalidated laws imposing ironclad oaths as professional qualifications on the ground that the measures were *intended* to impose punishment on Confederate sympathizers rather than simply to serve as bona fide occupational qualifications. Finally, Justice Stephen Field, sitting on circuit, expressly applied motive analysis to invalidate San Francisco's "queue ordinance," which required prisoners to cut their hair short—a measure that had plainly been inspired by anti-Chinese animus.[5]

Thus, in 1898, some precedent existed on both sides of the question of whether legislative motive was relevant to constitutionality. Yet the tradition of rejecting motive inquiries was preponderant. Indeed, had it seemed probable that a discriminatory motive could invalidate otherwise constitutional legislation, southern disfranchisers probably would have been more circumspect in their public statements.

As to the constitutionality of delegating broad discretion to registrars, the relevant precedent was *Yick Wo v. Hopkins* (1886), where the Court invalidated a San Francisco ordinance that required persons establishing laundries in wood buildings, but not in stone or brick ones, to secure permits from the board of supervisors. *Yick Wo* had two rationales. First, the ordinance contained no criteria to guide the supervisors' discretion. Second, in practice, the board had granted permits to essentially all Caucasian applicants, while denying them to all of the roughly 200 Chinese petitioners. Both aspects of *Yick Wo* were potentially relevant to black disfranchisement.

The purpose of circumscribing literacy tests with "good character" and "understanding" clauses was to invite discrimination by registrars.

Opponents had criticized such provisions as shams and had warned that courts would invalidate them. Yet even these vague standards were more than the laundry ordinance in *Yick Wo* had provided. Thus, *Yick Wo* did not dictate a result one way or the other in *Williams*, and the justices distinguished it on the unhelpful ground that it was not this case.

Broad administrative discretion can also be challenged as applied. The *Williams* decision rejected this claim as well, observing, "[I]t has not been shown that their [Mississippi's voter requirements] actual administration was evil; only that evil was possible under them."[6]

For the Court to reject an as-applied challenge in the absence of supporting evidence is unremarkable. The more interesting question is what standard of proof the Court would have applied had the issue been appropriately presented. *Yick Wo* would have been the most relevant precedent, but discrimination there was irrefutable. Had the standard been set this high, black litigants who challenged disfranchisement rarely could have met it. The *Plessy* era justices never resolved this question regarding disfranchisement, though they shed some light on it in the analogous context of jury discrimination, where the standard they applied proved virtually impossible to satisfy.

The Court's failure to resolve the standard-of-proof question was not due to the absence of an appropriate case. In *Giles v. Harris* (1903), the plaintiff alleged race discrimination in the administration of Alabama's "good character" and "understanding" clauses and sought an injunction compelling the registration of himself and others similarly situated.

Writing for the majority, Justice Oliver Wendell Holmes ruled that even if the allegations were proved, plaintiff was not entitled to the requested relief, for two reasons. First, if the allegation of rampant fraud were true, then for the Court to order registration would make it a party to the sham. Second, such an order would be "an empty form" if Alabama whites really had conspired to disfranchise blacks. The Court would be powerless to enforce such an injunction, and therefore the plaintiff's remedy must come from the political branches of the national government.

Holmes did not rule out a suit for money damages, but it would have to be heard before a jury, unlike an injunction suit. With blacks excluded from southern juries, such a suit was unlikely to succeed. In any event, when Giles brought a damages action, the Court in *Giles v. Teasley* (1904) rejected his claim on grounds similar to those on which it had dismissed the earlier suit. First, if the registration board were patently unconstitutional, then it could do Giles no harm. Second, the

Court could provide no effective relief against this sort of state political action.

The extraordinary *Giles* opinions are among the Court's most candid confessions of limited power. They suggest that even plain constitutional violations may go unredressed in the face of hostile public opinion. Yet, we should not read these decisions to suggest that the justices would have invalidated disfranchisement had they simply possessed the power to enforce such a ruling. The justices were probably no more supportive of black suffrage at this time than were most white Americans.

ltd. power

By 1900, most white southerners were determined to eliminate black suffrage, even if doing so required violence. In 1898, whites in Wilmington, North Carolina, concluded a political campaign fought under the banner of white supremacy by murdering a dozen blacks and driving 1,400 of them out of the city. Many southern blacks now abandoned politics. Northern and southern progressives came to view black disfranchisement as an enlightened effort to remove "the most fruitful source of bitterness between the races." Disfranchising blacks would alleviate the need to resort to alternatives, such as election violence and fraud.[7]

white hostility

reasons for tolerating disenfran- chisement

Many whites in the North now shared the view that the Fifteenth Amendment had been a mistake and that black suffrage was "the greatest self-confessed failure in American political history." The ideal of universal male suffrage had been undermined by concerns about enfranchising millions of southern and eastern European immigrants and by the imperialist adventures of the 1890s. The *Nation* noted the coincidence of *Williams v. Mississippi*, which sanctioned black disfranchisement, with the country's efforts to deal with the "varied assortment of inferior races in different parts of the world, which must be governed somehow, and which, of course, could not be allowed to vote."[8]

immigrants

This shift in public opinion regarding black suffrage was evident in Congress's posture toward disfranchisement. In 1893–1894, Democrats took advantage of their simultaneous control of Congress and the presidency for the first time since before the Civil War to repeal most of the 1870s voting rights legislation. When Republicans regained national control from 1897 to 1910, they made no effort to reenact these measures.

Moreover, Congress failed to remedy patent violations of section 2 of the Fourteenth Amendment, which *requires* reduction of a state's congressional representation if its adult male citizens are disfranchised for any reason other than crime. Because disfranchisement need not be racially motivated to trigger section 2, the difficulty blacks faced in proving

14th A, Sec 2

Fifteenth Amendment violations in court should have been no obstacle to congressional enforcement of section 2. Yet Congress took no action on proposed resolutions to reduce southern representation, and Republican presidents made it clear that they did not support efforts to penalize the South for disfranchising blacks.

The Court, like Congress, broadly reflects public opinion. As Congress was unwilling to enforce section 2, the reluctance of the justices to order remedies for less transparent violations of the Fifteenth Amendment is unsurprising. A contemporary observer concluded that, with the Court and Congress reflecting "the apathetic tone of public opinion," the Fifteenth Amendment, though still part of the Constitution in "the technical sense," was "already in process of repeal" as "a rule of conduct."[9]

JURY SERVICE

During Reconstruction and even into the 1880s, large numbers of southern blacks served on juries, especially in heavily black counties. As whites suppressed black voting, blacks disappeared from juries. Most southern whites found black jury service, which they conceived as a form of political officeholding, even more objectionable than black suffrage. As segregation spread across southern society, the jury box succumbed to its pressure. Black service on southern juries dwindled by the late 1880s and, after 1900, essentially no blacks sat on southern juries.

The Supreme Court first confronted race discrimination in jury service in *Strauder v. West Virginia* (1880), invalidating a law that barred blacks from juries. The significance of this decision was limited, however, because only a couple of states still formally barred blacks from jury service. The typical jury selection statute of the time required that jurors be of "good intelligence, sound judgment, and fair character." *Strauder* did not resolve how to handle allegations that blacks had been excluded from juries by administrative discrimination.[10]

In 1881, *Neal v. Delaware*, in dicta, implied that the complete absence of blacks from juries, despite Delaware's sizable black population, constituted prima facie evidence of discrimination. But *Neal*'s holding was more limited, as the Court reversed the conviction on the ground that Delaware had conceded discrimination in jury selection. A few years later, *Yick Wo* confirmed that discrimination through administration was just as unconstitutional as discrimination by statute. Yet in *Yick Wo*, the discrimination had been irrefutable. As of 1900, the Court still had not clarified the standards of proof for establishing racially discriminatory administration with regard to jury selection or any other matter.

In the absence of law on that subject, the Court's resolution was bound to be influenced by public sentiment. By the 1890s, southern whites were intensely opposed to black officeholding—including jury service—and they largely succeeded in eradicating it. The last black—prior to the 1965 Voting Rights Act—was elected to Virginia's legislature in 1891, Mississippi's in 1895, and South Carolina's in 1902. There were no black congressmen from the South between 1901 and 1972.

Northern whites were not committed to protecting southern black officeholding. Most had never been enthusiastic about the practice, which is why the Fifteenth Amendment did not expressly protect it. By early in the twentieth century, blacks were no longer serving in several northern state legislatures, and Republican presidents McKinley, Roosevelt, and Taft had drastically curtailed federal patronage appointments of blacks.

attitudes of Northern whites

The Court during the *Plessy* era effectively nullified *Strauder* by making race discrimination in jury selection virtually impossible to prove. *Yick Wo* notwithstanding, the Court refused to invalidate hopelessly vague jury selection statutes. Several decisions held that criminal defendants were entitled to hearings on motions to quash indictments only if they produced evidence, not mere allegations, of discrimination. What evidence the justices had in mind is unclear. Rejecting *Neal's* dicta, the Court ruled that the lengthy absence of blacks from a county's juries raised no inference of discrimination and that defendants bore the burden of overcoming the presumption that state officials have acted constitutionally. The justices also rejected as an inadequate proffer of proof a defendant's attempt to compel the testimony of jury commissioners.

Furthermore, where defendants offered proof that was rejected as inadequate by state courts, the justices deferred, unless the findings were clearly erroneous—the most lenient standard of appellate review. Because the Court had previously interpreted federal law to authorize the removal of jury discrimination claims to federal court only when a state *statute* discriminated, and because federal habeas corpus review of state convictions was almost completely unavailable at this time, state trial judges always made the initial findings on jury discrimination. By deferring to those findings, the justices virtually eliminated any possibility that jury discrimination claims would be heard in a forum not openly committed to white supremacy. Between 1904 and 1935, the Court did not reverse the conviction of even one black defendant on the ground of race discrimination in jury selection, even though blacks were universally excluded from southern juries.

SEPARATE AND UNEQUAL

Plessy sustained a statute that mandated "equal but separate" railroad accommodations. In practice, however, segregation in public education and in railroad travel afforded blacks nothing like equality. "[S]carcely fit for a dog to ride in" is how one black Marylander described Jim Crow railroad cars.[11]

funding for educ

Before black political power was nullified in the South, public funding for black and white education remained nearly equal. In South Carolina, per capita spending was equal until about 1880, and in North Carolina and Alabama, blacks actually received more than whites. Nashville's black teachers received equal pay until disfranchisement. As Congress lost interest and southern blacks lost voting rights, southern whites were liberated to follow their inclinations regarding black education. Most thought that it spoiled good field hands, encouraged competition with white labor, and rendered blacks dissatisfied with their subordinate status.

As southern whites became freer to implement their own views, unfavorable attitudes toward black education spread. In 1901, Georgia's governor, Allen D. Candler, stated: "God made them negroes and we cannot by education make them white folks. We are on the wrong track. We must turn back." A few years later, the governor-elect of South Carolina, Cole Blease, concluded, "[T]he greatest mistake the white race has ever made was in attempting to educate the free Negro." Many whites now accepted "scientific" evidence that purported to show that the black race was losing the Darwinian struggle for survival, that it was deteriorating and on the road to extinction, and that ameliorative efforts through education were futile. Many southern whites came to oppose black education entirely, while others supported rudimentary education for literacy and basic industrial and agricultural training; few supported equal educational opportunities.[12]

Yet southern law, independent of federal constitutional constraints, required equal black education. A typical state constitution mandated segregation but forbade racial distinctions in the distribution of public school funds. When some southern states in the 1880s authorized the funding of education from taxes segregated by race—that is, taxes raised from whites would be allocated to white schools and taxes paid by blacks would be allocated to black schools—courts promptly invalidated the measures.

By 1900, every southern state faced popular demands for the formal segregation of public school funds, as whites complained about their taxes subsidizing black education. Yet political campaigns to segregate school funds failed everywhere. Opponents predicted that courts would invalidate such schemes, and they questioned why formal separation was necessary when less direct methods had already achieved the same goal. *[campaigns to segregate funding]*

Beginning in the 1890s, southern states had subverted constitutional mandates for racial equality in education by granting local school boards discretion in allocating public funds. Such statutes frequently required school terms of the same length for blacks and whites but left other issues—teacher salaries and qualifications, student-teacher ratios, spending on physical plants and equipment—to the discretion of local officials. *[local discretion]*

The disfranchisement of blacks removed political constraints on the racially discriminatory administration of public school funds. Progressive educational campaigns, which swept the South from 1900 to 1915, poured much larger sums into public education, which administrators could then freely divert to white schools. The temptation to "rape . . . the Negro school fund" was great and was seldom resisted.[13]

Enormous racial disparities in educational spending ensued. By 1915, per capita spending on white pupils was roughly three times that on black pupils in North Carolina, six times in Alabama, and twelve times in South Carolina. Incredibly, these disparities were mild in comparison with other inequalities, such as spending on physical plants, equipment, and transportation. The formal segregation of public school funds could hardly have been more effective at diverting educational resources to whites. Yet these disparities were difficult to challenge in court. School officials had broad discretion in allocating public funds, and courts refused to presume discrimination.

The *Plessy* era Court's only case involving racial inequality in education was *Cumming v. Richmond County Board of Education* (1899). There, a Georgia county had ceased funding a black high school, while continuing to operate a high school for whites, on the ground that the limited funds available for black education were better spent on a larger number of children in primary schools (300) than a much smaller number in secondary education (60). The Court rejected the Fourteenth Amendment challenge to this separate-and-*un*equal scheme, reasoning that the board's action was not motivated by racial animus and that redistributing funds among black schools to maximize the educational opportunities of blacks as a group was reasonable. The author of the unanimous opinion was Harlan, the sole dissenter in *Plessy* and the Fuller Court justice most committed to protecting the civil rights of blacks.

It is not clear that in 1899 the Court would have invalidated a *statute* that provided high school education only to whites. The Fourteenth Amendment's guarantee of "equal protection of the laws" has never been interpreted to deny legislatures the ability to extend differential treatment to groups that are differently situated. In 1899, the justices likely believed that natural racial differences justified different educational opportunities for blacks and whites.

Nor would such an approach have been inconsistent with *Plessy*, which did *not* hold that the Constitution required racially separate facilities to be equal. The Louisiana statute, not the Court, had imposed the equality requirement in *Plessy*. Thus, the Court had had no occasion to decide whether separate and *un*equal could be constitutional. Language in the opinion suggested, however, that the Constitution required reasonableness, not equality. In 1899, the justices might easily have thought it unreasonable to provide blacks with inferior railroad accommodations, but not unreasonable to provide inferior educational facilities. They certainly would have thought this with regard to women.

Cumming did not have to resolve that question, however, as the inequality there derived from administrative discrimination. Georgia law granted county education boards discretion over establishing high schools. The Court's jury cases had refused to presume the discriminatory exercise of administrative discretion or to infer discriminatory purpose from disparate racial impact. Thus, even if this Court would have invalidated a discriminatory statute, it was not bound to overturn Richmond County's unequal expenditures.

Existing law permitted, but did not compel, the Court to invalidate the discrimination in *Cumming*. With the law indeterminate, the outcome probably depended on the justices' personal views, which likely reflected general societal attitudes. By 1900, most white Americans believed that education for blacks and whites served different purposes. Most southern whites opposed black education altogether or favored only industrial training; few endorsed black secondary schooling. Public high school education was still virtually nonexistent for southern blacks. In 1890, only 0.39 percent of southern black children attended high school, and in 1910 just 2.8 percent. The black public high school in *Cumming* was the only one in Georgia; there were only four in the whole South.

Northern whites, though more committed to black literacy, generally agreed that southern blacks needed to receive only limited education. Northern philanthropic organizations, such as the Peabody and Rosenwald funds, which heavily subsidized southern black education, supported industrial training to prepare blacks for the same "negro jobs" held by their parents: manual labor and service positions. President William McKinley, visiting the Tuskegee Institute, praised its industrial-education mission and its managers, who "evidently do not believe in attempting the unattainable." President William Howard Taft also endorsed primarily industrial training for southern blacks: "I am not one of those who believe it is well to educate the mass of Negroes with academic or university education." The justices likely shared this predominant white view of black education and thus found reasonable Richmond County's reallocation of limited black educational funds from the high school to primary schools.[14]

In all four settings considered thus far in this chapter—segregation, disfranchisement, black jury service, and separate-and-unequal education—traditional sources of constitutional law were sufficiently indeterminate to accommodate white supremacist preferences. National opinion had become more sympathetic to the perspective of southern whites, and so did the justices' rulings.

Beginning in the second decade of the twentieth century, however, the Supreme Court in several rulings vindicated the civil rights claims of blacks. The justices rendered these decisions in a racial context even more oppressive than that of the *Plessy* era. These decisions show that constitutional law is partly about law, not simply about politics. Even justices from whom the NAACP saw little hope of securing racial justice may have felt bound to invalidate transparent constitutional violations. Moreover, these decisions had a negligible impact on actual racial practices.

A brief look at two of these rulings—*Guinn v. Oklahoma* (1915) and *Bailey v. Alabama* (1911)—should suffice to illustrate these points. In *Guinn*, the Court ruled that the Fifteenth Amendment barred the grandfather clause—a device that insulated illiterate whites from disfranchisement by exempting from literacy tests those persons and their descendants who were enfranchised before 1867, when most southern blacks first received the vote.

The grandfather clause was such an obvious evasion of the Fifteenth Amendment that delegates to Louisiana's 1898 constitutional convention, the first to adopt such a measure, warned that courts would invalidate it as a "weak and transparent subterfuge." The convention conferred with the state's two U.S. senators, who confirmed that view; one declared the provision to be "grossly unconstitutional."[15]

The convention ignored this advice, as did several other states, which also adopted grandfather clauses, despite doubts about their constitutionality. Yet all of these states but one limited the duration of the grandfather clause, hoping to accomplish its purpose before litigation began. Only Oklahoma's grandfather clause, at issue in *Guinn*, was permanent.

Contemporary commentators regarded *Guinn* as an easy case for the justices. The *Washington Post* observed that the grandfather clause "was so obvious an evasion that the Supreme Court could not have failed to declare it unconstitutional." The *New York Times* thought "no other decision was possible" in *Guinn*, because the grandfather clause "had no reason for being unless it was for the purpose of nullifying the Fifteenth Amendment, and the court is not there to nullify the Constitution." A *Harvard Law Review* commentator similarly queried, "Is it not a trespass upon the dignity of a court to expect it to refuse to brush aside so thin a gauze of words?" Of the more than 55,000 blacks who resided in Oklahoma in 1900, only 57 came from states that had permitted blacks to vote before 1867.[16]

The Court's decision in *Bailey v. Alabama* (1911) is analogous. The Thirteenth Amendment provides that "[n]either slavery nor involuntary servitude, except as a punishment for crime . . . shall exist within the United States." In 1885, Alabama became the first southern state to adopt a false-pretenses law applying specifically to labor contracts. The statute criminalized entering into a labor agreement that provided advance wages with the fraudulent intent to subsequently breach.

Southern agricultural labor contracts typically lasted a year and almost always provided advance wages. Punishing fraud rather than the breach itself was essential, as lower courts were virtually unanimous in holding that the criminalization of ordinary contract breaches violated the Thirteenth Amendment and state constitutional prohibitions on imprisonment for debt. Thus, the Alabama Supreme Court interpreted the 1885 statute to require proof of fraudulent intent when the contract was signed.

A half dozen southern states, including Alabama, responded to this and similar rulings by adopting new false-pretenses laws early in the twentieth century. These statutes created presumptions of fraudulent intent from the fact of breach. Moreover, Alabama evidence law barred accused breachers from testifying about their uncommunicated motives.

The justices in *Bailey* invalidated the Alabama statute under the Thirteenth Amendment and the federal antipeonage statute. Because fraudulent intent was presumed from the breach and the defendant's testimony to the contrary was barred, Alabama had effectively criminalized the breach of any labor contract that paid advance wages—that is, essentially all long-term agricultural labor contracts. Once the justices accepted the nearly universal baseline proposition that the Thirteenth Amendment barred criminalizing ordinary contract breaches, how could they not invalidate Alabama's transparent subterfuge without countenancing southern nullification of the Constitution?

Guinn and *Bailey* not only invalidated patent constitutional violations, but they also had little ameliorative effect on the racial practices involved. *Guinn*'s implications for black suffrage were utterly trivial. Only Oklahoma had a permanent grandfather clause. By 1915, the grandfather clauses of all other southern states had achieved their purpose of insulating illiterate whites from the disfranchising effect of literacy tests and had been extinguished by sunset provisions. As a Richmond newspaper coolly observed after *Guinn*, such devices were "no longer vital to the South's protection."[17]

Moreover, the Court in *Guinn* explicitly noted that a literacy test uncorrupted by a grandfather clause was permissible—dicta that ensured that the ruling had no impact on black disfranchisement. Mississippi and South Carolina, disfranchisement pioneers, already had demonstrated that a literacy test without a grandfather clause could nullify black suffrage. So long as registrars committed to white supremacy exercised broad discretion in administering literacy tests, illiterate whites could generally register, while literate blacks could not.

Guinn also had no effect on other disfranchisement techniques, such as poll taxes, white primaries, complex registration requirements, fraud, and violence. For these reasons, a New Orleans newspaper confidently concluded that *Guinn* was "not of the slightest political importance in the South." One New York newspaper predicted that blacks would discover that "getting the right to vote from the Supreme Court in Washington is not exactly the same thing as getting the right from the election board in their own voting district." The *New York Times* assured readers that, *Guinn* notwithstanding, "The white man will rule his land. The only question left by the Supreme Court's decision is how he will rule it."[18]

In Oklahoma itself, *Guinn* had no effect on black voter registration, as the legislature responded by immediately "grandfathering" the grandfather clause. Under the new statute, voters in the 1914 congressional election, when the grandfather clause was in effect, were automatically registered. All other eligible voters, including essentially all blacks, had to register between April 30 and May 11, 1916, or be forever disfranchised. The federal government failed to challenge this patent evasion, and the justices had no opportunity to invalidate it until 1939.

Bailey had as little effect on peonage as *Guinn* did on black voting. For thirty more years, courts in Florida and Georgia enforced false-pretenses statutes with phony presumptions that were essentially identical to the law invalidated in *Bailey*. Yet after 1914, the Court decided no more peonage cases until World War II, when it finally invalidated these laws.

To be sure, some other southern legislatures repealed the statutory presumptions that *Bailey* had condemned, and some state courts invalidated those that remained on the books. But these states retained the basic false-pretenses laws which *Bailey* had approved. All-white juries still determined whether black agricultural workers had accepted advance wages with the fraudulent intent to subsequently breach contracts. Removal of the statutory presumption cannot have affected many case outcomes. Moreover, as few blacks would have relished testing their luck in court, most would have simply assumed that contractual breach would lead to prosecution and conviction.

Bailey also left undisturbed many alternative methods of coercing black labor: convict labor, convict lease, vagrancy laws, antienticement laws, and anti–labor-agent laws. Given the willingness of southern law enforcement officers to "manufacture" black criminals for convict labor and convict lease, contract-enforcement laws were unnecessary for coercing black labor. The highly visible, mostly black chain gang was a powerful inducement for blacks to abide by labor contracts rather than risk convictions for loitering or vagrancy. Moreover, many employers who coerced black labor made no pretense of legality: Blacks worked under shotguns, were locked up at night, and were tracked down with hunting dogs if they escaped.

At a time when many, perhaps most, southern whites still believed that they had a proprietary interest in black labor and that blacks would work only if coerced, judicial invalidation of a couple of peonage statutes was unlikely to prove efficacious. Many state judges, even if they felt legally obliged to invalidate a peonage statute, nonetheless sympathized with the legislature's "purpose of requiring the fickle laborers in our cotton country to reasonably observe their contracts." Moreover, blacks prosecuted under unconstitutional peonage laws were among the least likely defendants to be able to afford to appeal convictions to a tribunal not under the sway of local planters. Nor did the NAACP or any similar organization able to render legal or financial assistance operate in the rural South in the 1910s.[19]

The federal government's enthusiasm for prosecuting peonage did not last long, especially once the southern-sympathizing Wilson administration assumed office in 1913. In any event, successful prosecutions generally required the testimony of black witnesses, who were usually under the control, both economic and physical, of planters. Such witnesses were easy to intimidate. In one infamous Georgia case, a planter who was worried about a federal investigation into his peonage practices simply ordered the murder of eleven of his tenants who were potential witnesses.

federal prosecutions

For all of these reasons, *Bailey* had little effect on the prevalence of peonage in the South. In a 1921 report, the U.S. attorney general concluded that peonage continued to exist "to a shocking extent" in Georgia. That same year, the NAACP reported, "Throughout the South, . . . Negroes are held today in as complete and awful and soul destroying slavery as they were in 1860." The association's files for the 1920s are filled with letters from the South that describe black workers being whipped, beaten, and generally treated like slaves.[20]

peonage persisted

At a time when white southerners could get away with lynching blacks, disfranchising them, segregating them, and coercing their labor, the Court proved a barrier to schemes that came too close to formal constitutional nullification. Yet because the justices challenged only the form, not the substance, of southern racial practices, nothing significant changed for blacks.

Racial attitudes and practices in the United States, which had been trapped in a long downward spiral since the end of Reconstruction in the 1870s, finally began moving in a more progressive direction in the years following World War I. One momentous factor was southern black migration to the North, which exploded during the war. A half million southern blacks migrated in the 1910s, and another million in the 1920s. Between 1910 and 1930, Chicago's black population increased from 44,000 to 233,000, and Detroit's from 5,700 to 120,000.

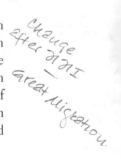

change after WWI — Great Migration

As blacks relocated from a region of pervasive disfranchisement to one that extended the suffrage without racial restriction, their political power grew. Northern blacks often held the balance of power between competitive political parties, especially after the New Deal reinvigorated the Democratic party in the North and liberated blacks from their historical propensity to vote solidly Republican.

In northern cities, blacks quickly reaped the rewards of their new-found political power: civil service positions proportionate to their share of the population, the appointment of black police officers, playgrounds and parks for black neighborhoods, and the election of black city council members and state legislators. Not long thereafter, blacks began influencing national politics—for example, successfully pressuring the House of Representatives in 1922 to pass an antilynching bill and the Senate in 1930 to defeat the nomination of Judge John Parker to the Supreme Court because of his earlier statements in defense of white political supremacy.

Blacks moved north mainly in search of better job opportunities, but their rising economic status also facilitated social protest. Larger black populations in northern cities provided a broader economic base for black entrepreneurs and professionals, such as teachers, ministers, lawyers, and doctors—groups that later supplied the resources and leadership for civil rights protest. Improved economic status also enabled blacks to use boycotts as leverage for social change, beginning with the "don't shop where you can't work" campaigns of the 1930s.

Migration to the North resulted in better education for blacks, which also facilitated subsequent social protest. In addition, more flexible racial mores in the North permitted challenges to the status quo that would not have been tolerated in the South. Only in the North could a protest organization such as the NAACP or a militant black newspaper such as the *Chicago Defender* develop and thrive. Because in the North, a black man could "[f]eel more like a man," blacks there were less likely to internalize racist norms of black subordination and inferiority, which posed major obstacles to creating a racial protest movement in the South.[21]

Before southern blacks migrated north, they moved from farms to cities within the South—a process that also greatly affected racial attitudes and practices. Better economic opportunities in cities eventually fostered a black middle class, which capitalized on the segregated economy to develop sufficient wealth and leisure time to participate in social protest. Many urban blacks were economically independent of whites and thus could challenge the racial status quo without endangering their livelihoods.

Blacks living in southern cities also enjoyed better education and, occasionally, access to the ballot. Because racial etiquette in the cities was somewhat less oppressive than in the countryside, urban blacks were also freer to participate in other forms of protest. Finally, because blacks in cities lived closer to one another, enjoyed better communication and transportation facilities, and shared social networks such as black colleges and churches, they found it somewhat easier to overcome the organizational obstacles confronting any social protest movement.

World War I had more immediate implications for race relations, including the ideological ramifications of a "war to make the world safe for democracy." W. E. B. Du Bois of the NAACP wrote in 1919: "Make way for Democracy! We saved it in France, and by the Great Jehovah, we will save it in the United States of America, or know the reason why." The war inspired blacks, who had borne arms for their country and faced death on the battlefield, to assert their rights. A black journalist noted, "The men who did not fear the trained veterans of Germany will hardly run from the lawless Ku Klux Klan." Returning black soldiers were treated as heroes in the black community, spoke to NAACP branches about their experiences, and demanded voting rights. Membership in the NAACP skyrocketed from 10,000 in 1917 to 91,000 in 1919.[22]

The Supreme Court's racial jurisprudence of the 1920s and 1930s reflected these broader changes in the social and political context. In several landmark decisions, the Court created new procedural rights for accused criminals and reversed the convictions of blacks who had been egregiously mistreated by the criminal justice system in the South. The Court interpreted the Due Process Clause of the Fourteenth Amendment to forbid convictions obtained through mob-dominated trials and to require the state appointment of lawyers for indigent defendants in capital cases. The Court also forbade convictions based on confessions extracted through torture and reversed convictions where blacks had been deliberately excluded from juries. Some of these decisions were in tension with earlier rulings, and all of them constituted new departures for a Court that had previously expressed little solicitude for criminal defendants, black or white.

Although the justices during the interwar years were willing to intervene against the worst abuses of Jim Crow, they refused to challenge the more routine but fundamental aspects of white supremacy, such as segregation and disfranchisement. After striking down two iterations of the white primary where state action was present, the justices drew back in *Grovey v. Townsend* (1935), unanimously finding no constitutional violation when blacks were excluded from Democratic primaries through the vote of a party convention. *Breedlove v. Suttles* (1937) rejected a constitutional challenge to the poll tax.

Nor did the Court in these years threaten racial segregation. Although this Court twice rejected invitations to overrule *Buchanan v. Warley* (1917), which had invalidated residential segregation laws, in *Corrigan v. Buckley* (1926), the justices dismissed a challenge to racially restrictive covenants and strongly hinted that judicial enforcement of such private agreements was not state action under the Fourteenth Amendment. *Gong Lum v. Rice* (1927) unanimously rejected a challenge to Mississippi's placement of Chinese-American students in black public schools rather than in white ones and strongly implied the permissibility of racial segregation in public education. And *Missouri ex rel. Gaines v. Canada* (1938), though it invalidated a state law that provided blacks who wished to pursue graduate or professional education with scholarships to attend universities outside the state, said nothing to suggest that separate-but-equal graduate education within a state was impermissible.

The years between the world wars marked a racial watershed as attitudes and practices became more progressive for the first time since Reconstruction. Several Court decisions reflected that progress, making new law for the protection of civil rights. Yet progress was minimal as compared with that which World War II would trigger.

2

World War II

World War II was a transformative event in the history of American race relations. The ideology of the war was antifascist and prodemocratic. President Franklin D. Roosevelt urged Americans to "refut[e] at home the very theories which we are fighting abroad." Frank Knox, the secretary of the navy, declared that "an army fighting allegedly for Democracy should be the last place in which to practice undemocratic segregation." Justice Frank Murphy informed his colleagues that statutory racial distinctions are "at variance with the principles for which we are now waging war."[1]

Yet many blacks were cynical about the purportedly democratic objectives of the war, spotting a paradox in America's fighting against world fascism with a segregated army. Blacks used their resentments constructively by adding a second front to the war, which became a fight against fascism at home as well as abroad. The *Pittsburgh Courier*, a leading black newspaper, observed a year before Pearl Harbor that "our war is not against Hitler in Europe, but against the Hitlers in America." In

1944, students at Howard University seeking to desegregate a restaurant in the District of Columbia carried signs that asked, "Are you for Hitler's Way or the American Way?" Many blacks reasoned that if they were good enough to die on the battlefield in this ostensibly democratic war, then they were "good enough to vote" and "good enough for organized baseball."[2]

During the war, blacks began more forcefully to demand their citizenship rights. Southern blacks registered to vote in record numbers and demanded admission to Democratic primaries. James Hinton, head of the National Association for the Advancement of Colored People (NAACP) in South Carolina, reported that blacks were "aroused as never before, and we expect great things to come from this awakening." Weary of Jim Crow indignities, many southern blacks refused to be segregated any longer on streetcars and buses, stood their ground when challenged, and thus provoked almost daily racial altercations. Hundreds of thousands of blacks channeled their militancy into NAACP membership, which increased ninefold during the war. Richmond newspaper editor Virginius Dabney observed that the war had "roused in the breasts of our colored friends hopes, aspirations, and desires which they formerly did not entertain, except in the rarest instances."[3]

World War II afforded unprecedented political opportunities for blacks to leverage concessions from the Roosevelt administration, which was determined to avoid divisive racial protest during wartime. The March on Washington movement sponsored by A. Philip Randolph, the head of the Brotherhood of Sleeping Car Porters, aimed to mobilize 100,000 blacks to march on the nation's capital in 1941 to protest race discrimination in the military and the defense industries. The prospect of such a march "scared the government half to death." Desperate to avoid such a spectacle, Roosevelt issued an executive order banning employment discrimination in defense industries and in the federal government and establishing a Fair Employment Practices Commission (FEPC) to monitor compliance.[4]

World War II also created valuable economic opportunities for blacks. Military conscription produced labor shortages, which induced many war industries to relax their restrictions on hiring black workers. Unemployment among blacks fell from 937,000 in 1940 to 151,000 four years later, and the number of skilled black industrial workers doubled. The average income of urban black workers rose more than 100 percent during the war, a hefty increase even adjusting for inflation. Black soldiers, though still suffering rampant discrimination, received skills training, education, and, for many, the first semblance ever of economic security. War-related economic opportunities helped to foster a black middle class, which proved instrumental to the postwar civil rights movement.

After the war, black soldiers returned home to fight for racial justice. A recently discharged black sailor in Columbia, Tennessee, reflecting the new mood, beat up a white radio repairman who had cursed and struck his mother during a disagreement over a repair job. A race riot ensued. Thousands of black veterans tried to register to vote, apparently sharing the view of one such veteran that "after having been overseas fighting for democracy, I thought that when we got back here we should enjoy a little of it." Thousands more joined the NAACP and helped to launch a postwar civil rights movement.[5]

Veterans were not the only blacks in a mood to fight for racial change. One white southerner observed with a sense of wonder, "It is as if some universal message had reached the great mass of Negroes, urging them to dream new dreams and to protest against the old order." The NAACP branch in Alexandria, Louisiana, informed an obstructionist voter registrar, "You do not seem to realize that the social order [has] changed [now that] over ten thousand Negro men and women died in World War II for 'World Democracy.'" Hundreds of blacks became plaintiffs in postwar lawsuits that demanded teacher pay equalization, the nondiscriminatory administration of voter registration requirements, an end to racial exclusion from public facilities, admission to white graduate and professional schools, and the equalization of grade schools.[6]

broad-based movement for civil rts

Blacks achieved even greater political influence after the war, now that hundreds of thousands of them lived in New York, Pennsylvania, Illinois, Michigan, Ohio, Maryland, and Missouri—states where blacks often held the balance of power between competitive political parties. The battle for black votes was intense in the 1948 presidential campaign. The Republicans adopted a progressive civil rights plank, and their presidential nominee, Thomas Dewey, had a strong record on race as governor of New York, including signing into law the nation's toughest fair-employment measure. President Harry S Truman proposed wide-ranging civil rights legislation and issued executive orders desegregating the military and the federal civil service. In the summer of 1948, the Democratic National Convention had a floor fight over civil rights, which the progressives won. Though the Democrats' racial activism produced a Dixiecrat revolt, the president and his political advisors correctly calculated that southern losses would be more than counterbalanced by northern gains. Indeed, had blacks voted roughly 2–1 for Dewey rather than for Truman, Republicans would have won the White House.

1948 Elections – black vote mattered

The Cold War, together with America's postwar emergence as an international superpower, also facilitated progressive racial change. As Americans and Soviets competed for the allegiance of a predominantly nonwhite Third World, U.S. race relations acquired international significance. In the ideological contest with communism, U.S. democracy was on trial, and southern white supremacy was its greatest vulnerability.

One State Department expert estimated that nearly half of all Soviet propaganda directed against the United States involved race issues. In 1946, Soviet foreign minister V. M. Molotov asked Secretary of State Jimmy Byrnes how Americans could justify pressing the Soviets to conduct free elections in Poland when America did not guarantee them in South Carolina or Georgia. In 1951, America's delegates to the United Nations were held to account for the rampaging white mobs driving blacks out of an apartment building in Cicero, Illinois. These and other similar racial atrocities received front-page newspaper coverage in communist and nonwhite nations around the world.

The Cold War imperative influenced the behavior of the federal government. The State Department, not known as a bastion of racial progressivism, strongly urged racial reform for Cold War reasons. Truman's civil rights committee observed, "The United States is not so strong, the final triumph of the democratic ideal is not so inevitable that we can ignore what the world thinks of us or our record." In embracing civil rights, Truman stressed "how closely our democracy is under observation," and he noted that the "top dog in a world which is half colored ought to clean his own house."[7]

The worldwide decolonization that followed the war was important not only because it helped to create a Cold War imperative for racial change but also because it provided an inspirational example to American blacks, who saw domestic racial reform as "part and parcel of the struggle against imperialism and exploitation in [the Third World]." Black leaders hoped that if the principle of self-determination for colonized peoples could be established, "a tide of change would rush forth that the United States could not resist." Thus, civil rights leaders attended the inaugural session of the United Nations in San Francisco in April 1945 with a dual agenda: racial equality at home and colonial self-determination abroad.[8]

The postwar social and political context of race was changing at all levels: national, southern, and northern. The national government's position on civil rights shifted dramatically during the 1940s, as reflected by the creation of the FEPC, the Justice Department's prosecution of lynchings, its submission of briefs in civil rights cases, the appointment of Truman's civil rights committee, civil rights bills proposed by the president, and executive orders desegregating the military and the federal civil service.

Changes in national racial practices also occurred outside of government. Perhaps of greatest symbolic significance was the desegregation of professional baseball, the national pastime, which took place in 1946–1947. By 1950, blacks were also playing in the National Football League and the National Basketball Association. In 1949, the American Medical Association accepted the first black physician into its House of Delegates; the American Nurses Association and the American Association of University Women also admitted blacks for the first time. By the late 1940s, church leaders of all denominations were condemning racial segregation, and Catholic parochial schools desegregated in many cities. For the first time, Hollywood began confronting racial issues, such as interracial marriage and lynching.

Not only had the national government become more committed to civil rights, but it had also developed a greater capacity to enforce that commitment. During Reconstruction, all that was available to enforce national racial policy in recalcitrant southern states was a downsized army. The federal bureaucracy then was minuscule, and federal grant-in-aid programs did not exist. The vast spending programs of the New Deal and the postwar national security state made the South more vulnerable to federal edicts on race.

The increased commitment of the national government to civil rights produced a backlash among southern whites, which culminated in the Dixiecrat revolt of 1948. Yet the most notable feature of that revolt may have been its failure. The Dixiecrats carried only the four Deep South states with the largest percentages of blacks, and even those were won only by seizing control of the Democratic party machinery. Outside of the Deep South, the New Deal/Fair Deal coalition held up well for Truman. The president won all of the other southern states, and in all of them but one, Dewey ran second. At the state level, with just a few exceptions, economically populist and racially moderate politicians continued to thrive by supporting expanded government services—education, roads, public health, old-age pensions—and downplaying race.

One reason that the Dixiecrats failed and that race-baiters at the state level generally were unsuccessful was the changing racial attitudes of southern whites. A contemporary political scientist concluded, "The failure of the Dixiecrats in 1948 and 1950 demonstrated that great masses of southerners would no longer be bamboozled by racist appeals." Though most white southerners remained adamantly opposed to grade school desegregation, their overall commitment to white supremacy was less intense than it had been. Many were now prepared to accept some racial reforms, such as the equalization of education spending, fairer legal treatment of blacks, greater black political participation, and occasionally even an end to segregation in some contexts, such as transportation.[9]

This liberalization of white racial opinion was a function of several changes sweeping the South: the rising education levels of both whites and blacks, urbanization, industrialization, and demographic shifts. As southern whites became better educated, their commitment to white supremacy gradually slackened. The level of education for blacks was rising even faster. In 1910, only 5,000 blacks attended college in the United States; in 1948, more than 88,000 did. A better-educated black population undermined one of Jim Crow's original justifications: protecting whites from being dragged down by illiterate freedmen. Did whites need to be insulated from an "inferior" race that produced, for example, Ralph Bunche, the Nobel Peace Prize winner?

Urbanization facilitated racial progress because cities had better schools and because urban racial mores proved to be less restrictive than those in the countryside. World War II had helped to erode southern insularity by exposing the region to novel external influences. Millions of southerners temporarily left home for military service and confronted different racial norms for the first time in their lives. Army surveys found that whites who served in integrated combat units underwent profound changes in their racial attitudes. Some white veterans, tired of seeing their black comrades-in-arms "crap[ped] all over," enlisted in progressive racial causes.[10]

Accelerating black emigration from the South also ameliorated the racial attitudes of white southerners. Historically, whites who lived in heavily black counties manifested the staunchest commitments to white supremacy. The number of such counties fell dramatically in the 1940s and 1950s.

Another important demographic force for progressive racial change was the growing migration to the South of northern whites, who were in search of greater economic opportunity and a more favorable climate. These migrants, most of them natives of New England or the upper Midwest, were disproportionately well educated and brought more egalitarian racial mores with them. In Florida and Virginia, these relocated northern whites were already affecting the politics of race by the early 1950s.

A final factor contributing to the changing racial attitudes of whites was the gradual erosion of Jim Crow's basic premise: that the black and white races were fundamentally different. By the 1930s, most scientists had repudiated theories of biological racial differences. By the 1940s, this shift in scientific paradigms was filtering down to popular opinion, assisted by the widespread revulsion against Nazism. Southern whites were resistant to the new understanding because of their heavy cultural investments in white supremacy. Still, by the 1940s, younger and better-educated whites in the South were having a harder time rationalizing Jim Crow.

Even those white southerners whose commitment to white supremacy remained undiminished found it harder after the war to preserve traditional racial practices. Distinctive regional mores, such as Jim Crow, are difficult to maintain in a nation that watches the same movies and television programs and is densely interconnected by highways, airplanes, and long-distance telephone wires. A more integrated nation was likelier to evolve a single set of racial practices and beliefs, probably some combination of the northern and southern varieties.

Moreover, the increasing social, economic, and cultural integration of the nation made it more costly to maintain aberrant regional practices. By resisting national trends toward greater racial equality, the South risked forfeiting industrial relocations, opportunities to host national conventions, and spring-training visits from the integrated Brooklyn Dodgers. The expansion of mass media also ensured that deviant southern racial practices received national—often international—attention. No longer could the news of southern racial atrocities be contained within the bounds of a generally sympathetic southern community.

In combination, these factors translated into genuine racial reform. Black voter registration in the South rose from roughly 250,000 in 1940 to 750,000 in 1948 and then to more than 1 million in 1952. In large cities such as New Orleans, Atlanta, and Memphis, blacks were able to qualify to vote almost as easily as in northern cities, and black voters occasionally held the balance of power in local elections. Even at the state level, black voters may have been the deciding factor in the narrow election victories in 1948 of economically populist and racially moderate politicians, such as Lyndon Johnson in Texas, Sid McMath in Arkansas, and Fuller Warren in Florida. By 1954, southern blacks served on eleven city councils and on fifteen boards of education.

Southern blacks used their newly secured suffrage rights to extract concessions from increasingly responsive local governments. Protection against police brutality was a top priority for many blacks, and dozens of southern cities hired their first black police officers after the war. Southern cities also began providing black communities with better public services and recreational facilities, and states increased their spending on black education (a response not just to growing black political power but also to the threat of desegregation litigation). Some counties appointed black voter registrars for black precincts.

Cracks in the walls of segregation began to appear in the border states and in parts of the peripheral South. Catholic parochial schools and public swimming pools desegregated in cities such as Baltimore, St. Louis, and Washington, D.C., in the late 1940s. Medical societies in these cities admitted their first blacks, and some theaters and department store lunch counters desegregated. Maryland repealed its Jim Crow transportation law in 1951. Austin, Texas, desegregated its public library, and Mount Sinai Hospital in Miami Beach, Florida, appointed its first black staff physician.

Other changes in racial practices penetrated even further into the South. Many southern cities, even in the Deep South, desegregated their minor league baseball teams. Some blacks in the upper South began playing football for formerly white colleges, and integrated gridiron contests against northern schools that fielded black players became more common throughout the South. In 1952, the Southern Historical Association desegregated its meeting in Knoxville, Tennessee. In 1953, Ralph Bunche spoke in unsegregated public auditoriums in Raleigh, Miami, and Atlanta. In New Orleans, Catholic universities, public parks, and the public library were desegregated in the early 1950s, and the first black Catholic priest in the Deep South was ordained in 1953. Most of these changes in southern racial practices would have been unthinkable before the war.

Significant shifts in racial attitudes and practices also occurred in the North. In the 1930s, northern liberals usually had little to say about race, but after the war, civil rights headed the liberal reform agenda. Hundreds of organizations devoted to improving race relations and promoting civil rights reform were established in northern cities in the late 1940s. Religious organizations in the North condemned race discrimination, and foundations financed studies by social scientists into the origins and the means of eradicating racial prejudice. Legal research in support of civil rights litigation became a favorite pro bono project of students at the Columbia University School of Law.

A barrage of civil rights legislation was enacted in the North after the war. A dozen or so states adopted fair employment measures, as did many cities. Though most of these laws had little practical effect, their passage symbolized the increased political power of northern blacks and the liberalization of white racial attitudes. Some northern states adopted far-reaching prohibitions on race discrimination in public accommodations, and a couple of them enacted novel measures that threatened to terminate state aid for school districts that were in violation of legal bans on segregation. These laws quickly desegregated schools in the southern counties of Illinois, Indiana, and New Jersey—years before the Court confronted southern school segregation in *Brown v. Board of Education*. In 1946, California repealed its statutory authorization for the segregation of Asians in public schools, and a federal judge invalidated the state's policy of segregating Mexican Americans.

desegregation

To be sure, not all social and political forces favored progressive racial reform in the postwar years. Northern whites proved to be nearly as committed to maintaining residential segregation as were southern whites. The McCarthyism of the early 1950s hindered the civil rights movement, as it did most social reform causes, by enabling opponents to brand reformers as communists. And the burgeoning political power of northern blacks was partially offset by the increasing independence of southern white voters, as manifested by the Dixiecrat revolt of 1948. Yet, notwithstanding these countervailing forces, the extralegal context during the postwar decade was as favorably disposed toward civil rights advances as it had ever been.

contd. resistance

Justices sitting on the high court during the World War II era proved remarkably supportive of progressive racial change. This development was largely fortuitous. By 1946, Presidents Roosevelt and Truman had entirely reconstituted the Court. In appointing new justices, both presidents had focused mainly on getting the Court to repudiate its *Lochner* era commitments to constraining federal power and limiting government regulation of the economy. Neither president manifested any significant interest in the racial views of his prospective nominees.

Roosevelt appointed to the Court a member of the NAACP's legal advisory committee, Felix Frankfurter, and a former Klansman, Hugo Black. He appointed Frank Murphy, another NAACP advisor and a former governor of Michigan, who enjoyed the support of Catholics, Jews, blacks, and labor unions. Yet he also appointed Jimmy Byrnes, a typical white supremacist senator from South Carolina, who had filibustered against antilynching legislation and would later mount a last-ditch defense of school segregation as the governor of his state. Black Americans lauded the appointments of Frankfurter and Murphy and criticized those of Black and Byrnes. Roosevelt seems not to have cared either way.

FDR judicial appmts

Truman appeared almost equally indifferent to the racial views of his Court nominees. He appointed the liberal former mayor of Cleveland,

Truman's choices

Harold Burton, who supported the NAACP and, as a senator from Ohio, endorsed anti–poll-tax legislation and a permanent FEPC. But Truman also appointed southern politicians who shared the racial views of the southern white elite: Fred Vinson of Kentucky and Tom C. Clark of Texas. Truman cared mainly about the willingness of his nominees to sustain the constitutionality of New Deal/Fair Deal economic policies (though political cronyism was also important). Race seems not to have entered the president's calculations. How Truman's appointees would vote on civil rights issues was anybody's guess.

Albeit not by design, the justices appointed by Roosevelt and Truman proved to be remarkably supportive of civil rights. Frankfurter and Murphy reflected the values and interests of core New Deal constituencies. Frankfurter, a Jewish immigrant from Austria who taught at the Harvard Law School, was so liberal on civil rights and civil liberties that his Court appointment had generated significant conservative opposition. During World War I, Frankfurter had encouraged President Woodrow Wilson to pardon the West Coast radical Tom Mooney, who was convicted on slim evidence of planting a bomb that killed ten people at the Preparedness Day Parade in San Francisco in 1916. In the 1920s, Frankfurter had supported the commutation of the death sentences of the Massachusetts anarchists Nicola Sacco and Bartolomeo Vanzetti. The appointment of Frankfurter to the high court reflected the changing composition of the Democratic party; he represented the civil libertarian views of Jews, Catholics, blacks, labor unions, and liberal intellectuals.

Murphy was a hero to many blacks because of his performance as the trial judge in a celebrated 1925 case in Detroit in which blacks were prosecuted for killing a member of a white mob that had sought to drive them from the home they had purchased in a white neighborhood. According to NAACP leaders, Murphy had presided over the trial with "absolute fairness"—no mean accomplishment given the extent of Klan influence in Detroit at that time. As a trial judge and later as the mayor of Detroit and the governor of Michigan, Murphy reflected the views and the values of traditional New Deal constituencies. As Roosevelt's attorney general in 1939, he created the first civil liberties unit in the Justice Department.[11]

Roosevelt's other appointees from the North, such as Robert H. Jackson and William O. Douglas, were not career politicians like Murphy and thus may not have shared his visceral political predisposition in support of civil rights. Neither Jackson nor Douglas had had much occasion to think deeply about race issues before their appointments to the Court. Both were staunch New Dealers and probably shared the tendency of prewar liberals to consider economic issues to be more important than racial ones. However, because they lacked strong racial preconceptions, Jackson and Douglas easily evolved in the same racially egalitarian direction as most members of the northern socioeconomic elite in the 1940s.

Truman made four Court appointments: two southerners (Vinson and Clark) and two northerners (Harold Burton and Sherman Minton). All four were not only New Deal/Fair Deal devotees but also ardent Cold Warriors. Their voting records on civil liberties issues—such as freedom of speech, search and seizure, and coerced confessions—were reactionary compared to those of their colleagues. Yet their performances in race cases were progressive.

The best explanation for these seemingly conflicting voting patterns may be the Cold War imperative for racial change. The predisposition of these justices to defer to the government in speech or criminal procedure cases may have inclined them to support racial equality claims, which came to the Court with the imprimatur of the federal government. In Court briefs, the Justice Department repeatedly invoked the Cold War imperative for racial change, which must have been music to these justices' ears.

In the 1940s, the South remained an important Democratic constituency, which had to be acknowledged in appointments to the Court, yet the white southerners appointed by Roosevelt and Truman did not prove to be significant impediments to racial reform. Jimmy Byrnes, who might have proved to be such an obstacle, fortuitously retired after just one year's service (1941–1942) to help Roosevelt run the war. Black, who was initially derided as "Justice K.K.K. Black," quickly proved to be an unlikely champion of racial equality.[12]

The other southern appointees of Roosevelt and Truman hailed from border states or the peripheral South—Reed and Vinson from Kentucky and Clark from Texas—and thus their commitment to white supremacy was probably somewhat attenuated. All three had served in important administration positions, which probably made them better attuned than most southern politicians to the critical role played by northern blacks in the New Deal coalition. As we shall see, in the 1950s, these three justices manifested varying degrees of sympathy for grade school segregation. However, on most other race issues—for example, white primaries, segregation in graduate and professional schools, and judicial enforcement of racially restrictive covenants—they showed little hesitation about joining or even authoring opinions in support of racial equality. Though their positions did not mirror those of most white southerners, they may have been consistent with those held by well-educated, relatively affluent, southern white lawyers.

The new justices were personally more supportive of racial equality, and so were the Court's revised institutional commitments. As Roosevelt began reconstituting the Court in the late 1930s, the justices abandoned their protection of contract and property rights, granting legislatures a free hand in economic regulation. However, rather than extending across the board this newfound deference to legislatures, the justices began assuming a special role in protecting rights integral to the democratic process, such as voting and free speech, and the equality rights of "discrete and insular" minorities.

Carolene Products footnote

The Court first explicitly articulated this new judicial role in a footnote to a 1938 opinion, *United States v. Carolene Products Co.* There, Justice Harlan Fiske Stone observed that the ordinary presumption of constitutionality applying to legislation was inoperable when a law "restricts those political processes which can ordinarily be expected to bring about repeal of undesirable legislation" or implicates "prejudice against discrete and insular minorities . . . which tends seriously to curtail the operation of those political processes ordinarily to be relied upon to protect minorities." In the following years, the justices incorporated this "political process" theory of judicial review into constitutional doctrine, rendering landmark decisions that expanded the equality rights of blacks and the First Amendment rights of political dissidents, religious minorities, and labor unions.[13]

VOTING

white primary

The most significant suffrage issue for the Court during this period was the white primary. *Grovey v. Townsend* (1935) had unanimously ruled that the exclusion of blacks from Democratic primaries by party resolution did not qualify as state action under the Fourteenth or Fifteenth amendments. In *Smith v. Allwright* (1944), the justices voted 8–1 to overrule *Grovey* and invalidate the white primary. The Court emphasized the many ways in which Texas regulated parties and primaries, including setting the date of primary elections, requiring that they be conducted in certain ways, and subjecting them to state oversight. *Smith* also observed that Texas could not escape responsibility by "casting its electoral processes in a form which permits a private organization to practice racial discrimination in the election."[14]

This shift, within the short span of nine years, from a unanimous decision sustaining white primaries to a near-unanimous ruling invalidating them, is unprecedented in U.S. constitutional history. One might attribute the turnabout to Roosevelt's nearly complete reconstitution of the Court, but this would be to miss the fundamental importance of World War II. With black soldiers dying on battlefields around the world, the justices must have been tempted to help move America, as the *New York Times* put it, "a little nearer to a more perfect democracy, in which there will be but one class of citizens."[15]

Another reason that *Smith* may have proved relatively easy for the justices—as a matter of politics, if not law—was that most Americans would have supported it. Northern opinion regarding poll-tax repeal supports this surmise; a 1940s Gallup poll revealed that nearly 70 percent of Americans favored repealing the tax, and northern congressional representatives voted overwhelmingly to abolish it for federal elections. Northerners had little reason to feel differently about white primaries and poll taxes, both of which restricted suffrage in only seven or eight southern states by the mid-1940s.

Even southern whites were far less committed to preserving black disfranchisement than they were to maintaining school segregation. A white Democrat in South Carolina wrote to Thurgood Marshall, the head of legal operations for the National Association for the Advancement of Colored People, to distance himself from his party's efforts to exclude blacks, which "profane the Bill of Rights." A white Democrat in Alabama criticized her party's proscription of blacks as a "cruel and shameful thing." By the late 1940s, opinion polls showed a clear southern majority in favor of abolishing poll taxes.[16]

Smith did not definitively resolve the white primary issue. To the extent that the outcome in *Smith* turned on the extensive regulation of parties and primaries by the state of Texas, deregulation was a natural response. Within a fortnight, the governor of South Carolina, Olin Johnston, convened a special legislative session to repeal all 150 state statutes regulating parties. Other Deep South states watched and waited, as lower courts wrestled with South Carolina's efforts at circumventing *Smith*.

In *Elmore v. Rice* (1947), federal district judge J. Waties Waring invalidated the exclusion of blacks from Democratic primaries in South Carolina, notwithstanding the legislature's efforts at political deregulation. Waring emphasized the determinative nature of Democratic primaries and the extent to which state law had regulated parties prior to the recent deregulation. Waring thought it "pure sophistry" to suggest that legislative deregulation had altered political realities. He also denied that "the skies [would] fall," as predicted, if

Democrats permitted blacks to participate in their primaries. The Fourth Circuit Court of Appeals affirmed Waring in a less flamboyant opinion. Probably delighted to have southern judges running interference on a sensitive racial issue, the justices denied review. Other states in the Deep South now abandoned thoughts of deregulation.[17]

One more variation on the white primary remained for the justices' consideration. In Fort Bend County, Texas, the Jaybird Democratic Association had been excluding blacks from its pre-primary selection of candidates since 1889. The association, whose membership consisted of all whites who resided in the county, selected candidates who invariably became the Democratic nominees and then were elected to office. Similar schemes operated in other East Texas counties. Though the Jaybirds were not created to circumvent *Smith* and *Elmore*, it is easy to imagine much of the South following suit if the Court were to sustain this scheme. Justices at the conference discussion of *Terry v. Adams* (1953) expressed concern that "[i]f this is approved it will be seized upon."[18]

The difficulty for the justices, though, was that finding state action in the Jaybirds' scheme risked eliminating any protection for private political association. Several justices had worried in *Smith* that extending the ban on race discrimination from government to political parties would interfere with the freedom of political association. In *Terry*, they were being asked to go further and forbid discrimination by a political club that state law did not regulate. Would they be asked next to prohibit individuals from mobilizing their friends in support of candidates who espoused white supremacy? Justice Jackson expressed a concern that others shared: Did not the "people have some rights" to political affiliation?[19]

The conflict felt by the justices over whether to protect associational rights or to safeguard their earlier white primary rulings from nullification is apparent in *Terry*'s seesaw history. The initial conference vote was 5–4 to *reject* the constitutional challenge. A second vote was 4–4, with Frankfurter passing. During the conference discussion, Frankfurter had said that he "can't see where [the] state comes in." He then changed his vote without explanation, thus creating a 5–4 majority to invalidate the Jaybirds' scheme. But four justices—Vinson, Reed, Minton, and Jackson—remained slated to dissent. Jackson, worried about infringing on private associational behavior and doubting whether the Jaybirds' electoral success was relevant to the state-action question, drafted a dissent that lambasted his colleagues for sacrificing "sound principle[s] of interpretation" in their haste to inter the "hateful little local scheme."[20]

Yet, when *Terry* was announced, only Minton dissented. Once their position no longer commanded a majority, Jackson, Reed, and Vinson apparently preferred subordinating "sound principle[s] of interpretation" to sustaining an abhorrent disfranchisement scheme. That same year, the justices confronted a similar law-politics dilemma on the more explosive issue of school segregation. As in *Terry*, they agonized over the conflict before deciding to elevate politics over their understanding of the law.

[handwritten margin note: final vote — one dissent]

HIGHER EDUCATION

Southern states historically provided blacks with no graduate or professional education, a seemingly flagrant violation of separate but equal. Beginning mainly in the 1930s, several southern states established out-of-state scholarships to finance higher education for their black citizens in those northern universities that were willing to accept them. *Missouri ex rel. Gaines v. Canada* (1938) invalidated such programs on the ground that states were constitutionally obliged to provide equal services to blacks *within* their boundaries. As a result, a few border and peripheral southern states began offering some graduate courses for blacks. Only Maryland and West Virginia integrated any programs. Most southern states continued to offer nothing. Ten years after *Gaines*, not a single southern state admitted blacks to a Ph.D. program, and only one accredited law school and one medical school in the South accepted blacks.

[handwritten margin note: Started a prof. opps. for blacks in the south]

The NAACP initially hoped that higher education litigation would pressure southern states to appropriate sufficiently large sums for equalizing black opportunities that they would eventually capitulate by integrating. Those hopes were quickly dashed, as southern legislatures after *Gaines* declined to significantly increase appropriations for black higher education. The small increase in funding that did occur was for out-of-state scholarships, which many states now adopted for the first time, even though *Gaines* had ruled them unconstitutional. Lower courts generally interpreted *Gaines* narrowly. Rather than ordering the immediate admission to white universities of black applicants who were being denied higher education, courts gave southern officials time to establish equal black facilities after a demand had been made for them.

[handwritten margin note: result of Gaines]

No more higher education cases reached the Court in the decade after *Gaines*. (Lloyd Gaines himself mysteriously disappeared, disrupting

NAACP plans to challenge Missouri's evasive response to the Supreme Court's ruling.) The NAACP had serious financial problems in the late 1930s; plaintiffs proved difficult to locate; and prospective suits were held in abeyance during World War II.

A slew of higher education lawsuits were filed immediately after the war, however, as black veterans took advantage of the GI Bill of Rights to apply to white universities. Southern states, anticipating or reacting to such suits, enacted laws that required education officials to establish, on demand, separate-and-equal programs of advanced education for blacks, and they appropriated significant sums for these programs. State judges, impressed with such legislative efforts, generally found these separate black institutions to be adequate, though the NAACP called them "Jim Crow dumps."[21]

In 1946, Heman Sweatt applied to the all-white University of Texas School of Law. During the litigation, Texas first set up an interim black law school and, later, a permanent one. The NAACP challenged the adequacy of this arrangement, and it also directly attacked the constitutionality of segregation in higher education. The Court declined to confront the latter question on the ground that the case could be more narrowly resolved. Yet the reasoning used by the justices to find the black law school unequal essentially nullified segregation in higher education.

The inferiority of Texas's black law school was not so obvious as to go uncontested. The admissions requirements and curricula of the black and white schools were the same; the three instructors at the black law school also taught at the University of Texas; and the smaller student body of the black law school afforded some pedagogical advantages. A former president of the American Bar Association testified that the schools offered equal educational opportunities.

The Court thought otherwise. The justices noted tangible features of the black school that were obviously inferior: the size of the faculty, the number of books in the library, and the absence of opportunities for law review and moot court. They also emphasized intangible differences "incapable of objective measurement but which make for greatness in a law school . . . [:] reputation of the faculty, experience of the administration, position and influence of the alumni, standing in the community, traditions and prestige." Finally, the justices observed that segregating Sweatt denied him the opportunity to interact with whites, who were 85 percent of the population in Texas and accounted for most of its lawyers, witnesses, and judges. Equal legal education was impossible with "such a substantial and significant segment of society excluded." Because equal protection rights are "personal," the Court refused to tolerate the delay that creating an equal black law school would require; instead, it ordered the immediate admission of Sweatt to the University of Texas.[22]

Vinson's opinion for the unanimous Court in *Sweatt v. Painter* (1950) refused to reconsider *Plessy*. Yet, a newly created black law school could not possibly have achieved equality with regard to the intangible factors identified in *Sweatt*. Indeed, the justices' concern that attending the black law school would deny Sweatt interaction with Texas's numerically dominant whites was impossible to reconcile with segregation. Thus, most commentators thought that *Sweatt* had nullified segregation in higher education, and some believed that it had left the separate-but-equal doctrine generally "a mass of tatters."[23]

popular understudies of decision

On the same day as *Sweatt*, the Court in *McLaurin v. Oklahoma* (1950) ordered a graduate education school to cease segregating—in classrooms, the library, and the cafeteria—the black man it had admitted pursuant to federal court order. The justices declared that segregation restrictions impaired George McLaurin's ability to learn his profession. As he was receiving a tangibly equal education, the justices were apparently no longer prepared to accept segregation *within* an institution of higher education. *Sweatt* had proscribed segregation in *separate* institutions. That seemed to leave nowhere left for segregation to remain.

McLaurin

Both *Sweatt* and *McLaurin* represented clear changes in the law. *Gaines* had simply insisted that blacks receive something, but the 1950 rulings interpreted "equality" so stringently that segregation in higher education became impossible. Had separate but equal always meant this, the South could not have constructed a social system around it. The briefs of Oklahoma and Texas had simply urged the Court to follow precedent. The lower court decisions in these cases had insisted that tangible factors be equalized, but they had rejected on the basis of precedent the direct challenge posed to segregation. The Court's focus on intangibles was unprecedented.

significant shift

These rulings were not as easy for the justices as the unanimous outcomes might suggest. Several of them were troubled by the departures from precedent and original intent. The two Kentuckians, Reed and Vinson, were initially inclined to reject Sweatt's challenge. At conference, Vinson opined that the original understanding of the Fourteenth Amendment did not cover public education, and he listed numerous precedents that sustained separate-but-equal education. Reed likewise thought that it was "hard . . . to say something that has been constitutional for years is suddenly bad. The 14th Amendment was not aimed at segregation."[24]

Jackson was similarly troubled by *Sweatt*. He observed at conference that he could "find no basis for [the] idea that [the] Fourteenth

[Amendment] reached schools." In correspondence, Jackson worried that *Sweatt* required the Court not merely to "fill gaps or construe the Amendment to include matters which were unconsidered" but "to include what was deliberately and intentionally excluded." Yet, even though he believed that the Court was essentially "amending the Constitution," Jackson ultimately supported Sweatt's claim.[25]

Sweatt and *McLaurin*, inconsistent with legal sources that were generally considered binding by these justices, are best explained in terms of social and political change. By 1950, major league baseball had been desegregated for three years—a salient development for several of the justices, who were huge fans. The military was undergoing gradual desegregation, pursuant to Truman's 1948 executive order. The Court's first black law clerk, William T. Coleman, had served two terms earlier and authored a memo to Frankfurter urging that *Plessy* be overruled. Coleman demonstrated by his very presence at the Court that segregated legal education could no longer be defended on the basis of black inferiority.

Several justices probably shared Jackson's conviction that "the segregation system [in higher education] is breaking down of its own weight and that a little time will end it in nearly all States." Clark observed that "the forces of progress in the South" were already eroding segregation in higher education. The assistant attorney general of Oklahoma conceded at oral argument in *McLaurin* that there might not be "much point" any longer to such segregation, which he predicted would be gone within a decade in his state.[26]

The Truman administration intervened in these cases to urge that *Plessy* be overruled; the attorney general told the justices that "[u]nless segregation is ended, a serious blow will be struck at our democracy before the world." Burton received a letter applauding his opinion in a 1950 case invalidating segregation in railroad dining cars (discussed below), because it "deprives communist agitators of one more weapon in their war upon our free society." The justices' unanimity in all three 1950 race cases—an impressive accomplishment for this ordinarily splintered Court—is most plausibly attributable to the influence of this Cold War imperative.[27]

Furthermore, the justices were aware that white southerners were no longer universally hostile to the desegregation of higher education. When a black woman sought admission to the University of Oklahoma Law School in 1946, a thousand white students demonstrated in her support. Two thousand white students and faculty members rallied in support of Sweatt's suit against the University of Texas Law School, and

[margin annotations: "factors leading to decisions to end segregation"; "Truman admin."; "popular opinion"]

white students there organized a college chapter of the NAACP—the only all-white branch in the country. Opinion polls conducted at these universities showed substantial—even majority—support among students for integration. Faculty members overwhelmingly supported it.

Thus, the justices had no reason to expect violence or school closures in response to their decisions, which would certainly not be so with regard to *Brown v. Board of Education*. Clark dismissed as "groundless" the parade of horrors invoked in the brief of the southern attorneys general. Vinson observed that "no great harm would come from association in professional schools." In fact, the southern reaction to these rulings was almost entirely nonviolent, and many white students extended blacks a warm welcome. White reaction might have been rather different a decade earlier, when law students at the University of Missouri had predicted that Lloyd Gaines would be "treated like a dog" if admitted.[28]

Finally, the justices tend to reflect the opinions of a cultural elite more than those of the general public. By 1950, that elite, even in the South to a certain extent, had repudiated segregation in higher education. One amicus brief in *Sweatt*, which urged that *Plessy* be overruled, was signed by 187 law professors and deans—the sort of people whose opinions the justices were likely to share. Deans of some of the most prestigious law schools in the country had testified on the NAACP's behalf at trial, denying that separate black law schools could possibly be equal.

academic elite

The Court's functional overruling of *Plessy* in higher education did not necessarily predict the result in *Brown*. The intangible factors emphasized in *Sweatt*, such as faculty reputation and alumni standing, are more important in law schools than in grade schools. In a 1950 memo, Clark pointed out to his colleagues that "it is entirely possible that Negroes in segregated grammar schools being taught arithmetic, spelling, geography, etc., would receive skills in these elementary subjects equivalent to those of segregated white students."[29]

Moreover, the justices had strong practical reasons for declining to extend the 1950 rulings to grade schools. Southern white resistance to the desegregation of higher education was minimal outside of the Deep South. Very few blacks were involved, and those whites most directly affected tended to be young (male) adults, not impressionable children, and also were those with the most progressive racial attitudes (because they were the best educated).

grade schools vs grad schools

By contrast, grade school desegregation would involve huge numbers of blacks and whites, including the youngest, and would cut across class and gender lines. The justices were fully aware that, however placid the reaction to the 1950 rulings, grade school desegregation "would involve a social revolution." Thurgood Marshall was not confident that the justices would make the leap from graduate schools to grade schools any time soon. The solicitor general, Philip B. Perlman, who favored the administration's involvement in the 1950 cases, drew the line at grade school segregation.[30]

Internal deliberations in the 1950 cases revealed that the justices had yet to decide how far to go. Justice Black thought it possible to distinguish between segregation in grade schools and in graduate schools on the ground that segregation in higher education was "wholly unreasonable"; he left open the door to "reasonable segregation." Clark likewise distinguished the two sorts of educational segregation and opposed extending *Sweatt* "at this time." He said that he did not know how he would vote in grade school cases, and "[s]hould they arise tomorrow, I would vote to deny certiorari or dismiss the appeal." Minton, too, preferred to avoid that issue, noting, "[W]e can meet grade and high schools whenever we get to it." The result in *Brown* was apparently anything but a foregone conclusion in 1950.[31]

RESIDENTIAL SEGREGATION

Corrigan v. Buckley (1926) rejected a constitutional challenge to racially restrictive covenants on the ground that state action was absent, while it strongly hinted that even judicial enforcement of such agreements would not violate the Constitution. The NAACP persisted in treating the latter issue as unresolved, and several efforts over the next twenty years to secure clarification failed, as the justices refused to grant review in restrictive covenant cases.

By the late 1940s, however, the justices may have felt that they could no longer responsibly evade the issue. The lack of new housing construction during the Great Depression and World War II, combined with the massive increases in urban populations that were a result of internal migration, had led to severe housing shortages. In some northern cities, a huge percentage of the housing stock was covered by racially restrictive covenants. Black populations that had multiplied several times over were confined to ghetto neighborhoods that had barely expanded in space. Racial conflict over scarce housing was pervasive and helped to cause a deadly race riot in Detroit in 1943. By the end of World War II, hundreds of lawsuits throughout the nation sought to enforce racially restrictive covenants, while defendants challenged the constitutionality of judicial enforcement.

Shelley v. Kraemer (1948) was an injunction suit to prevent a black family from taking possession of property covered by such a covenant. The defense was that judicial enforcement would violate the Equal Protection Clause. Precedent on this issue was about as clear as it ever gets: All nineteen state high courts that had considered the issue had rejected the constitutional challenge. By 1946, the Court of Appeals for the District of Columbia Circuit had ruled seven times that the Constitution permitted judicial enforcement of racially restrictive covenants. Chief Justice Vinson had participated as a lower court judge in one of those decisions. Thurgood Marshall was reluctant to press the restrictive covenant issue, given the clarity of the precedents and the number of NAACP defeats in lower courts, but the association was unable to control the litigation. Given hostile precedent, the NAACP's brief relied mainly on sociological data regarding the inadequacy of ghetto housing and on vague and legally nonbinding sources, such as the Atlantic Charter and the UN charter.

Precedent notwithstanding, the Court in *Shelley* barred judicial enforcement of racially restrictive covenants. Vinson's opinion explained that judicial orders, like legislation and executive action, can qualify as state action—a point that nobody disputed. The Court had ruled many times that judges engaged in jury selection or in devising common-law rules, such as restrictions on union picketing, were state actors bound by the Constitution. The question in *Shelley* was different: Did judicial enforcement of *private* racially discriminatory agreements violate the Fourteenth Amendment? Vinson failed to appreciate the difference between these issues: judges discriminating themselves and judges enforcing private discriminatory contracts just as they would any other agreement.

Taken seriously, Vinson's rationale in *Shelley* threatened to obliterate the private sphere, as *all* behavior occurs against a backdrop of state-created common-law rules. For example, a discriminatory exclusion of certain people from one's home would be unconstitutional on this theory, once the police were summoned or a trespass prosecution commenced to vindicate property rights. Thus, *Shelley* would have been a revolutionary decision, had subsequent cases taken it seriously, which they never did.

By 1948, public attitudes toward race discrimination specifically and toward state responsibility for private wrongs generally had changed enough to enable the justices to decide *Shelley* as they did. The Great Depression and the New Deal had helped to alter conceptions of government's responsibility for conduct occurring in the private sphere. The

Four Freedoms of the Atlantic Charter included freedom "from want" and "from fear"—not typical negative liberties against government interference, but affirmative rights to government protection from privately inflicted harms. Similar conceptions were implicit in the economic bill of rights touted by Roosevelt in the 1944 election, which asserted government responsibility for providing citizens with decent jobs, health care, housing, and education. Truman invoked this notion of expanded government responsibility in a 1947 speech in which he declared that "the extension of civil rights today means not protection of the people *against* the Government, but protection of the people *by* the Government." The justices responded to such changed understandings of government responsibility by expanding the state-action concept.[32]

Perhaps even more important to *Shelley*'s outcome were changes in racial attitudes. Specifically with regard to racially restrictive covenants, many Americans apparently shared one newspaper's view that a "nation that has poured out its blood and treasure in a war billed as a contest against racism can hardly afford the luxury of forcing its own citizens to live in ghettos." Truman's civil rights committee had recommended legislation to prohibit racially restrictive covenants, and it successfully urged the administration to intervene in litigation challenging judicial enforcement of them. Moreover, restrictive covenants, unlike many racial issues, directly affected other minority groups—Jews, Asians, Latinos, and Native Americans, among others—whose collective interests were likely to command the attention of New Deal Democrats, who dominated the Court at this time.[33]

Before 1948, the constitutionality of judicial enforcement of racially restrictive covenants seemed certain. Nearly twenty state high courts had so ruled, and the justices would not even review such cases as late as 1945 because the law seemed so clear. In 1948, however, they unanimously invalidated the practice (though only six of them participated in the decision, apparently because three of the justices owned property covered by such covenants). Rarely have the justices changed their minds about an issue so swiftly and unanimously. But then, rarely has public opinion on any issue changed as rapidly as did public opinion on race in the postwar years.

TRANSPORTATION

In the wake of World War II, the Court decided two cases involving segregation and discrimination in transportation. *Henderson v. United States*

(1950) raised the question of whether discrimination against black railroad passengers in dining car facilities violated the ban in the Interstate Commerce Act on "undue prejudice or disadvantage." This ruling was relevant to constitutional law, because the Court had long interpreted that statute to impose on private railroads the same equality rules that were mandated for states by the Constitution.

When Henderson's case arose in 1941, the Southern Railway's practice was to set aside two tables for blacks behind a curtain in an eleven-table dining car, but to seat whites there if no blacks had yet appeared for service. Blacks who arrived while whites were occupying the "black" tables had to wait until they were completely empty to be seated, whereas whites continued to be accommodated at all tables. Under these rules, Henderson was unable to secure a dining car seat during his entire journey.

By the time the litigation reached the Interstate Commerce Commission (ICC), the railroad had changed its policy, and the commission ruled that, even though the old practices were discriminatory, Henderson was unlikely to suffer from them any more. Under the new rules, once a black person had requested dining car service, the stewards were to cease placing whites at the "black" tables. The ICC found this practice substantially equal, but the district court disagreed, as blacks were still not guaranteed service on the same terms as whites, because whites could potentially sit at any table, and blacks could not.

The railway then changed its policy again, this time allocating one table behind a wood partition exclusively to blacks. The ICC upheld this practice on the ground that blacks, though generating less than 5 percent of the dining car demand, were receiving 9 percent of the seating space. The district court affirmed, but the Supreme Court reversed.

Henderson did not involve the total exclusion of blacks from luxury services, which an earlier case had. Moreover, under the railroad's latest dining car policy, blacks were receiving *more* space than their racial demand warranted. Yet the case was still relatively easy for the justices. Several high court precedents had insisted that equal protection rights are personal—that is, they belong to individuals, not groups. Thus, the relevant question in *Henderson* was not whether blacks received the same average benefits as whites, but whether particular blacks received the same benefits as particular whites. The answer was clearly not. If a black person entered the dining car when the "black" table was full, he would be denied service, while a white person arriving simultaneously might be served. This was racial inequality, as the justices had previously defined it.

Yet *Henderson* did not stop there. Though the justices declined an invitation to explicitly reconsider *Plessy*, the opinion implicitly condemned segregation. Relying on *McLaurin*, which was decided on the same day, Burton's opinion for the unanimous Court criticized the wood partition separating the "black" table because it highlighted "the artificiality of a difference in treatment which serves only to call attention to a racial classification of passengers." Because all forms of segregation would seem vulnerable to that objection, *Henderson* hinted at broader implications.[34]

If *Henderson* was easy legally, it was a laugher politically. The justices had not hesitated to condemn race discrimination in railroad accommodations in 1941 (in *Mitchell v. United States*), before the war had crystallized a national civil rights consciousness. A decade later, public opinion was much less tolerant of race discrimination in transportation. In 1949, the administration actually proposed legislation to forbid segregation in interstate transportation. The attorney general, J. Howard McGrath, made a rare Court appearance in *Henderson* and asked the justices to overrule *Plessy*.

The facts made the case even more compelling. Henderson was an FEPC field representative, who was denied service while returning from Birmingham, Alabama, where he had helped to organize local hearings on employment discrimination. The justices could not have been favorably disposed toward sustaining railroad discrimination against federal government employees, especially given the valuable propaganda opportunities it afforded the Soviets.

Though law and politics made *Henderson* easy, the justices remained ambivalent about the broader segregation issue. As in *Sweatt* and *McLaurin*, they declined invitations to overrule *Plessy*. Yet the rationales of all three decisions raised doubts about the continuing validity of segregation.

The best explanation for why the justices would articulate rationales inconsistent with segregation, while refusing to openly overrule *Plessy*, is that they were divided. At one pole, Douglas was so adamant that *Plessy* be overruled that until virtually the last minute he contemplated concurring separately in *Henderson*. By contrast, Stanley F. Reed stated at the *Henderson* conference that it was "impossible to say that segregation *per se* is prohibited by [the] Constitution." Jackson likewise declared that "we must amend [the Constitution] if we ban segregation." Frankfurter thought it "inconceivable" that the authors of the 1887 Interstate Commerce Act had intended to bar segregation. Thus, in 1950, several of the justices remained reluctant to overrule *Plessy*, even with regard to transportation, where white southerners were less heavily invested in segregation.[35]

The justices actually did condemn segregation in transportation, but under the Dormant Commerce Clause, not the Equal Protection Clause. As early as the 1820s, the Court had ruled that the Commerce Clause of the Constitution is not only an affirmative grant of power to Congress but also a constraint on state power. Determining which state laws so impair interstate commerce as to violate the Constitution has perplexed the justices for nearly two centuries. On the one hand, states have obvious and legitimate interests in regulating behavior that occurs within state boundaries and affects the lives of state citizens. On the other hand, inconsistent state laws regulating national commerce could potentially destroy it, and states have political incentives to engage in economic protectionism, which incites retaliation and could possibly ignite escalating trade wars. By 1946, the Court's efforts to reconcile such competing considerations had produced scores of decisions under the Dormant Commerce Clause — rulings that had proved impossible for the justices or commentators to reconcile. Many of these involved state regulation of railroads.

The application of state laws *forbidding* race discrimination in public accommodations to interstate railroads and ships had provoked constitutional challenges since the 1870s. *Hall v. DeCuir* (1878) invalidated under the Dormant Commerce Clause a Louisiana public accommodations law, as applied to a Mississippi River steamboat, which was carrying interstate travelers. Though the Court never invalidated inverse legislation — measures *requiring* segregation on interstate carriers — dicta in several decisions assumed that such laws would be equally unconstitutional, and the Court consistently construed ambiguous public accommodations laws to cover only *intra*state passengers. Thus, by the time *Morgan v. Virginia* reached the Court in 1946, the law seemed clear: The Dormant Commerce Clause permitted states to segregate intrastate, but not interstate, passengers. The justices could invalidate Virginia's law simply by invoking *DeCuir*.

Yet constitutional law is rarely that simple. The complication in *Morgan* was that the Roosevelt Court had begun to transform doctrine under the Dormant Commerce Clause and was permitting states greater regulatory freedom. The same justices who objected to *Lochner* era constraints on state economic regulation imposed under the guise of substantive due process tended to find pre-1937 Dormant Commerce Clause doctrine too restrictive. For example, in *South Carolina State Highway Department v. Barnwell Brothers* (1938), the Court sustained a state's stringent regulation on the size of trucks, despite the severe burden it imposed on interstate commerce by forcing large vehicles to circumvent the state's highways. The justices had previously invalidated many less burdensome regulations on railroads, which suggests that *Barnwell Brothers* represented a new departure under the Dormant Commerce Clause. Thus, although *DeCuir* clearly indicated that Virginia could not segregate interstate passengers, in 1946, *DeCuir* was not obviously still good law.

Nevertheless, the justices in *Morgan* ruled that Virginia could not segregate interstate bus passengers—a result that is most plausibly explained by their growing solicitude for civil rights. Although the justices were not yet ready to invalidate state-mandated segregation under the Equal Protection Clause—a ruling that would have been difficult to confine to transportation—they were willing to bend Dormant Commerce Clause doctrine to accomplish the same result.

By 1946, the justices had little sympathy for racial segregation in transportation. Extralegal forces that supported progressive racial change in other legal contexts were equally operative in the transportation field. The NAACP's brief in *Morgan* reminded the justices that the nation was just emerging from a "death struggle against the apostles of racism." A Gallup poll conducted in the late 1940s revealed that national opinion opposed racial segregation in interstate transportation by 49 percent to 43 percent.[36]

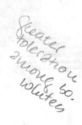

Perhaps more important, the justices appreciated that most southern whites could tolerate an end to segregation in interstate transportation. Interracial contact on buses was transitory, impersonal, and generally involved adults, not children—all features distinguishing it from grade school education. During the war, Virginius Dabney, the racially moderate editor of the *Richmond Times-Dispatch*, advocated desegregating local transportation in Virginia. A few years after *Morgan*, Armistead Boothe, a moderate Virginia legislator who believed that judicially compelled school desegregation would be the "keynote to tragedy," proposed a repeal of the statute that mandated segregation on common carriers. (*Morgan* had required ending segregation only for *inter*state travelers.) One liberal white journalist who favored the measure observed that while public school desegregation "is not seriously considered" by most Virginians, many whites thought that forcing blacks, no matter how "distinguished," to the back of the bus was "idiotic and evil." The justices might well have predicted (rightly) that most southern whites could tolerate the result in *Morgan*.[37]

The availability of a nonracial doctrine such as the Dormant Commerce Clause to achieve a result that the justices found politically appealing may have proved to be irresistible. Reliance on this doctrine enabled the justices to avoid singling out for criticism southern racial policy, as the Dormant Commerce Clause rationale would also condemn the application to interstate transportation of northern laws *forbidding* segregation on common carriers. Perhaps more significant, this rationale forbade segregation only in interstate travel and thus did not directly threaten other forms of segregation. The NAACP appreciated that the justices were probably not ready to invalidate school segregation and thus did not raise the equal protection challenge in *Morgan*. That choice was probably wise, as Frankfurter later observed that he would not have supported a school segregation challenge in the mid-1940s.

3

Brown v. Board of Education

In the spring of 1951, black students at segregated Moton High School in Prince Edward County, Virginia, commenced a strike against overcrowding and other unequal conditions in their school. This sort of youthful black militancy, though it was not uncommon in the postwar South, was a stunning departure from white expectations of black subservience in rural Southside, Virginia.

Local leaders of the National Association for the Advancement of Colored People initially tried to discourage the protest because Prince Edward County seemed like such an inhospitable environment in which to challenge Jim Crow education. When the students would not be dissuaded, however, the association's lawyers agreed to sponsor a lawsuit, but only on the condition that the students and their parents directly attack segregation, which had not been their initial intention. This lawsuit became one of the five consolidated cases that became known to history as *Brown v. Board of Education.*

Student Strike

NAACP

When cases that challenged the constitutionality of racial segregation in public schools reached the Supreme Court in 1951–1952, the social and political context had changed dramatically since 1927, when the justices had last (obliquely) considered the question. Several million blacks had migrated from southern farms to northern cities in search of greater economic opportunities and relative racial tolerance. One largely unintended consequence of this migration was black political empowerment, as blacks relocated from a region of pervasive disfranchisement to one of relatively unrestricted ballot access.

Demographic shifts, industrialization, and the dislocative impact of World War II had produced an urban black middle class with the education, disposable income, and lofty expectations conducive to involvement in social protest. Economic gains enabled blacks to challenge the racial status quo by freeing them from white control and by creating a powerful lever—the economic boycott—for extracting racial reforms. Urbanization facilitated social protest because cities generally had looser restrictions on black suffrage, less repressive racial mores, and superior transportation and communication facilities.

Ideological forces had also helped to transform American racial attitudes and practices. The war against fascism impelled many Americans to reconsider their racial preconceptions in order to clarify the differences between Nazi Germany and the Jim Crow South. The ensuing Cold War pressured Americans to reform their racial practices in order to convince nonwhite Third World nations that they should not equate democratic capitalism with white supremacy. Finally, developments in transportation and communication—television, interstate highways, the expansion of air travel—bound the nation into a more cohesive unit. The homogenization of the United States hindered the white South from maintaining deviant social practices such as Jim Crow.

Potent as these background forces for racial change were, by the early 1950s they had yet to produce any dramatic changes in southern racial practices. Black voter registration in the South had increased from roughly 3 percent in 1940 to about 20 percent in 1952, but 80 percent of southern blacks remained voteless, and many Deep South counties with black majorities still disfranchised blacks entirely. Many southern cities had instituted less offensive racial seating practices on buses, but none had desegregated them. Many other cities had desegregated their police forces and minor league baseball teams, and disparities in the public funding of black and white schools were diminishing. Yet racial segregation in public grade schools remained completely intact in the southern and border states. Preserving school segregation was a top priority of white supremacists. For the Court to invalidate it was certain to generate far greater controversy and resistance than had striking down the white primary or segregation in interstate transportation.

The justices were unenthusiastic about confronting so quickly the issue that they had deliberately evaded in the 1950 university segregation cases. Moreover, these five cases were quite unrepresentative of the southern school segregation issue. Three were from jurisdictions—Kansas, Delaware, and the District of Columbia—where whites were not deeply committed to segregation, and judicial invalidation would probably not cause great disruption. The other two cases, however, came from Clarendon County, South Carolina, and Prince Edward County, Virginia, where blacks were 70 percent and 45 percent of the populations, respectively. Broad forces for racial change had barely touched these counties, where judicial invalidation of school segregation might well jeopardize public education. The NAACP's executive secretary, Roy Wilkins, later confided that Clarendon County "would be the last place on Earth he would pick" to integrate.[1]

Yet, ironically, the NAACP's decision in 1950 to no longer accept equalization cases pushed blacks in these counties to convert their grievances against inferior schools and lack of bus transportation into broad desegregation challenges. The association was not willing to abandon courageous blacks who were willing to challenge Jim Crow under oppressive conditions, but it did pressure them to attack segregation directly, which they would probably not have otherwise done. Some civil rights leaders questioned the wisdom of pushing a desegregation suit on the Court at this time. Why run the risk, they wondered, if narrower challenges to racial inequality were virtually certain to succeed? Even Thurgood Marshall, the NAACP's general counsel, had doubts as to whether the justices were prepared to invalidate school segregation.

On May 17, 1954, the decision in *Brown v. Board of Education* unanimously invalidated racial segregation in public schools. The Court's opinion emphasized the importance of public education in modern life and refused to be bound by the views of the drafters of the Fourteenth Amendment, most of whom had held more benign views of segregation. Segregated public schools were "inherently unequal" and thus violated the Equal Protection Clause of the Fourteenth Amendment. Because a practice that the Court had just invalidated in the states could not possibly be permitted in the capital of the free world, the justices ruled in the companion case of *Bolling v. Sharpe* that the Due Process Clause of the Fifth Amendment imposed identical restrictions on the District of Columbia.

Brown's unanimity can be misleading, because the justices at first were deeply conflicted. When the school segregation cases were first argued in the fall of 1952, the outcome was anything but certain.

Fred M. Vinson began the justices' conference discussion, as the chief justice traditionally does. Vinson was from Kentucky, a border state with southern leanings and a long tradition of segregated education. There is a "[b]ody of law [in] back of us on separate but equal," Vinson announced, and "Congress has not declared there should be no segregation." It is "[h]ard to get away from [the] long continued interpretation of Congress ever since the Amendments." Public schools in the District of Columbia "have long been segregated."[2]

Figure 3.1. The justices who deliberated on *Brown v. Board of Education* in the 1952 term. *Standing, left to right*: Tom C. Clark, Robert H. Jackson, Harold H. Burton, and Sherman Minton. *Seated, left to right*: Felix Frankfurter, Hugo L. Black, Chief Justice Fred M. Vinson, Stanley F. Reed, and William O. Douglas. Photograph by Fabian Bacrach, Collection of the Supreme Court of the United States.

Vinson was making two points in these introductory remarks. First, a long line of judicial precedents upheld segregation as constitutional. Second, the same Congress that wrote the Fourteenth Amendment and was responsible for its enforcement had segregated schools in the District of Columbia for more than eighty years, which implied that it considered segregation to be constitutional.

Vinson continued: "Harlan in his dissent in *Plessy* does not refer to schools." That the lone justice who had condemned railroad segregation in 1896 had implied that school segregation was acceptable was "significant" to the chief justice. Vinson found it hard to "get away from that construction by those who wrote the amendments and those who followed." He also worried that the "complete abolition of public schools in some areas" was a serious possibility if the Court invalidated segregation. Though others "said we should not consider this," Vinson believed that "we can't close our eyes to [the] problem." He also thought it "would be better" if Congress acted.

To maintain confidentiality and preserve fluidity, the justices decided not to take even a tentative vote at conference. Yet several of them kept informal tallies, and all but one of those recorded that Vinson would probably vote to reaffirm *Plessy*.

As the senior associate justice, Hugo Black spoke next. He was the only justice from the Deep South—Alabama. Black predicted "violence if [the] court holds segregation unlawful," and he warned that "states would probably take evasive measures while purporting to obey." He thought that South Carolina "might abolish [its] public school system." Black worried that if the justices invalidated school segregation, district courts "would then be in the firing line for enforcement through injunctions and contempt," and he did not favor "law by injunction."

Yet Black was certain that the intention of segregation laws was "to discriminate because of color," whereas the "basic purpose" of the Fourteenth Amendment was the "protection of the negro against discrimination." He was inclined to hold that "segregation per se is bad *unless* the long line of decisions bars that construction of the amendment." Black declared his willingness to "vote . . . to end segregation," but he expressed doubt about whether his colleagues would do the same.

Stanley F. Reed, like Vinson, was from Kentucky. Of all the justices, he was the most supportive of segregation, in terms of both policy and constitutionality. Reed took a "different view" from Black, declaring that "state legislatures have informed views on this matter." "Negroes have not thoroughly assimilated," he said, and states "are authorized to make up their minds." "[A] reasonable body of opinion in the various states

Black

concerns about so. reaction

intent of segregation

Reed. deference to states

[was] for segregation," which was "for [the] benefit of both [races]." After noting the "constant progress in this field and in the advancement of the interests of the negroes," Reed concluded that "states should be left to work out the problem for themselves."

Because he did not believe that the Constitution's meaning was "fixed," Reed asked, when are "the changes to be made?" He answered: when the "body of people think [segregation is] unconstitutional." He could not "say [that] time [has] come," when seventeen states still mandated racial segregation in their schools. Reed predicted, "Segregation in the border states will disappear in 15 or 20 years." But in the Deep South, "separate but equal schools must be allowed." He thought that "10 years would make [the schools] really equal" in Virginia, and he urged his colleagues "to allow time for equalizing." Until then, he "would uphold separate and equal." Reed's statement was unambiguous: *Plessy* was good law and should be reaffirmed.

Felix Frankfurter was an Austrian Jew, who immigrated to the United States as a child. He taught law at Harvard for a quarter century before President Franklin D. Roosevelt appointed him to the Court in 1939. Frankfurter and Black had feuded before over the meaning of the Fourteenth Amendment—specifically, whether it "incorporated" the Bill of Rights and made those guarantees applicable to the states, rather than simply to Congress, as intended at the founding. Reminiscent of that dispute, Frankfurter now wondered how Black could "know the purpose of the 14th amendment." Frankfurter had "read all of its history and he can't say it meant to abolish segregation." He also wanted "to know why what has gone before is wrong." He was reluctant to admit that "this court has long misread the Constitution." Moreover, he "can't say it's unconstitutional to treat a negro differently than a white."

Yet Frankfurter also discussed the remedy that the Court might impose if it invalidated segregation: "These are equity suits. They involve imagination in shaping decrees. [I] would ask counsel on reargument to address themselves to problems of enforcement." Frankfurter appears not to have made up his mind, conceding that he "can't finish on [the] merits and would reargue all [of the cases]."

Frankfurter had no similar doubts regarding the District of Columbia case, which he thought "raise[d] very different questions." To permit school segregation in the nation's capital was "intolerable," and Frankfurter was prepared "to vote today that [it] violates [the] due process clause." Paradoxically, Frankfurter was quicker to bar segregation where the legal argument against it was weaker. The Fourteenth Amendment binds states, not Congress, and the many slave owners who endorsed the Fifth Amendment, which does constrain Congress, presumably would not have condemned segregation in public schools, had such schools existed when the amendment was ratified in 1791. What Frankfurter found compelling was the moral, not the legal, argument against segregation in the nation's capital.

In the end, Frankfurter favored "put[ting] all the cases down for reargument," which he insisted was not "delaying tactics" but a "further maturing process." Even the D.C. case should be reargued to allow the Eisenhower administration time to fulfill the president's campaign promise to end racial segregation in areas under federal control through administrative action, which Frankfurter thought would produce "enormous . . . social gains" over judicial intervention.

William O. Douglas grew up in the state of Washington, where few black people lived. Then he traveled east to attend law school at Columbia University, after which he became a law professor, first at Columbia and then at Yale. In 1936, Roosevelt appointed him to the Securities and Exchange Commission, a position that afforded few opportunities to ponder racial issues. As a justice, Douglas often had little trouble resolving legal problems that vexed his colleagues, and segregation was no exception. "Segregation is an easy problem," Douglas stated, and the answer was "very simple." He explained:

> No classifications on the basis of race can be made. [The] 14th amendment prohibits racial classifications. So does [the] due process clause of the 5th [amendment]. A negro can't be put by the state in one room because he's black and another put in the other room because he's white. The answer is simple though the application of it may present great difficulties.

Nobody could have doubted where Douglas stood on *Brown*.

Robert H. Jackson was raised in upstate New York, another region with few blacks and no school segregation. Jackson admitted that his upbringing afforded him "little personal experience or firsthand knowledge by which to test many of the arguments advanced in these cases." He was "not conscious of the [race] problem" until he moved to Washington, D.C., in the 1930s to join the Roosevelt administration. Jackson's conference statement began bluntly:

> [There is] [n]othing in the text that says this is unconstitutional. [There is] nothing in the opinions of the courts that says it's unconstitutional. Nothing in the history of the 14th amendment [says it's unconstitutional]. On [the] basis of precedent [I] would have to say segregation is ok.

Jackson ridiculed the NAACP's brief as "sociology," not law. He also noted that New York law mandated school segregation in the 1860s, when the Fourteenth Amendment was passed, and still did so in the 1890s, when *Plessy* was decided.

Jackson thought that "it will be bad for the negroes to be put into white schools" and doubted whether one can "cure this [race] situation by putting children [of different races] together." He would not "say it is unconstitutional to practice segregation tomorrow." Yet he predicted that "segregation is nearing an end. We should perhaps give them time to get rid of it and [I] would go along on that basis. There are equitable remedies that can be shaped to the needs."

What Jackson meant by these final words is unclear, but he apparently could imagine joining a decision that invalidated segregation or that threatened to do so unless certain conditions were met. Jackson also wanted to invite the Judiciary Committees of the U.S. House of Representatives and Senate to participate in the reargument, because "if stirred up . . . [,] they might abolish [segregation]." Still, the thrust of his remarks suggests that Jackson was dubious as to the legal basis for invalidating segregation.[3]

Harold H. Burton was the sole Republican justice in 1952, though he had been appointed by Democrat Harry S Truman. Burton had been a senator from Ohio and, before that, the mayor of Cleveland, a city long known for its relative racial egalitarianism. Burton spoke briefly and to the point at conference: *Sweatt* "crossed the threshold of these cases. Education is more than buildings and faculties. It's a habit of mind." Burton continued: "With [the] 14th amendment, states do not have the choice. Segregation violates equal protection. [The] total effect is that separate education is not sufficient for today's problems. [It is] not reasonable to educate separately for a joint life." Though Burton "would give plenty of time in this decree," he plainly favored invalidating segregation in public education.

Tom C. Clark was from Texas, a peripheral South state. Few blacks lived in West Texas, where the commitment of whites to preserving segregation was relatively thin. East Texas, however, resembled the Deep South; many counties there had majority or near-majority black populations, and most whites were deeply invested in Jim Crow.

Clark declared that the "result must be the same in all the cases" — a statement that probably evinced the typical sensitivity of southern whites to perceived antisouthern prejudice. He meant that if the Court invalidated segregation in South Carolina and Virginia, it must do so as well in Delaware and Kansas. Clark observed that "the problem [in

Texas] is as acute as anywhere. Texas also has the Mexican problem. [A] Mexican boy of 15 is in a class with a negro girl of 12. Some negro girls get in trouble" (read: pregnant). After this brief digression into Texas's social history, Clark got to the point:

> If we can delay action it will help. [The] opinion should give lower courts the right to withhold relief in light of troubles. [I] would go along with that. Otherwise [I] would say we had led the states on to think segregation is OK and we should let them work it out.

defer to states

Clark's statement is ambiguous. His willingness to "go along" with an opinion affording lower courts discretion to withhold relief indicates a possible vote against segregation. Yet his concern that the Court "had led the states on to think segregation is OK" and thus perhaps should "let them work it out" suggests an opposite vote. Clark, like Frankfurter and Jackson, was probably undecided.

Sherman Minton was from Indiana, a northern state with predominantly southern racial views. He and Truman had been cronies in the Senate—apparently an important criterion for Truman's Court appointments. Like Burton, Minton was brief and to the point at the conference: "[A] body of law has laid down [the] separate but equal doctrine. That however has been whittled away in these cases [referring to *Sweatt* and *McLaurin*]. Classification on the basis of race does not add up. It's invidious and can't be maintained."

Minton

With regard to the District of Columbia case, Minton also observed: "Congress has authorized segregation but it's not legal. Our decree will cause trouble but the race carries trouble with it. The negro is oppressed and has been in bondage for years after slavery was abolished. Segregation is per se illegal." Minton left no doubt that he was voting to end school segregation.

This is approximately what the nine justices said as they first collectively considered the School Segregation Cases. Figuring out how these statements would have translated into votes requires speculation, as the justices decided, contrary to their usual practice, not to vote after speaking. In the absence of a formal tally, commentators have disagreed as to how the justices would have voted in December 1952. My view is that four of them—Black, Douglas, Burton, and Minton—thought that school segregation was plainly unconstitutional. But Court majorities require five, and no other justice was equally certain. Two of them—Vinson and Reed—probably leaned toward reaffirming *Plessy*. The other three—Frankfurter, Jackson, and Clark—were apparently ambivalent.

initially no vote

Before trying to explain how a 4–3–2 split became a 9–0 ruling against segregation, let us look more closely at each justice and speculate as to why he held the views that he did. Black's ready condemnation of segregation was perhaps the most surprising position taken by any of the justices. In 1952, he was the only member of the Court from the Deep South, and he had been a Klan member in the mid-1920s. Black appreciated better than could his colleagues how fiercely white southerners would resist judicial invalidation of school segregation. The consequences of that resistance would also be more personal for Black, whose immediate family members living in Alabama would feel the repercussions of his vote.

One cannot know for sure why Black concluded that school segregation was unconstitutional. He often claimed to be a textual literalist, but a constitutional injunction to states not to deny "equal protection of the laws" does not plainly forbid separate-but-equal schools. Nor does the legislative history of the Fourteenth Amendment clearly do so. Thus, the legal sources to which Black usually claimed allegiance seem to have better supported an opposite result in *Brown*. Accordingly, if he is to be taken at his word about his method of constitutional interpretation, Black's personal views about segregation, not his legal interpretation, must explain his vote.

But why did Black personally condemn segregation at a time when few white Alabamans his age did so? Maybe Black was just idiosyncratic; he certainly had a contrarian personality. Another possibility is that Black was so chastened upon his appointment in 1937 by public criticism of his former Klan membership that he dedicated his judicial career to rebutting it. Soon after joining the Court, Black hired a Catholic secretary and a Jewish law clerk, apparently to dispel suspicions of religious prejudice flowing from his Klan affiliation. Not long thereafter, he wrote the landmark opinion in *Chambers v. Florida* (1940), which reversed a black man's conviction because of a coerced confession and celebrated the Court's role as savior of oppressed minorities. Perhaps Black was like John Marshall Harlan, the former Kentucky slave owner who seems to have partially dedicated his judicial career to gainsaying Radical Republican criticism of his appointment by resisting the Court's post-Reconstruction retreat from racial equality.

Douglas's vote may be the easiest to explain. He was less committed than the other justices to maintaining a distinction between the law and a judge's values, which is why Douglas frequently found to be easy issues that troubled his colleagues. For him, the immorality of segregation was the beginning and the end of the legal inquiry. If segregation was wrong, then it was unconstitutional.

Douglas had revealed no special racial sensitivity in his pre-Court years, but he was a quintessential northern liberal. Before World War II, such people were generally more interested in economic issues than racial ones. By the late 1940s, however, racial egalitarianism had become a defining characteristic of theirs. By 1952, the immorality of segregation was no longer debatable for someone of Douglas's political ilk.

The antisegregation votes of Burton and Minton are harder to explain. Neither was as liberal as Douglas. Their personal histories regarding race are thin. The little surviving evidence suggests that they shared neither Reed's support for segregation nor Frankfurter's passion for racial equality. On civil liberties issues generally, they were the most conservative justices, nearly always siding with the government and celebrating judicial restraint.

Why would Burton and Minton, generally averse to civil liberties claims, have been so receptive to the civil rights claim in *Brown*? Perhaps the answer lies in a consideration that was emphasized in the briefs, the oral arguments, and the newspaper reactions but was never mentioned at conference: the Cold War imperative for racial change. Burton and Minton were fierce judicial Cold Warriors. Their enthusiasm for judicial restraint was most evident in cases challenging government loyalty and security programs, where they almost never found a constitutional violation.

In *Brown*, the Cold War imperative put them in the unusual position of siding with individual-rights claimants and the federal government against state legislatures. The Justice Department's brief invoked the Cold War imperative as a principal justification for invalidating school segregation: "Racial discrimination furnishes grist for the Communist propaganda mills." Reed's law clerk recalled that his justice observed that he was hearing much on this subject and it was causing him to think, though he believed that it should be irrelevant. After *Brown*, supporters of the decision boasted that U.S. leadership of the free world "now rest[ed] on a firmer basis" and that U.S. democracy had been "vindicat[ed] . . . in the eyes of the world." Perhaps Burton and Minton, ever heedful of national security, concluded that barring segregation was service to that cause.[4]

Frankfurter and Jackson may have been the justices who were most conflicted over *Brown*, which posed for them a clash between law and politics. Both justices abhorred segregation, but both were committed to maintaining the distinction between the law and the personal values of judges. Traditional legal sources to which they looked for guidance—text, original intent, precedent, and custom—pointed more toward reaffirming than overruling *Plessy*. Thus, as Jackson conceded, invalidating segregation could be defended only in "political" terms. *Brown* required these justices to choose between their aversion to segregation and their aversion to political decision making by judges. We shall further explore that conflict in a moment.

Two justices, Vinson and Reed, were leaning toward reaffirming *Plessy*. Both came from Kentucky, which legally mandated school segregation, and Reed endorsed segregation as social policy. In 1947, he refused to attend a Court party because black messengers were invited, and in 1952, he was appalled that "a Negro" might sit down beside Mrs. Reed at a restaurant after the Court had interpreted an old civil rights statute to require the desegregation of public accommodations in the District of Columbia.[5]

Less is known about Vinson's racial views, though he was probably more tolerant of segregation than were northern justices such as Burton and Minton. Thus, although these Kentuckians were equally committed Cold Warriors, their support for (or lesser aversion to) segregation may explain why they were less influenced by the Cold War imperative. They were also less committed in general to protecting individual rights than were Black or Douglas. School segregation was not a vexing constitutional problem for Vinson or Reed because their general inclination was to defer to legislatures; traditional legal sources supported segregation; and the policy was congenial, or at least not adverse, to their personal preferences. With law and politics aligned, Vinson and Reed could readily reaffirm *Plessy*.

In December 1952, only four justices were clearly prepared to invalidate school segregation. Two were inclined to sustain it, and three appeared to be undecided. The justices' informal head counts confirm that deep divisions existed. In a memorandum to the files that he dictated the day *Brown* was decided, Douglas observed:

> In the original conference, there were only four who voted that segregation in the public schools was unconstitutional. Those four were Black, Burton, Minton and myself. Vinson was of the opinion that the *Plessy* case was right and that segregation was constitutional. Reed followed the view of Vinson, and Clark was inclined that way.[6]

Frankfurter and Jackson, according to Douglas, "viewed the problem with great alarm and thought that the Court should not decide the question if it was possible to avoid it," though both believed that "segregation in the public schools was probably constitutional."

Frankfurter distinguished between school segregation in the District of Columbia, which he thought violated the Due Process Clause, and in the states, where he thought that "history was against the claim of unconstitutionality."

In Douglas's estimation, in 1952 "the vote would [have been] five to four in favor of the constitutionality of segregation in the public schools in the States with Frankfurter indicating he would join the four of us when it came to the District of Columbia case." Douglas's dislike of Frankfurter may have colored his perception of his colleague's likely vote, but his interpretation is consistent with the conference notes.

Other justices who were counting heads reached roughly similar conclusions. In a letter written to Reed just days after *Brown* was decided, Frankfurter noted that he had "no doubt" that a vote taken in December 1952 would have invalidated segregation by five to four. The dissenters would have been Vinson, Reed, Jackson, and Clark, but not himself, and the majority would have written "several opinions." On another occasion, Frankfurter bragged that he had filibustered the decision in 1952–1953 "for fear that the case would be decided the other way under Vinson." After the initial conference, Reed reported to his law clerk that Vinson would probably join him in dissent, as would at least one other justice (Jackson or Clark). Burton and Jackson counted between two and four dissenters if the decision were rendered in 1952–1953. These roughly similar head counts confirm that the justices were deeply divided. Possibly, a bare majority existed to reaffirm *Plessy*.[7]

Worried about the "catastrophic" impact of a divided decision, Frankfurter suggested having the cases reargued on the pretext that the justices required further briefing on issues such as the original understanding of the Fourteenth Amendment and the remedial options that would be available should they invalidate segregation. The justices were far less interested in the answers to these questions than in securing additional time to resolve their differences. Five of them—Black, Frankfurter, Jackson, Burton, and Minton—voted for reargument, and on June 8, 1953, the cases were rescheduled for the next term.[8]

Then, in September 1953, Vinson died suddenly. Frankfurter recorded his death as "the first indication I have ever had that there is a God." President Dwight D. Eisenhower replaced Vinson with Earl Warren, the governor of California, to whom he felt politically indebted from the 1952 Republican convention. Eisenhower did not appoint Warren to influence the outcome of *Brown*. Apparently, he briefly considered appointing instead John W. Davis, the lawyer who had defended segregation for South Carolina in the Supreme Court.[9]

conference
Warren's
observations

Brown was reargued in December 1953. Warren opened the conference following the argument by proposing another informal discussion without a vote. On the merits, he declared that the "separate but equal doctrine rests on [the] basic premise that the Negro race is inferior. That is [the] only way to sustain *Plessy*." Yet the "argument of Negro counsel proves they are not inferior."[10]

Warren continued: "[W]e can't set one group apart from the rest of us and say they are not entitled to [the] same treatment as all others. [The] 13th, 14th and 15th Amendments were intended to make equal those who once were slaves." Acknowledging that this view "causes trouble perhaps," Warren could not "see how segregation can be justified in this day and age." Recognizing that the "time element is important in the deep south," Warren concluded, "we must act but we should do it in a tolerant way."

shift in
majority

Anyone counting heads—and all of the justices were—would have immediately recognized that the outcome in *Brown* was no longer in doubt. Warren, together with the four who had already indicated their support for overruling *Plessy*, made a majority. Warren may have been instrumental not just to securing unanimity in *Brown*, but also to determining its outcome.

With the result settled, two factors pushed toward unanimity. First, the justices anticipated that white southerners would receive *Brown* belligerently and perhaps violently. Resisters would be sure to exploit any hint of internal Court dissension. Justices who disagreed with the outcome thus felt pressure to suppress their convictions for the good of the institution.

Warren and others persuaded Reed not to dissent for this reason, even though he remained convinced that segregation was constitutional. Years earlier, Frankfurter had observed, "Reed was a soldier and glad to do anything that the interest of the Court might require." Three days after *Brown*, Frankfurter wrote to Reed to praise him for resolving the "hard struggle . . . involved in the conscience of your mind" in a manner that was conducive to the nation's "great good." Jackson left his hospital bed, where he was recovering from a heart attack, to be on the bench when *Brown* was announced, thus illustrating the importance that the justices attached to demonstrating their unanimity.[11]

A second factor may also have fostered unanimity. As we have seen, the more ambivalent justices, such as Frankfurter and Jackson, experienced *Brown* as a conflict between law and politics: They loathed segregation but doubted whether it was unconstitutional. After December 1953, they were irrelevant to the outcome, whereas a year earlier they had controlled it. Perhaps they could have endured a disjunction between their personal predilections and their constitutional views if it affected the outcome, but not for the sake of a dissent. If a majority were committed to invalidating segregation, they would acquiesce and suppress their legal doubts.

Though speculative, this interpretation draws support from the internal history of *Terry v. Adams* (1953), which was decided almost contemporaneously with *Brown*. The issue there was whether the exclusion of blacks by the Jaybird Democratic Association of Fort Bend County, Texas, qualified as "state action" under the Fourteenth or Fifteenth amendments. The justices in *Terry* initially voted 5–4 to reject the constitutional challenge. Even after Frankfurter immediately switched sides, a closely divided decision seemed imminent. Vinson, Reed, Minton, and Jackson planned to dissent, and the latter drafted an opinion that criticized the majority for sacrificing "sound principle[s] of interpretation."[12]

Yet when *Terry* came down, only Minton dissented. Apparently, the other three prospective dissenters, once deprived of control over the outcome, were unwilling to subordinate their political preferences to their legal principles. Similar considerations may explain the unanimity in *Brown*.

Brown was hard for justices who approached legal decision making as Frankfurter and Jackson did, because for them it posed a conflict between law and politics. The sources of constitutional interpretation that they usually invoked—text, original understanding, precedent, and custom—seemed to indicate that school segregation was permissible. By contrast, the personal values of these justices condemned segregation as (in Justice Black's words) "Hitler's creed." Their quandary was how to reconcile their legal and moral views.[13]

Frankfurter's self-identity as a judge required that he separate his personal views from the law. He preached that judges must decide cases on "the compulsions of governing legal principles," not "the idiosyncrasies of a merely personal judgment." In a memorandum he wrote in 1940, Frankfurter noted, "No duty of judges is more important nor more difficult to discharge than that of guarding against reading their personal and debatable opinions into the case." In another case, he declined to invalidate a death sentence, despite his personal opposition to capital punishment, because of "the disciplined thinking of a lifetime regarding the duty of this Court."[14]

Frankfurter undoubtedly abhorred racial segregation. More than that of any other justice, his personal behavior evinced egalitarian commitments. In the 1930s, he had served on the NAACP's National Legal Committee, and in 1948, he had hired the Court's first black law clerk,

William Coleman. Yet in a memorandum he wrote while *Brown* was pending, Frankfurter insisted that his personal views on segregation were of limited relevance to the constitutional question:

> However passionately any of us may hold egalitarian views, however fiercely any of us may believe that such a policy of segregation as undoubtedly expresses the tenacious conviction of Southern States is both unjust and shortsighted[, h]e travels outside his judicial authority if for this private reason alone he declares unconstitutional the policy of segregation.[15]

The Court could invalidate segregation, Frankfurter believed, only if it were legally as well as morally objectionable.

Yet Frankfurter had difficulty finding a legal argument for striking down segregation that convinced him. His law clerk Alexander Bickel spent a summer reading the legislative history of the Fourteenth Amendment, and he reported to Frankfurter that it was "impossible" to conclude that the Thirty-Ninth Congress had either intended or foreseen that the amendment would bar segregation.[16]

Frankfurter was no doctrinaire originalist; he believed that the meaning of constitutional concepts changes over time. But this did not mean that judges were free to simply write their own moral views into the Constitution. In the early 1950s, twenty-one states and the District of Columbia still had mandatory or optional school segregation. Thus, Frankfurter could hardly maintain that evolving social mores condemned segregation.

Precedent strongly supported the practice. Of forty-four challenges to school segregation adjudicated by state appellate courts and lower federal courts between 1865 and 1935, not a single one had succeeded. Frankfurter ordinarily celebrated the rule of precedent, calling it "the most influential factor in giving a society coherence and continuity." At conference, Frankfurter conceded that, based on legislative history and precedent, "*Plessy* is right."[17]

Brown presented a similar dilemma for Jackson. He too found segregation to be anathema. In a 1950 letter, Jackson, who had left the Court for a year in 1945–1946 to prosecute Nazis at Nuremberg, wrote to a friend: "You and I have seen the terrible consequences of racial hatred in Germany. We can have no sympathy with racial conceits which underlie segregation policies." Yet, like Frankfurter, Jackson thought that judges were obliged to separate their personal views from the law, and he disfavored the frequent overruling of precedents.[18]

Jackson revealed his internal struggles in a draft concurring opinion which began: "Decision of these cases would be simple if our personal opinion that school segregation is morally, economically or politically indefensible made it legally so." But when he turned to the question of whether "existing law condemn[s] segregation," he had difficulty answering in the affirmative:

> Layman as well as lawyer must query how it is that the Constitution this morning forbids what for three-quarters of a century it has tolerated or approved. He must further speculate as to how [we can justify] this reversal of its meaning by the branch of the Government supposed not to make new law but only to declare existing law. . . . Can we honestly say that the states which have maintained segregated schools have not, until today, been justified in understanding their practice to be constitutional?[19]

Jackson's constitutional analysis began with the text, but he could find there "no explicit prohibition of segregated schools." A ban on school segregation could "only be supplied by interpretation." Regarding the original understanding of the Fourteenth Amendment, Jackson observed that among the amendment's supporters

> may be found a few who hoped that it would bring about complete social equality and early assimilation of the liberated Negro into an amalgamated population. But I am unable to find any indication that their support was decision, and certainly their view had no support from the great Emancipator himself.

He summed up the legislative history:

> It is hard to find an indication that any influential body of the movement that carried the Civil War Amendments had reached the point of thinking about either segregation or education of the Negro as a current problem, and harder still to find that the amendments were designed to be a solution.

Turning from words to deeds, Jackson could "find nothing to show that the Congress which submitted these Amendments understood or intended to prohibit the practice here in question." The same Congress that passed the Fourteenth Amendment and every Congress since had supported school segregation in the District of Columbia. In the late 1860s, Congress had required southern states to ratify the Fourteenth Amendment as a condition of regaining their congressional representation, but it had never intimated that school segregation violated that condition of readmission. Jackson thought that the behavior of states ratifying the amendment was "equally impossible to reconcile with any understanding that the Amendment would prohibit segregation in schools." Eleven northern and border states ratifying the amendment had segregated schools, as did all of the reconstructed southern states.

As to precedent, northern state courts, as well as a Supreme Court dominated by northerners, had concluded that the Fourteenth Amendment did not prohibit segregation: "Almost a century of decisional law rendered by judges, many of whom risked their lives for the cause that produced these Amendments, is almost unanimous in the view that the Amendment tolerated segregation by state action."

Having canvassed the legal sources that he considered to be most relevant to constitutional interpretation, Jackson concluded:

> Convenient as it would be to reach an opposite conclusion, I simply cannot find in the conventional material of constitutional interpretation any justification for saying that in maintaining segregated schools any state or the District of Columbia can be judicially decreed, up to the date of this decision, to have violated the Fourteenth Amendment.

Jackson's draft opinion candidly admitted his difficulty in legally justifying a judicial ban on school segregation—a bit too candidly, in the estimation of his law clerk E. Barrett Prettyman. Prettyman's memorandum responding to Jackson's draft noted that the nation must believe that the *Brown* decision was "honestly arrived at, confidently espoused, and basically sound." If the country could "be made to feel . . . that it is a decision based upon *law*," then segregation

> should die in relatively short order, no matter how many legal skirmishes ensue. On the other hand, if the country feels that a bunch of liberals in Washington has finally foisted off their social views on the public, it will not only tolerate but aid circumvention of the decision.[20]

Prettyman thought that Jackson's opinion should begin not with doubts and fears, but with a clear statement of his legal position. Yet Jackson's rationale for invalidating segregation occupied just two pages near the end of a twenty-three-page opinion, and it read as if it were "almost an afterthought." He advised that Jackson not "write as if you were ashamed to reach [this result]."

Prettyman nicely captured Jackson's dilemma: The justice was, in a sense, "ashamed" of the result he reached. Jackson admitted to his colleagues his difficulty in "mak[ing] a judicial basis for a congenial political conclusion." Unable to "justify the abolition of segregation as a judicial act," he agreed to "go along with it" as a "political decision."[21]

Jackson hesitated to invalidate segregation for another reason as well. He had become skeptical of judicial supremacy, not only because he thought it was inconsistent with democracy, but also because he feared that courts were bad at it. Jackson worried that unenforceable judicial decrees bred public cynicism about courts. In a posthumously published book, he wrote: "When the Court has gone too far, it has provoked reactions which have set back the cause it was designed to advance, and has sometimes called down upon itself severe rebuke."[22]

In 1954, Jackson wondered if the Court was up to the task of transforming southern race relations. His draft opinion asked: Why has separate but equal "remained a dead letter as to its equality aspect?" His answer was that the doctrine had been "declared and supported heartily only by the judicial department which has no power to enforce its own decrees." Blacks had to sue to enforce equality. But "[t]his was costly, it was time consuming and it was impossible for a disadvantaged people to accomplish on any broad scale."[23]

Jackson feared that a judicial ban on segregation would be even harder to implement. Litigants would quickly discover "that devices of delay are numerous and often successful," especially as enforcement would require coercing "not merely individuals but the public itself." Because a ruling against one school district would not bind any other, every instance of recalcitrance would necessitate separate litigation. Individual blacks would bear this burden, as the Justice Department was unlikely to sue, and even if it wished to, Congress would probably not appropriate the necessary funds. Jackson preferred legislative action to judicial, not from "a mere desire to pass responsibility to others," but because it went "to the effectiveness of the remedy and to the use to be made of the judicial process over the next generation."

Other justices shared Jackson's anxiety about invalidating a practice that was apparently sanctioned by traditional sources of constitutional interpretation. Clark conceded that he "always [had] thought that the 14th amendment covered the matter and outlawed segregation. But the history shows different." Vinson, like Jackson, observed that the same congressional representatives who had passed the Fourteenth Amendment approved segregation in the District of Columbia's schools. Several justices worried about overruling an unbroken line of precedent that dated back to the 1860s. Clark thought that the Court had "led the states on to think segregation is OK," and even Black confessed that perhaps "the long line of decisions bars [the antisegregation] construction of the amendment."[24]

It is not surprising that the nine justices who were sitting in 1952—even those who drew the law-politics line differently than Frankfurter and Jackson did or who were less committed to maintaining any such distinction—would be uneasy about invalidating segregation. All of them were appointed by Presidents Roosevelt and Truman on the assumption that they supported, as Jackson put it, "the doctrine on which the Roosevelt fight against the old court was based—in part, that it had expanded the Fourteenth Amendment to take an unjustified judicial control over social and economic affairs."[25]

For most of their professional lives, these men had criticized untethered judicial activism as undemocratic—the invalidation of the popular will by unelected officeholders who were inscribing their social and economic biases on the Constitution. This is how all nine of them understood the *Lochner* era (1905–1937), when the Court had invalidated minimum wage, maximum hour, and protective labor legislation on a thin constitutional basis. The question in *Brown*, as Jackson's law clerk William H. Rehnquist noted, was whether invalidating school segregation would eliminate any distinction between this Court and the *Lochner* era one, except for "the kinds of litigants it favors and the kinds of special claims it protects."[26] Thus, several justices wondered if the Court were the right institution to forbid segregation. Several expressed views similar to Vinson's: If segregation were to be condemned, "it would be better if [Congress] would act." Even Black confessed that "[a]t first blush I would have said that it was up to Congress."[27]

In 1950, Jackson had observed that he "would support the constitutionality of almost any Congressional Act that prohibited segregation in education." Now he cautioned:

> However desirable it may be to abolish educational segregation, we cannot, with a proper sense of responsibility, ignore the question whether the use of judicial office to initiate law reforms that cannot get enough national public support to put them through Congress, is our own constitutional function. Certainly, policy decisions by the least democratic and the least representative of our branches of government are hard to justify.

"[I]f we have to decide the question," Jackson lamented, "then representative government has failed."[28]

In the end, even the most conflicted justices voted to invalidate segregation. How were they able to overcome their initial doubts? All judicial decision making involves extralegal, or "political" considerations, such as the judges' personal values, social mores, and external political pressure. But when the law—as reflected in text, original understanding, precedent, and custom—is clear, judges will generally follow it. And in 1954, the law—as understood by most of the justices—was reasonably clear: Segregation was constitutional. For the justices to reject a result so clearly indicated by the conventional legal sources suggests that they had very strong personal preferences to the contrary.

Why were these justices so repulsed by segregation at a time when national opinion was divided roughly down the middle? One possibility is fortuity: Integrationists just happened to dominate the Court in 1954. Had there been five Stanley Reeds, *Plessy* would probably have been reaffirmed.

A more satisfying explanation emphasizes the systematic differences that exist between the justices and ordinary Americans. Two prominent ones are level of education and economic status. Justices are very well educated, having attended both college and law school—and often the most elite ones. (Jackson was a rare exception, having become a lawyer without attending law school.) They are also relatively wealthy.

On many policy issues that become constitutional disputes, opinion correlates heavily with socioeconomic status, with elites tending to hold more liberal views on certain social issues, though not on economic ones. Early in the twenty-first century, such social issues include gay rights, abortion, and school prayer. In 1954, racial segregation was such an issue: 73 percent of college graduates approved of *Brown*, but only 45 percent of high school dropouts did so. Racial attitudes and practices were changing dramatically in postwar America. As members of the cultural elite, the justices were among the first to be influenced.

As they deliberated over *Brown*, the justices expressed astonishment at the extent of the recent changes in racial attitudes and practices. Jackson treated such changes as constitutional justification for eliminating segregation. In his draft opinion, he wrote that segregation "has outlived whatever justification it may have had." Jackson noted:

> Certainly in the 1860's and probably throughout the Nineteenth Century the Negro population as a whole was a different people than today. Lately freed from bondage, they had little opportunity as yet to show their capacity for education or even self-support and management.

However, he continued, "Negro progress under segregation has been spectacular and, tested by the pace of history, his rise is one of the swiftest and most dramatic advances in the annals of man." This advance "has enabled him to outgrow the system and to overcome the presumptions on which it was based." Black progress was sufficient for Jackson to conclude that race "no longer affords a reasonable basis for a classification for educational purposes."[29]

Other justices made similar observations. Frankfurter noted "the great changes in the relations between white and colored people since the first World War," and he remarked that "the pace of progress has surprised even those most eager in its promotion." Burton recorded the encouraging trend toward desegregation in restaurants and the armed forces, and Minton detected "a different world today."[30]

The southern justices were no less cognizant of change, though they were more inclined to treat it as a justification for staying their hand. Clark noted "much progress" in voting and education. Even Reed recorded the "constant progress in this field [public schooling] and in the advancement of the interests of the negros."[31]

The attitudes of the justices' law clerks may be the strongest evidence of this culturally elite bias favoring desegregation. With post-*Brown* polls revealing a nation split down the middle, the clerks almost unanimously favored judicial invalidation of segregation, notwithstanding any difficulties in the legal justification for such a result. Of the fifteen to twenty young men clerking during the 1952 term, only Rehnquist seems to have favored reaffirming *Plessy*. Even those clerking for southern justices, some of whom had grown up with segregation, favored overturning it. Reed reported that he stopped discussing the issue with his clerks because they were so adamant that *Plessy* be overruled. By the 1950s, most highly educated, relatively privileged young adults—even those from the South—apparently had difficulty sympathizing with segregation.

The justices did not possess the youthful antisegregation bias of their clerks, but they did share the socioeconomic bias. Could Reed, who thought that segregation was constitutionally permissible and morally defensible, have been persuaded to join *Brown* had his culturally elite status not diminished the intensity of his segregationist sentiment? Even he conceded that, "of course," there was no "inferior race," though perhaps blacks had been "handicapped by lack of opportunity." It speaks volumes that an upper-crust Kentuckian who had spent much of his adult life in the nation's capital would have said such a thing. Most white southerners—less well educated, less affluent, and less exposed to the nation's cultural elite—would have demurred.[32]

The culturally elite biases of the justices increased the likelihood that they would invalidate segregation before national opinion had turned against it. Yet the potential gap between the attitudes of the justices and those of the public is limited; the justices are part of the larger culture and inhabit the same historical moment. As little as ten years before *Brown*, racial attitudes in the nation had probably not changed enough for even a culturally elite institution such as the Court to condemn segregation. The NAACP was wise not to push school desegregation challenges before 1950, as the justices would probably have rejected them. Frankfurter later noted that he would have voted to sustain school segregation in the 1940s, because "public opinion had not then crystallized against it."[33]

By the early 1950s, powerful political, economic, social, and ideological forces for progressive racial change had made judicial invalidation of segregation conceivable. Slightly more than half of the nation supported *Brown* from the day it was decided. Thus, *Brown* is not an example of the Court's resistance to majoritarian sentiment, but rather of its conversion of an emerging national consensus into a constitutional command. By 1954, the long-term trend against Jim Crow was clear. Justices observed that segregation was "gradually disappearing" and that it was "marked for early extinction." They understood that *Brown* was working with, not against, the current of history.[34]

Given the long-term trend in race relations and the Court's historical tendency to construe the Constitution to reflect contemporary mores, perhaps it was inevitable that the justices would eventually invalidate school segregation. Jackson predicted, "Whatever we might say today, within a generation [segregation] will be outlawed by decision of this Court because of the forces of mortality and replacement, which operate upon it." If Reed was right that segregation would disappear in the border states within fifteen or twenty years even without judicial intervention, then the propensity of constitutional law to suppress isolated practices might have ensured an eventual ruling against segregation. A subsequent generation of justices, who probably would have found segregation even more abhorrent than their predecessors had, would have been sorely tempted to apply an ascendant national norm against segregation to shrinking numbers of holdout states.[35]

But *Brown* was not inevitable in 1954, when seventeen states and the District of Columbia still segregated their schools and four more states permitted local communities to adopt segregation at their discretion. *Brown* did not simply bring into line a few renegade states. Reed, who conceded that the Constitution's meaning was "not fixed," thought that the Court could invalidate an established practice only when the "body of people" had deemed it unconstitutional, which could not plausibly be said about school segregation in 1954.[36]

Lower courts were not blazing new trails on this issue, as they often do before the high court's momentous constitutional rulings. Prior to *Brown*, only a single California federal judge had repudiated the voluminous body of precedent that sanctioned separate but equal. As we have seen, significant legal hurdles confronted those justices who were personally inclined to invalidate segregation. The Court might easily have written an opinion that echoed John W. Davis's oral argument in defense of segregation: "[S]omewhere, sometime to every principle comes a moment of repose when it has been so often announced, so confidently relied upon, so long continued, that it passes the limits of judicial discretion and disturbance."[37]

Moreover, the probable consequences of invalidating segregation weighed heavily on the justices. The Court had never done anything like this before. Frankfurter observed that, although individuals had brought these cases, the justices were effectively being asked "to transform statewide school systems in nearly a score of States." He cautioned that a "declaration of unconstitutionality is not a wand by which these transformations can be accomplished." Jackson similarly noted that individual lawsuits were "a weak reed to rely on in initiating a change in the social system of a large part of the United States." Several justices worried that issuing unenforceable orders might "bring the court into contempt and the judicial process into discredit." Invalidating segregation would probably also produce violence and school closures. Vinson cautioned, "We can't close our eyes to [the] problem in various parts of [the] country. . . . When you force the complete abolition of public schools in some areas then it is most serious."[38]

In the early 1950s, several southern states were undertaking crash equalization programs that promised a rapid redress of educational inequalities in black schools. Some justices were tempted to see if southern leaders, such as their friend and former colleague Jimmy Byrnes, who had recently been elected governor of South Carolina, could deliver on such promises. Vinson observed that in Clarendon County, South Carolina, "you have equal facilities. [But it] took some time to make them equal." Reed pleaded with his colleagues to stay their hand, as "10 years would make [black schools] really equal." Many southern white moderates likewise urged the Court to give equalization a chance, while warning that invalidating school segregation would jeopardize racial progress in the South.[39]

The justices were not oblivious to these arguments against invalidating segregation. In December 1952, there was no secure majority yet for overruling *Plessy*. The *Brown* decision was not inevitable. Roy Wilkins of the NAACP was wise to prepare two different press releases as he awaited the ruling. The association could not be certain that it would win its case.

4

Brown II and Subsequent Desegregation Developments

The Court invalidated school segregation on May 17, 1954, but it ordered no immediate remedy and deferred reargument on that issue until the following term. The remedial issue posed several questions for the justices. First, should they order immediate desegregation or allow a gradual transition, and should they impose any deadlines for beginning or completing desegregation? Second, how detailed should the remedial decree be? The Court could dictate specifics about the desegregation process, remand to district courts to formulate decrees, or appoint a special master to take evidence and propose orders. Third, should the justices treat the lawsuits as class actions or limit relief to the named plaintiffs?

In *Brown II*, decided on May 31, 1955, the justices resolved in favor of vagueness and gradualism. They remanded the cases to district courts to issue decrees in accordance with "local conditions" while keeping in mind the "flexibility" of traditional "equitable principles." They required a "prompt and reasonable start toward full compliance," with additional time allowed if "consistent with good faith compliance at the earliest practicable date." District courts were to order the admission of "parties to these cases" to public schools on a nondiscriminatory basis "with all deliberate speed."[1]

The National Association for the Advancement of Colored People had pressed for immediate desegregation, with a completion deadline of the fall of 1956, which it called "generous in the extreme." Proponents of immediate relief warned that gradualism would encourage resistance, "greatly weaken the court's moral position," and unjustly condemn "half a generation of Negro school children to a segregated system." Yet the justices never seriously considered ordering immediate desegregation. Several considerations inclined them toward gradualism.[2]

Some justices had insisted on gradualism as their price for voting to invalidate segregation in *Brown I*. The federal government had suggested this compromise between immediate desegregation and reaffirmation of *Plessy*, and it apparently worked. In the justices' internal deliberations, Robert H. Jackson had said that he would invalidate segregation but "won't be a party to immediate unconstitutionality," and Tom C. Clark had said that he would "go along" if the opinion "g[a]ve lower courts the right to withhold relief in light of troubles." Even less ambivalent justices, such as Hugo L. Black and William O. Douglas, agreed to "give plenty of time" and to "put off enforcement awhile." Immediate desegregation was never in the cards if these justices did not favor it.

Another factor in favor of gradualism was the perceived importance of avoiding unenforceable orders. Justice Black declared that "nothing could injure the court more than to issue orders that cannot be enforced," while Justice Sherman Minton urged that the Court not "reveal its own weakness" with a "futile" decree. The more specific and immediate the relief ordered, the greater the chances of defiance. Vague commands are notoriously difficult to defy, because their meaning is so elusive. Moreover, President Dwight D. Eisenhower and the Justice Department were publicly backing gradualism, and the enforcement of judicial decrees ultimately depends on the support of the executive branch.

The justices also feared that immediate desegregation would cause violence and school closures. White southerners campaigned to convince them of this. Voters in South Carolina, Georgia, and Mississippi had sent messages by adopting constitutional amendments that authorized legislatures to end public education in response to court-ordered desegregation. Public officials in Deep South states declined the Court's invitation to file amicus briefs in *Brown II*, thus signaling their intention not to be legally or morally bound by the decision, and they warned of the dire consequences of immediate desegregation. North Carolina, which did submit an amicus brief, reported a poll of local police chiefs that found that 193 out of 199 predicted violence in response to immediate integration.

By the time *Brown II* was decided, violence was no longer simply an abstract possibility. In September 1954, hundreds of angry white parents in Milford, Delaware, forced the closing of a desegregated school and the abandonment of integration; the episode received national publicity. Such ferocious resistance in a border state did not bode well for desegregation in the Deep South.

The NAACP's lawyers responded to such warnings of violence by noting that southern officials had predicted similar outbreaks as a result of the university desegregation rulings of 1950, but none had occurred. The justices were unpersuaded. Justice Black noted that the Deep South "would never be a party to allowing white and negro to go to school together"—a statement that made a "deep impression" on some of his colleagues. Stanley F. Reed also thought that "our order may result in public schools being abolished." Felix Frankfurter, who was in direct contact with his "warm friend" Jimmy Byrnes, conveyed news of "chaotic" conditions in South Carolina.[3]

Sympathy toward the plight of white southerners also inclined the justices toward gradualism: They felt guilty about undermining the expectations of those who had assumed the legitimacy of separate but equal based on past Court rulings. Jackson had wondered in *Brown I* if "we honestly [can] say that the states which have maintained segregated schools have not, until today, been justified in understanding their practice to be constitutional." Even Black had worried that the "long line of decisions" might prevent the Court from overturning segregation. If they were going to reject "an almost universal understanding that segregation is not constitutionally forbidden," Jackson observed, then "consideration of that in framing the decree would be just."[4]

Several justices also thought that they could diminish the resistance of southern whites by appearing sympathetic and accommodating. Frankfurter especially believed that "how we do what we do in the Segregation cases may be as important as what we do." He emphasized the "largely educational" effect of Court opinions and cautioned against their being "self-righteous." Jackson had warned that "it would retard acceptance of [*Brown I*] if the Northern majority of this Court should make a Pharisaic and self-righteous approach to this issue." On this subject, the justices' thinking mirrored that of President Eisenhower, who intervened in the brief writing in *Brown II* to urge that the feelings of white southerners be "met with understanding and good will."[5]

The law clerks who were assigned to work on the remedial order overwhelmingly embraced this view. Gradualism "would indicate to the South that the Court understands and is sympathetic to the problems which the decision raises in their states" and that it was "not trying to jam a new social order down their throats." By contrast, a "meat-ax decree ordering immediate integration" would be like "castor oil . . . forced on a child" and would probably produce "both confusion and lasting resentment." The clerks urged the justices to heed the view of southern moderates, such as newspaper editors Harry Ashmore and Hodding Carter, who predicted that the immediate desegregation of schools would be disastrous.[6]

Among the justices, only Black seemed to appreciate that white southerners were "going to fight this" no matter what the Court said. Yet Black, too, endorsed a form of gradualism for fear of the Court's issuing a futile order. He and Douglas favored immediate integration but only for the named plaintiffs. Justice Black declared that he was "not fond of class suits," nor was he "sure how many students would want their names in this litigation." If only "5 or 10" were admitted, most problems would "disappear." Though the other justices thought that these suits were obviously class actions and a draft order treated them as such, *Brown II* ultimately required the admission only of "parties to these cases." Reed apparently had persuaded a majority that "[t]hese are class suits but nothing should be said about it in the decree."[7]

Finally, racism may partially explain the gradualism of *Brown II*. The justices seemed to empathize more with white southerners, "who are to be coerced out of [segregation]," than with blacks, "who are coerced into [it]." How else can one explain Jackson's view that the immediate enforcement of blacks' constitutional rights was "needlessly ruthless"? Not all of the justices were convinced that segregation could be casually dismissed as "Hitler's creed." Reed noted a "reasonable body of opinion" in support of segregation, and Jackson did not "deny the sincerity and passion with which many feel that their blood, lineage and culture are worthy of protection by enforced separatism of races." The justices decided *Brown* as a new epoch in U.S. race relations was dawning; it is hardly surprising that remnants of the preceding, less egalitarian era would still infect their thinking.[8]

Whether the relief granted should be immediate or gradual was not the only issue to be resolved in *Brown II*. The justices also had to decide whether to impose deadlines for beginning and/or completing desegregation, which might embolden district judges who faced local pressure for delay. (Deadlines and gradualism are not the same issue, as deadlines can be immediate or delayed.) The NAACP urged immediate desegregation or at least a deadline of September 1956. The Justice Department suggested that district judges require school boards to submit desegregation plans within ninety days, but it opposed completion deadlines.

The justices rejected deadlines altogether. Earl Warren began the conference by repudiating them. Reed thought that the Court should "[f]ix no definite time," and Douglas "[w]ould not suggest a date." One argument against deadlines was that they would become an excuse for failing to act earlier. Another was that precision enabled defiance, which the justices desperately wished to avoid. Frankfurter worried that any deadline would be "arbitrary"—a judicial fiat—which would "tend to alienate instead of enlist favorable or educable local sentiment."[9]

The justices also believed that administrative problems genuinely justified some delay. Desegregation required the redrawing of district lines and school attendance zones, consolidating schools, reassigning teachers and administrative staff, arranging student transportation, improving the conditions of ramshackle black schools, and accommodating students' disparate achievement levels. Thus, the justices had plausible reasons for eschewing deadlines. Yet by requiring desegregation with "all deliberate speed" and compliance "at the earliest practicable date," they invited delay by recalcitrant school boards and district judges and provided inadequate political cover for those who were willing to comply in good faith.

Another issue for the justices was how much guidance to provide district judges in formulating their decrees. The president and the Justice Department, sources that were likely to influence the justices, urged decentralization—that is, returning cases to district judges with limited guidance. Proponents of this approach within the Court argued that district judges were better informed about "local difficulties and variations" and would not "be thought of as carpetbaggers." Their rulings would appear less "the mere imposition of a distant will." In addition, most of the justices disapproved of federal courts—Supreme or otherwise—"operating as a super–school board." To the extent possible, elected officials and education experts should continue to assign students. A law clerk of Justice Harold H. Burton stated the prevalent view: "[W]e should not lose sight of the fact that this Court is a member of the judicial branch of the government."[10]

The justices were not completely naive. They understood that district judges would face enormous pressure to postpone and minimize desegregation. Justice Black noted that district courts would be "in the firing line," as states "took evasive measures while purporting to obey."

Warren thought that to "let them flounder" without guidance would be "rather cruel." Frankfurter conceded that decentralizing the desegregation process "would unload responsibility upon lower courts most subject to community pressures without any guidance for them except our decision of unconstitutionality." This might result in "drawn-out, indefinite delay without even colorable compliance." If the Court gave them "something to rely on, they [could] better resist undesirable local pressures" by "point[ing] to a superior authority in undertaking what [would] often be unpopular action."[11]

Yet the justices disagreed over how much guidance to provide. Black doubted the need for any opinion to accompany the decree: "[T]he less we say the better off we are." Because "[t]here will be deliberate effort[s] to circumvent the decree, [i]t becomes desirable to write as narrowly as possible." Minton agreed, but the others felt obliged to offer lower courts some guidance. Yet none of them was prepared to impose the detailed rules that would have been necessary to constrain evasion or to insulate district judges from local pressure. Frankfurter wanted the impossible—an opinion that had "enough 'give' to leave room for variant local problems" but was not so "loose [as] to invite evasion." Warren, too, wished to give district courts "as much latitude as we can, but also as much support." These goals were irreconcilable.[12]

The justices ultimately adopted loose phraseology that could neither constrain evasion nor bolster compliance: "good faith" implementation, an order to begin "as soon as practicable," and desegregation with "all deliberate speed." They said nothing about the permissibility of a wide array of desegregation policies that could be used to circumvent *Brown*: freedom-of-choice plans, which allowed parents to choose among several schools; pupil placement schemes, which assigned students to schools based on a long list of ostensibly race-neutral criteria; transfer options, which permitted parents to move their children out of desegregated schools; and grade-a-year plans, which started desegregation in the first or twelfth grade and then expanded it to one additional grade every year. The justices were aware of all of these issues, but they chose to allow the district courts to "carry the ball."[13]

Moreover, the justices did not take seriously the one reasonably clear instruction they did provide—that community disagreement with the constitutional principles announced by the Court could not justify delay. The justices thought that district courts *should* consider local resistance in determining the timing of desegregation, but they worried that saying so would "put a premium upon lawlessness." Justice Black thought that "attitudes should not be mentioned in [the] decree but

BROWN V. BOARD OF EDUCATION AND THE CIVIL RIGHTS MOVEMENT

they cannot be ignored." Frankfurter stated, "[The a]ttitude of the south is a fact to be taken into consideration as much as administrative difficulty." Can the justices have believed that district judges would take the instruction to ignore community sentiment more seriously than they took it themselves?[14] Jackson had warned early in 1954:

> I will not be a party to . . . casting upon the lower courts a burden of continued litigation under circumstances which subject district judges to local pressures and provide them with no standards to justify their decisions to their neighbors, whose opinions they must resist.

With Jackson dead in 1955, his colleagues did just that.[15]

Brown II was a clear victory for white southerners. Although they did not convince the Court to repudiate *Brown I* or to explicitly authorize district judges to delay desegregation based on hostile community sentiment, they won on every other issue. The Court approved gradualism, imposed no deadlines for beginning or completing desegregation, issued vague guidelines, and entrusted (southern) district judges with broad discretion.

When informed of the decision, Florida legislators broke into cheers. A Louisiana legislator declared, "It was the mildest decree the Supreme Court possibly could have handed down." A Mississippi politician celebrated the fact that a native Mississippi judge would determine what was "as soon as feasible." Other white southerners expressed relief that the Court did not really intend to foist integration on them any time soon. Southern legislators opined that desegregation might be "feasible" in another fifty or one hundred years.[16]

Black leaders were disappointed with the decision, though they generally tried not to show it. One rationalized that a fixed deadline would only have excused delay. Another opined that the Court had given "even the most recalcitrant southern states an honorable way to conform to the decision." The NAACP implausibly claimed to be "gratified" by the Court's "clear-cut determination" that blacks were to have their rights to nonsegregated education "as soon as practicable."[17]

But some blacks could not hide their disappointment. An NAACP officer in Mississippi lamented, "It looks like the Supreme Court doesn't believe in our constitution." One prominent black journalist, James L. Hicks, noted that he was "deeply disappointed" and could not "fool [him]self into believing that we have won a great victory." Another black newspaperman, John H. McCray, admitted that he "can't find too

[handwritten margin note: So. response]

[handwritten margin note: Black response]

much to cheer about in [the decision]," and he criticized the Court for "seek[ing] to do business" with diehard southern segregationists.[18]

The justices had conceived of gradualism partly as a peace offering to white southerners—an invitation to moderates to meet them halfway. Some southern politicians understood this, observing that the Court had "intended to appeal to the states to help work out this problem," "to correct an obnoxious decision," and to fix its "mistake." Many applauded the justices for their "moderate and reasonable" decision, which was "something to be thankful for." The *Tampa Tribune* predicted that the ruling would "dissipate the thunderhead of turmoil and violence which had been gathering in Southern skies since the Court held school segregation unconstitutional." Several legislatures suspended their consideration of bills to block desegregation, and other states canceled plans for special legislative sessions.[19]

Yet others put a different spin on *Brown II*, perceiving it as weakness or backtracking. A Florida segregationist thought the Court had "realized it made a mistake in May and is getting out of it the best way it can." A Texas legislator declared that the "Court got hold of a hot potato and didn't know what to do with it." Some southern observers believed that the threats of school closures and violence had intimidated the justices, and over the following months many predicted that patient determination on the part of white southerners would convince the Court and the nation to abandon southern blacks as they had during Reconstruction.[20]

That *Brown II* was a mistake from the Court's perspective was quickly apparent. The justices' conciliatory gesture inspired defiance, not accommodation. Within months, new organizations called "citizens' councils" were formed, and they endorsed all methods short of violence to preserve white supremacy. Several southern legislatures passed "interposition" resolutions, denouncing *Brown* as an "illegal encroachment" and declaring it "null, void and of no effect." Early in 1956, most southern congressional representatives signed the Southern Manifesto, which condemned *Brown* as a "clear abuse of judicial power" and pledged the South to all "lawful means" of resistance.[21]

To say that *Brown II* was misguided is not to say that the justices calculated foolishly. They operated without the aid of historical hindsight, and their prediction that conciliation on their part would strengthen southern moderates and encourage compliance was shared by many contemporary commentators. The mostly restrained southern reaction to *Brown I* and the early steps taken toward compliance in the border states may have induced the justices to underestimate the commitment of white southerners to preserving school segregation.

Yet, instead of encouraging compromise, *Brown II* seems to have inspired defiance and undermined those moderates who were already taking preliminary steps toward desegregation. In retrospect, the justices should have taken the advice of one of Justice Burton's law clerks, who pointed out that a "firm forceful policy . . . impresses people with the fact that you mean what you say." Yet in May 1955, correctly anticipating little support from the political branches and overestimating their ability to manage southern resistance, the justices opted for conciliatory vagueness.[22]

Did their miscalculation matter much? Probably not. For reasons explored in a subsequent chapter, certain features of southern politics and the political dynamics of the segregation issue virtually ensured massive resistance. *Brown II*, by instilling hope among white southerners that *Brown I* could be overturned, did not help. But an order for immediate desegregation also would have been bitterly resisted. Most white southerners would oppose desegregation until they were convinced that resistance was costly and futile. The Court was powerless to make that showing on its own.

The justices backed off after *Brown II*. With the notable exception of the Little Rock case—discussed later in this chapter—they distanced themselves from school desegregation for the next eight years.

In 1955–1956, the justices twice endured humiliation from southern state courts rather than further entangle themselves in racial controversy. First, they confronted a challenge to Virginia's law barring interracial marriage. A Chinese man and a white woman had tried to circumvent this law by marrying in North Carolina. After returning to Virginia, the woman later sought an annulment under the antimiscegenation law, which her husband challenged as unconstitutional. The trial court granted the annulment, and the Virginia Court of Appeals affirmed and sustained the statute.

Naim v. Naim was the last case the justices wished to see on their docket in 1955. Many southern whites had charged that the real goal of the NAACP's school desegregation campaign was "to open the bedroom doors of our white women to the Negro men" and "to mongrelize the white race." To strike down antimiscegenation laws so soon after *Brown* risked appearing to validate those suspicions. Moreover, opinion polls in the 1950s revealed that over 90 percent of whites, even outside the South, opposed interracial marriage. Frankfurter later explained that one reason *Brown* was written as it was—emphasizing the importance of public education rather than condemning all racial classifications— was to avoid the miscegenation issue.[23]

The justices' problem was that *Naim* seemed to fall within the Court's mandatory jurisdiction. In the 1950s—unlike today—the Court was *required* by federal statute to grant appeals when state courts had rejected federal claims that were not "insubstantial." To say that antimiscegenation laws posed an insubstantial constitutional question would have been disingenuous. The importance was "obvious," law clerk William A. Norris (later a judge on the U.S. Court of Appeals for the Ninth Circuit) told Justice Douglas, and "[f]ailure to decide the case would blur any distinction remaining between certiorari and appeal." Burton's clerk agreed that the Court could not honestly avoid the case, though he would have preferred to "give the present fire a chance to burn down."[24]

Both clerks underestimated the desperation and creativity of the justices, several of whom searched for an escape route. Clark suggested one: The plaintiff should be estopped from invoking the antimiscegenation law because she had deliberately evaded it when marrying. Burton suggested another: The Court could dismiss the case on the ground that the Naims were never legally married because Virginia required residents to marry within the state—a plainly erroneous reading of Virginia law.

Of all the justices, Frankfurter felt the gravest anxiety about the case. If this had been a certiorari petition, he would have rejected it, as "due consideration of important public consequences is relevant to the exercise of discretion in passing on such petitions." (Indeed, in 1954, the Court had denied certiorari in another southern miscegenation case.) But *Naim* was an appeal, and Frankfurter admitted that the challenge to antimiscegenation laws "cannot be rejected as frivolous." Still, the "moral considerations" for dismissing the appeal "far outweigh the technical considerations in noting jurisdiction." To thrust the miscegenation issue into "the vortex of the present disquietude" would risk "thwarting or seriously handicapping the enforcement of [*Brown*]."[25]

Frankfurter's proposed solution, which the justices adopted, was to remand the case to the Virginia Court of Appeals with instructions to return it to the trial court for further proceedings in order to clarify the parties' relationship to the commonwealth, which was said to be uncertain from the record; clarification might obviate the need to resolve the constitutional question. On remand, the Virginia jurists refused to comply with the Court's instructions; they denied that the record was unclear and that state law permitted returning final decisions to trial courts in order to gather additional evidence. Virginia newspapers treated the state court's response as an instance of nullification.

The petitioner then returned to the Supreme Court, asking that the case be set for argument. Douglas's law clerk Norris now identified three options that were available. The Court could summarily vacate the state judgment to "punish" Virginia for its disobedience. Norris thought that this solution would be "intemperate and would unnecessarily increase the friction between this Court and the southern state courts." Second, the justices could circumvent the recalcitrant state high court and remand the case directly to the trial court. Finally, they could take the appeal, which would be a "tacit admission that the Court's original remand was unnecessary." Norris favored the last option and warned, "It will begin to look obvious if the case is not taken that the Court is trying to run away from its obligation to decide the case."[26]

Norris failed even to imagine the option chosen by a majority—dismissing the appeal on the ground that the Virginia court's response "leaves the case devoid of a properly presented federal question." A majority of the justices apparently preferred to be humiliated at the hands of truculent state jurists rather than to stoke further the fires of racial controversy.[27]

Georgia had its turn at humiliating the justices around the same time. *Williams v. Georgia* (1955) raised an important question of federal courts doctrine: When does a state criminal defendant's failure to comply with state procedural rules, which leads the state court to refuse to consider his federal constitutional claim, constitute an "adequate and independent" state ground that bars Supreme Court review on the merits? Two years earlier, in *Avery v. Georgia*, the Court had overturned a black man's conviction because of possible race discrimination in jury selection. Jurors were supposed to be randomly selected by drawing tickets from a box, yet the names of whites were on tickets of a different color than those used for the names of blacks. *Avery* was decided by the justices after Williams's conviction, but the ruling of the state supreme court in *Avery*, which criticized the practice of different color tickets while declining to overturn Avery's conviction, had come down well before Williams's trial. Williams's lawyer, who was "guilty of almost criminal negligence," failed to raise the *Avery* challenge at trial or on the initial appeal, and the Georgia courts then ruled that the defendant had waived his right to have it considered.[28]

Williams appealed his death sentence to the Supreme Court. Three justices—Warren, Black, and Douglas—voted to reverse his conviction outright: Georgia could not execute Williams based on the verdict of a jury that had been selected via obviously unconstitutional procedures simply because his lawyer had failed to object. To remand the case, Warren warned, was to invite the Georgia jurists to invent a different basis for denying Williams a new trial. The chief justice declared that he would not "have this man's life on my conscience" because of a "procedural dodge." Justices Black and Douglas likewise opposed sending the case back to the Georgia courts "to take another crack."[29]

However, a majority did not support outright reversal, preferring to give the Georgia court an opportunity to correct its own error. John Marshall Harlan, who thought that the "aggravating facts" justified "straining to vindicate" Williams's rights, suggested remanding the case to the Georgia court with a reminder that state law seemed to permit discretionary grants of new trials even after procedural defaults. Hopefully, the Georgia court would get the message and reconsider its decision. Frankfurter wanted to go even further and remand the case in a way that "would not give [Georgia] much room to stand pat."[30]

Frankfurter wrote the Court's opinion, observing that where state law grants courts discretion to order new trials in extraordinary cases, the U.S. Supreme Court has jurisdiction to ensure that the discretion is not exercised so as to frustrate constitutional rights. The Court declined to reverse outright, but it strongly hinted that it might do so if Georgia refused to order a new trial.

On remand, the Georgia court declined to "supinely surrender [the] sovereign powers of this State," accused the Supreme Court of violating the Tenth Amendment by asserting jurisdiction, and reaffirmed its earlier ruling. In essence, the Georgia jurists told the justices "to go to hell."[31]

When *Williams* returned to the Court six months later, those justices who had previously favored outright reversal now reconsidered. Justice Black warned that challenging Georgia might precipitate a constitutional crisis. Nobody favored Frankfurter's suggestion that they at least respond to the insubordinate challenge made by the Georgia jurists to the Supreme Court's jurisdiction. All nine justices now voted to deny certiorari, and Georgia executed Williams shortly thereafter. The growing belligerence of southern states over school desegregation since *Brown II* must explain the justices' change of heart; they did not want to compound their desegregation difficulties by unnecessarily alienating southern courts. The justices apparently discounted the possibility that by capitulating in cases such as *Williams*, they might encourage resistance by appearing craven rather than conciliatory.

The justices also avoided further confrontation over school desegregation until 1963 by denying full review in the many cases that were appealed, with the sole exception of the Little Rock case, *Cooper v. Aaron* (1958). The justices apparently decided to say no more on the subject until they received some signal of support from the political branches.

That signal was not immediately forthcoming. President Eisenhower repeatedly refused to say whether he endorsed *Brown*, insisting that his duty was to enforce Court decisions, not to approve or disapprove of them. Eisenhower preached moderation, urged that desegregation difficulties be resolved locally, and denied a role for the federal government in the "ordinary normal case of keeping order and preventing rioting." Asked by reporters for a message to youngsters on desegregation, he repeated the mantra of southern whites that "it is difficult through law and through force to change a man's heart."[32]

The administration's failure in 1956 to enforce desegregation orders against local resistance in several southern cities encouraged similar violence elsewhere. Civil rights leaders beseeched Eisenhower to publicly condemn the "violence and terror in certain southern communities." Instead, he criticized "extremists on both sides," morally equating NAACP leaders, "who want to have the whole matter settled today," with the Ku Klux Klan. Eisenhower privately noted that *Brown* was a foolish decision that "set back progress in the south at least 15 years." When rumors of his private views circulated, he refused to deny them. Not until 1959 did Eisenhower publicly declare that segregation was "morally wrong."[33]

Democrats who were seeking to replace Eisenhower as president in 1956 were not much more supportive of *Brown*. Senator Estes Kefauver of Tennessee allowed that he would be "very shy" about using federal troops to enforce desegregation and that he would do so only in a "very severe case." The most liberal Democratic presidential candidate, Governor Averell Harriman of New York, declared, "No responsible person could propose the use of federal troops." The eventual Democratic nominee, Illinois's former governor, Adlai Stevenson, urged cautious federal action in enforcing *Brown*. Stevenson preferred education and suasion to force, and he observed, "[You] do not upset habits and traditions that are older than the Republic overnight."[34]

Congress did not support the Court either. Throughout the 1950s, liberal representatives failed in their efforts to pass symbolic statements affirming that *Brown* was the law of the land (not even that it was rightly decided). Congress did pass tepid civil rights legislation in 1957, but it covered only voting rights, and even that it did ineffectively. A proposal to empower the attorney general to bring desegregation suits was eliminated from the final bill with the president's assent. The clear implication of this excision, as the celebrated political commentator Walter Lippmann noted, was that the right against school segregation was "not to be enforced by the executive power of the Federal Government."[35]

The gradualism of politicians simply mirrored that of their constituents. Polls revealed that national majorities of nearly 4–1 preferred gradualism to immediate action, especially after desegregation led to violence in 1955–1956. In the NAACP chapter of the City College of New York—a strongly integrationist group, one would suppose—twice as many members favored gradualism as immediate integration.

Early in 1956, *Life* ran an editorial entitled "Go Slow, Now," which urged southern blacks to be patient and to "avoid needless scraping of Southern sensitivities and emotions." Eleanor Roosevelt also defended gradualism, pointing out that "[g]o slow doesn't mean, don't go." The *St. Louis Globe-Democrat*, another *Brown* supporter, suggested that the NAACP "make haste slowly," because racial tolerance must evolve gradually and traditional mores could not be changed overnight.[36]

We have little direct evidence as to what the justices were thinking in 1955–1957. Desegregation orders were producing violent resistance— described in chapter 9—even in peripheral South states such as Tennessee and Texas. The political branches of the national government had done virtually nothing to support *Brown* or to intervene against violent resistance. Southern white moderates were urging a "cooling-off period" and warning that aggressive implementation of *Brown* "could set off violence and bloodshed." Even liberal northern Democrats supported gradualism. In this political environment, the justices may have calculated that further intervention on their part could do no good.[37]

The Court reentered the fray only after the Little Rock crisis. In September 1957, Governor Orval Faubus used the state militia to block enforcement of a court order desegregating Central High School. To avoid a contempt citation, Faubus later withdrew the state troops, but a white mob then filled the vacuum, forcing black students out of the integrated school. After enduring weeks of criticism from Democrats and civil rights leaders for being "wishy-washy" and refusing "to take a strong stand," Eisenhower nationalized the state militia and sent in the army's 101st Airborne Division.[38]

Ironically, Eisenhower had helped to foment the crisis through his previous statements and inaction. In September 1956, when Governor Allan Shivers used Texas Rangers to block enforcement of a desegregation order as whites rioted in Mansfield, reporters asked Eisenhower how he planned to respond. The president pleaded ignorance of these events, while insisting that the federal government could not intervene in ordinary instances of rioting. During the summer of 1957, Eisenhower stated, "I can't imagine any set of circumstances that would ever induce me to send federal troops . . . into any area to enforce the orders of a federal court." Faubus was justifiably surprised when the 101st Airborne appeared in Little Rock.[39]

Several blacks attended Central High under military guard during the 1957–1958 school year. The situation was chaotic. Hundreds of white students were suspended for harassing blacks, and there were more than twenty bomb threats. Early in 1958, the Little Rock school board petitioned district judge Harry J. Lemley for a reprieve of two and a half years to allow community resistance to subside. Lemley acquiesced, stating that the court could not "close its eyes and ears to the practical problem with which [the] board is confronted." Noting the "chaos, bedlam, and turmoil" at Central High and the "deep seated popular opposition in Little Rock to the principle of integration," Lemley concluded that the right of black students to nondiscriminatory admission to public schools had to be balanced against the public inter-

district judge

Figure 4.1. A member of the Arkansas National Guard blocks four of the Little Rock Nine from entering Central High School on September 4, 1957. *Left to right*: Carlotta Walls, Gloria Ray, Jane Hill, and Ernest Green. Arkansas History Commission.

est in a smoothly functioning educational system. The Eighth Circuit Court of Appeals, sitting en banc, reversed by a vote of 6–1. The justices then convened in special session in the summer of 1958 to determine whether a district judge could delay desegregation, once it had begun, because of community resistance.[40]

Cooper v. Aaron (1958) was easy for the justices, who could appreciate as well as segregationists that to reward violent resistance in Little Rock by postponing desegregation would encourage similar behavior elsewhere. A Louisiana legislator had observed that Lemley's decision "shows that massive resistance really works. This gives us a powerful new weapon with which to protect our schools." Other southern officials evidently agreed, as reaction to Lemley's "wonderful" decision was "immediate and jubilant." One federal judge in Virginia announced that if the Court affirmed Lemley, he would permit Norfolk to continue segregating its schools, and another judge awarded Prince Edward County an extended deadline partly based on Lemley's ruling. The Court had to intervene or else desegregation would have ground to a halt.[41]

In addition, the justices must have understood the importance of demonstrating support for a president who had run political risks by dispatching troops to an American city. After *Brown*, they had anxiously awaited some sign of support from the political branches. Now that the president had finally provided it, the justices had no choice but to back him up.

The Court's opinion in *Cooper* was more forceful and condemnatory than *Brown* had been—"judicial rhetoric that expressed displeasure amounting to anger," according to one contemporary observer. The justices blamed Faubus and the Arkansas legislature for the violence at Central High School. In dicta, they criticized the efforts of Arkansas public officials not only to nullify *Brown* but also to evade it, such as by allowing public school funds and buildings to be used by segregated private schools.[42]

Based on the vehemence of *Cooper*, one might have guessed that the justices would now aggressively monitor the desegregation process, but this was not so. The apparent boldness of the interventions by the president and the Court was misleading. Eisenhower had used federal troops only after the blatant defiance of a desegregation order by a governor whom he suspected of lying to his face. The justices had acted primarily to support the president. Neither party had abandoned gradualism.

Justice Clark, who nearly dissented in *Cooper* because the Court had departed from its customary procedures in order to issue a quick ruling, reminded his colleagues that *Brown* had not contemplated desegregation "through push button action." Most of the other justices agreed. The draft opinion of Justice William J. Brennan, who had joined the Court in 1956, had required school boards to formulate deadlines for desegregation. When other justices objected to such rigidity, deadlines were removed. The final opinion in *Cooper* also referred to "desegregation" rather than "integration," because white southerners found the former "a shade less offensive." Even in the face of blatant defiance by the white South, a majority of the justices was inclined toward accommodation and gradualism.[43]

For several more years after *Cooper*, the justices continued to abstain as white southerners defied or evaded *Brown*. The NAACP deplored the Court's refusal to grant review in cases challenging laws that were "designed to impede and frustrate full implementation of [*Brown*]."[44]

2 subsequent rulings

The Court took two noteworthy actions in desegregation cases in 1958–1959. In December 1958, just months after *Cooper*, the justices in *Shuttlesworth v. Birmingham Board of Education* summarily affirmed a lower court decision that rejected a facial challenge to Alabama's pupil placement law. One year later, they denied review of a decision upholding Nashville's grade-a-year desegregation plan, which included a minority-to-majority transfer option.

The summary affirmance in *Shuttlesworth* departed from the Court's usual pattern of denying review in school desegregation cases. Perhaps the justices felt obliged to grant review in this case because it was an appeal from a three-judge trial court, which falls within the Court's mandatory jurisdiction, unless the constitutional issue is plainly insubstantial. A summary affirmance indicates agreement with the ruling below. By 1958, pupil placement had become a preferred method of avoiding desegregation; every southern state had adopted such a scheme. The justices carefully left open the possibility that plaintiffs could prove discriminatory administration, but they declined to invalidate pupil placement on its face.

pupil placement

A contrary ruling would have been easy to defend. Alabama's placement law was part of a massive resistance package that scarcely disguised the legislature's intention to defy *Brown*. Indeed, Alabama legislators had explicitly declared that if the pupil placement plan failed to block integration, they could then abolish the public schools. Just months earlier, Governor John Patterson had announced, "[W]e are going to maintain segregation in the public schools." The lower court in *Shuttlesworth* refused to "lightly reach [the] conclusion" that Alabama was intent on nullification, but nothing had been left to inference.[45]

Even aside from the Alabama legislature's generally defiant purpose, the patent motive behind pupil placement was to frustrate desegregation by inviting the surreptitious consideration of race by school boards and then by confounding blacks who were dissatisfied with their placements in a maze of administrative appeals. The lower court in *Shuttlesworth* refused to consider legislative motive, but that position was debatable by 1958 and would be rejected by the Court in a school desegregation case a few years later.

Another possible objection to pupil placement schemes was that they presumptively allocated students to their current (segregated) schools and placed the burden on them to request transfers. This was not obviously a sufficient remedy for past segregation. Federal courts in Louisiana and Virginia had invalidated placement schemes for such reasons. After these rulings, Governor James Coleman of Mississippi had expressed concern that his state was "legally naked and legally defenseless" against a desegregation suit, because its pupil placement law seemed to be doomed. Although the placement laws of Louisiana and Virginia were not identical to Alabama's, they were broadly similar, and it would not have been hard for the justices to have written a persuasive opinion invalidating the Alabama law. As the battle over massive resistance climaxed in 1958–1959, however, the justices apparently had no desire to invalidate a scheme that was being used in some jurisdictions to achieve at least token desegregation.[46]

In a private memorandum, Douglas revealed that the justices were divided in *Shuttlesworth*. He and Warren thought the law "was a palpable device to avoid integration" and favored granting full review. Justice Potter Stewart (recently appointed to the Court by President Eisenhower to replace Justice Burton) objected that "Alabama in good faith was seeking to comply with our decisions." Douglas reported:

> That naive viewpoint so riled me that I prepared a memo for the court showing the purpose of the law. I also pointed out that this law, if not struck down, would be hard to knock out in its application. No purpose to discriminate on racial grounds would be shown in any application; it could be proved—as in the jury cases—only by showing a systematic discrimination that would be avoided by having token integration. I said that the case we could knock out would be a long time coming. The C[hief] J[ustice] spoke up and said, "not until we are long dead."

According to Douglas, Black "thought we were right; but he said nothing would be done anyway for a generation or more." The other justices were unwilling to invalidate the law on its face. Warren and Douglas chose not to dissent from the Court's summary affirmance for fear that doing so "would underline the defeat or setback which school integration had suffered as a result of this decision."[47]

The setback was clear even without their dissent. Alabama officials were "jubilant" over *Shuttlesworth*, which Governor Patterson saw "as an indication that the Supreme Court is going to let us handle our own affairs." Senator Russell Long of Louisiana deemed the decision to be "the most encouraging thing for the South in some time," as it "shows a willingness of the court to settle for token integration." State senator Willie Rainach of Louisiana thought *Shuttlesworth* indicated that "[t]he court's position may well have deteriorated to the point that it would like to compromise."[48]

The other important case around this time involved Nashville's desegregation plan, which was one of the first to adopt grade-a-year desegregation. Nashville's scheme also offered a transfer option to students who were assigned to schools where their racial group was in the minority. This ensured that no whites would be compelled to attend a majority-black school and encouraged blacks, through a variety of formal and informal pressures, to transfer out of racially mixed schools to which they had been assigned. School officials throughout the South closely monitored the Nashville case and signaled their intention to adopt similar policies should the Court endorse them.

In *Kelley v. Board of Education of Nashville* (1959), the Court denied review of the Sixth Circuit decision upholding Nashville's plan—an action that ordinarily implies no view on the merits. Yet given the obvious importance of the case, and the unusual decision of three justices—Warren, Douglas, and Brennan—to publicly dissent from the Court's denial of review, the justices had plainly considered the issues carefully.

The headline in the *Southern School News* read, "Court Backs Stairstep." White southerners generally concluded that *Kelley* had sanctioned grade-a-year plans and minority-to-majority transfer options. Nashville's school superintendent announced that he was "immeasurably pleased" with the decision. A prominent southern journalist, John Temple Graves, wrote that the Court had given "clear hope that it begins to see that massive integration won't work," and he urged the white South now to endorse token desegregation in order to enable the justices to "save face." Martin Luther King, Jr., later observed that the Court "had granted legal sanction to tokenism."[49]

The justices' thinking in *Shuttlesworth* and *Kelley* can be reconstructed with some guesswork. Between 1957 and 1959, southern battle lines were drawn around outright defiance of *Brown* and token compliance. The extremism of post-*Brown* southern politics—discussed in a subsequent chapter—had eliminated meaningful integration as an option. Eisenhower's use of troops at Little Rock demonstrated that schools could not remain segregated after courts had ordered them desegregated. But did they have to remain open? Massive resisters had been threatening to close schools as their final resort since 1954. Now they were put to the test. In 1958, Governor Faubus closed Little Rock's four high schools, and Governor J. Lindsay Almond of Virginia closed several schools that courts had ordered desegregated in Charlottesville, Norfolk, and Warren County. Other states with similar school-closing legislation watched and waited as events in Arkansas and Virginia unfolded.

In this struggle, "moderate" southern politicians fought to keep schools open by promising to restrict integration to token levels. In 1957, Republican Ted Dalton ran for governor of Virginia, repudiating massive resistance and school closures and endorsing the use of pupil placement for limited integration. That same year, LeRoy Collins of Florida became the first Deep South governor to oppose massive resistance. Collins condemned the legislature's interposition resolution as a "cruel hoax," insisted that some desegregation was inevitable, and promised that it could be delayed and controlled through the pupil placement law. In 1958, Malcolm Seawell, the attorney general of North Carolina, endorsed similar policies.[50]

These were risky positions for southern politicians to embrace at the time. Dalton was labeled an "integrationist." Collins was attacked for "surrendering" and called a "weakling." Seawell was pilloried for his "abject surrender" and compared to Judas Iscariot, even though only thirteen blacks attended desegregated schools in all of North Carolina—"eye-dropper integration," according to the NAACP.[51]

For the Court to have invalidated gradualist policies such as pupil placement, minority-to-majority transfer, and grade-a-year desegregation might have destroyed these moderate politicians, especially after the use of federal troops at Little Rock had already weakened them. Diehard segregationists would have seized upon such rulings as proof that no middle ground existed between massive resistance and massive integration. The justices closely followed southern politics, and since 1954, they had sought to bolster moderates, many of whom were explicitly appealing to the Court after Little Rock for a "cooling-off" period. The decisions in *Shuttlesworth* and *Kelley* suggest that the justices were not deaf to such appeals.

Internal Court documents indirectly support this interpretation. While the Little Rock case was pending, Frankfurter told Harlan that the justices' duty was to "serve as exemplars of understanding and wisdom and magnanimity" to southern moderates. He thought that the recent victory of moderate candidates in school board elections in Little Rock had "important implications . . . which are relevantly to be kept in mind by us in the procedures we adopt, when choice is open, and in how we express what we do." A few months later, Frankfurter urged his colleagues to deny the NAACP a stay in a Florida case that required it to turn over its membership lists to a legislative investigating committee, because the state court had behaved moderately and refrained from "breathing . . . defiance." So long as state jurists had produced "a creditable judicial document" and had deferred to high court authority "in terms that . . . are appropriately respectful," Frankfurter wanted to reward them.[52]

In a 1959 case that challenged Virginia's anti-NAACP laws, Black observed that "having originally adopted gradualism, I think we have to recognize the policy." He noted that even *Brown*'s defenders "mainly support gradualism" and that the recent victory of moderates in Little Rock counseled judicial restraint. Thus, Black wanted to give the high court of Virginia a chance to construe these state laws before the U.S. Supreme Court decided whether to invalidate them.[53]

The words and the deeds of the executive branch may also have influenced the justices' reaffirmation of gradualism. In August 1958, Eisenhower denied a magazine report that he had privately criticized *Brown*, while admitting that he might have "said something about 'slower.'" (Thurgood Marshall quipped in response, "If we slow down any more, we'll be going backward.") Editing a desegregation speech of his attorney general, William Rogers, Eisenhower urged that he avoid "the impression that the Federal government is looking for opportunities to intervene," refrain from suggestions that integration "will necessarily be permanent," and hint that an acceptable desegregation plan need not be completed within five or even ten years. The Justice Department resumed its policy of noninvolvement after Little Rock and declined to prosecute those who were accused of agitating disturbances at Central High School, thereby encouraging further resistance and undermining the school board.[54]

As massive resistance ended in Virginia early in 1959, the administration rushed to applaud the tokenism that ensued: Twenty-one students were attending seven "integrated" schools in two cities. Eisenhower complimented Virginians on their "heartening" desegregation, which made him "very proud." Attorney General Rogers noted the "tremendous development in the thinking of the people" of Virginia over the past few months and explained that the administration would not press for "extreme" civil rights legislation—such as empowering the attorney general to bring desegregation suits—which "might do more harm than good." "In light of Virginia's experience," he noted, "we should keep our eyes open and wait." One year later, with fewer than one black school child in a thousand attending an integrated school in the South, Rogers made the extraordinary statement that the pace of desegregation is "surprisingly good when compared with the legal problems involved." Nothing that the administration said or did encouraged the Court to reject tokenism.[55]

The justices had one additional reason for not pressing desegregation in 1958–1959: They already faced withering assaults from several directions. The Court's "Red Monday" decisions of 1957—which limited congressional and state legislative investigations of alleged communists, as well as federal criminal prosecutions of them—were extremely controversial. Senator James Eastland of Mississippi, who had an ulterior motive, accused the justices of having "woven a web of protection around the Communist party." Yet even many people without segregationist impulses criticized these rulings. In 1958, Congress barely defeated bills that would have overturned several of these "procommunist" decisions and deprived the Court of jurisdiction over related issues.[56]

That same year, the Conference of State Chief Justices voted 38–8 to criticize the Court for lacking self-restraint and invading the legislative field. Those members of the conference whose votes were not motivated by Brown may have been reacting partly against the Court's recent expansion of federal habeas corpus jurisdiction, which authorized federal trial judges to reverse the criminal rulings of state supreme courts—a development that was unlikely to win friends for the Court among the ranks of state chief justices. In addition, a couple of 1957 high court decisions that reversed criminal convictions—harbingers of the Warren Court's criminal procedure revolution—had rankled the law enforcement lobby. White southerners, of course, had been after the Court since Brown.

Rarely in U.S. history have the justices proved oblivious to sustained and powerful external criticism. The 1950s was no exception. In a pair of 1959 rulings, the justices appeared to back down on the communist issue. They may have chosen to acquiesce in token school desegregation for similar reasons.

Not until 1963 would the justices reenter the school desegregation fray to express their impatience with the concept of "all deliberate speed." By then, many lower court judges, responding to the explosion in direct-action protest that began in 1960, had already begun to reject gradualist methods that produced only token integration. National politicians were voicing dissatisfaction with the glacial pace of desegregation, and Congress was debating proposals to force quicker change in school districts that received federal funds. Late in 1962, Deputy Attorney General Nicholas Katzenbach criticized the "wide gulf" that lay between the Court's pronouncements and the social reality of continuing school segregation. In a special civil rights message to Congress in February 1963, President John F. Kennedy declared *Brown* to be "both legally and morally right" and criticized the pace of desegregation as "too slow, often painfully so."[57]

Reflecting this changed political and social climate, in the spring of 1963, the justices hinted at a new desegregation policy. In *Watson v. Memphis*, the Court rebuked a federal judge for applying the formula of "all deliberate speed" to the desegregation of public parks, and it warned that desegregation plans that "eight years ago might have been deemed sufficient" were no longer so. This was the justices' first commentary on the pace of desegregation since *Brown II*, and it came in the same month that Birmingham street demonstrations made civil rights the nation's top political priority.[58]

One week later, the decision in *Goss v. Board of Education* invalidated the same minority-to-majority transfer scheme that the justices had declined to review in 1959. *Goss* ruled that a one-way transfer option was a racial classification perpetuating segregation, and it observed that the context for construing "all deliberate speed" had been "significantly altered" since *Brown II*. The next year, the Court declared, "The time for mere 'deliberate speed' has run out"; "[t]here has been entirely too much deliberation and not enough speed."[59]

The Court now intervened in the school desegregation process much more aggressively than would previously have been imaginable. In the mid-1950s, there had been much doubt as to whether courts had the authority to forbid state officials from closing—for segregationist reasons—public facilities that the Constitution did not require the state to operate in the first place. Justice Reed had stated during *Brown II* deliberations that the Court "can't require public school systems." But in 1964, the justices in *Griffin v. County School Board* strongly hinted that on the remand in the Prince Edward County case the district judge should order public schools reopened.[60]

In 1968, the justices unanimously invalidated a freedom-of-choice plan that they would probably have been delighted to sustain in the mid-1950s. Several years earlier, even the U.S. Civil Rights Commission, which was reliably more liberal on race issues than was the Court, had thought freedom of choice obviously constitutional. In *Swann v. Charlotte-Mecklenburg Board of Education* (1971), the justices sustained busing to achieve desegregation, and they approved a sweeping plan that effectively undid the effects of housing segregation. It is safe to say that in 1954 no justice had ever dreamed of such a thing.

These decisions, though dramatic departures from 1950s constitutional doctrine, were consistent with the political climate that had developed by the time they were rendered (the 1971 decision in *Swann* may be an exception). The Justice Department urged the Court to invalidate minority-to-majority transfers in *Goss*. By 1964, Prince Edward County had become a national and international embarrassment, as 1,700 black youngsters went largely uneducated for several years. The Johnson administration urged the justices to reopen the county's public schools, and Attorney General Robert Kennedy called the situation "unnatural and unsatisfactory." The Court's invalidation of freedom of choice in *Green v. County School Board* (1968) on the ground that it produced insufficient integration tracked executive branch guidelines that imposed a similar results-based test for determining whether school districts should forfeit their federal education funds.[61]

Although the success of the civil rights movement probably explains much of the justices' more aggressive posture on desegregation in the 1960s, they may also have simply become fed up with the intransigence and disingenuousness of southern whites. One cannot know for sure, but massive resistance may have come back to haunt white southerners. Moderate critics had predicted that massive resistance would eventually produce massive integration, and they may have been right. The justices eventually grew tired of the endless evasion and bad faith, and they adjusted constitutional and other doctrines in response.

In an unprecedented 1961 ruling, *NAACP v. Gallion*, the justices, exasperated at the bad faith of Alabama jurists, ordered them to quickly hold a hearing on the NAACP's right to operate in the state or else forfeit jurisdiction to the federal district court. For similar reasons, *McNeese v. Board of Education* (1963) abandoned the traditional requirement that litigants exhaust their state administrative remedies before suing in federal court. In *Griffin*, the Court invalidated school closures partly because of the illicit motivation behind them: defiance of a federal court desegregation order. Traditional constitutional doctrine disfavored judicial inquiries into legislative motives, but years of massive resistance had changed the justices' minds.

By 1964, the justices were so irritated by delays in Prince Edward County, where desegregation litigation had commenced in 1951, that they refused to afford state courts the usual opportunity to resolve state constitutional questions before the federal courts ruled on federal issues—the opposite of what they had done in an important NAACP case from Virginia in 1959. They also approved the district court's order to the county to levy taxes for the operation of public schools—a virtually unprecedented decision, about which several justices had doubts. Who knows whether they would have overcome those doubts had it not been for the county's extraordinary defiance of *Brown*, which had lasted for an entire decade?

expanded role of fed. cts

Similarly, because the justices no longer trusted white southerners to do what they were told or to be honest about what they were doing, beginning in 1968 the Court evaluated desegregation plans based on actual results—how many blacks attended mixed schools. Contrast this with 1955, when many justices apparently believed that compliance with *Brown* need not require a great deal of integration. Burton, for example, had stated that "nonsegregation . . . may here and there result in some presence of more than one race." In *Green*, however, the justices explained that freedom of choice had to be evaluated against the backdrop of thirteen years of resistance and evasion.[62]

In 1954, the Court had played a vanguard role in school desegregation. Half of the nation supported *Brown* from the day it was decided, but it was the justices who had put the issue on the map. Many of them had to overcome serious legal doubts to invalidate segregation, but fundamental changes in the extralegal context of race relations had rendered a contrary result too unpalatable to most of them.

Brown II then authorized a relaxed transition. Gradualism appealed to the justices because it enabled them to maintain their unanimity, avoid issuing unenforceable orders, assuage their consciences, and appeal to southern moderates. White northerners generally endorsed gradualism, while many white southerners interpreted the Court's willingness to be accommodating as a sign of weakness. Southern politics moved far to the right, as the region made a concerted effort at massive resistance.

Given the intensity of white opposition to desegregation in the South and the president's indifference, the justices doubted that further intervention on their part to accelerate the process would prove constructive, and they feared that it might undermine southern moderates. Aside from their condemnation of outright defiance in the Little Rock case, the justices withdrew almost entirely from the school desegregation arena for nearly a decade. When they reentered in 1963–1964, they were following, not leading, national opinion. The civil rights movement had overtaken the school desegregation process, and the political branches of the national government were now playing the vanguard role. The contribution of *Brown* to these developments is the topic of the following chapters.

5

Brown's Direct Effects

Many commentators have called *Brown* the most important Court decision of the twentieth century, perhaps the most important ever. Yet judicial decisions can matter in many different ways. This chapter considers *Brown's* direct consequences: How much school desegregation did it produce? The following chapters examine a variety of possible indirect effects.

Even before *Brown*, a couple of northern states that had some formerly segregated school districts began to desegregate, in response to social and political forces emanating from World War II. In 1947, New Jersey passed a constitutional amendment that barred school segregation, and the governor ordered aggressive enforcement of it, including the withholding of state funds from districts that continued to segregate. In 1949, Illinois enacted a similar funds-withholding law. By the early 1950s—before *Brown*—officially sponsored segregation had largely disappeared from both states, showing that school desegregation could occur without a mandate from the Supreme Court.

Four western states—Arizona, New Mexico, Kansas, and Wyoming—which permitted local communities to impose segregation at their discretion (local option) had similar experiences. These states had begun eradicating segregation before *Brown*, and the Court's intervention simply accelerated the process. The Arizona legislature replaced compulsory segregation with local option in 1952, but state trial courts invalidated the new law even before *Brown*. Tucson, which had never segregated high schools, desegregated its elementary schools several years before *Brown*, and Phoenix allowed blacks to attend neighborhood schools in 1953. Smaller Arizona cities desegregated quickly and easily after *Brown*. In New Mexico, which had a tiny black population, the few communities that segregated schools under local option desegregated the year before *Brown* or in the months following. In the fall of 1954, the state school superintendent reported that segregation "has been on the wane for many years."[1]

In the early 1950s, a couple of small Kansas cities that had segregated schools under local option voluntarily desegregated. The Topeka school board, which was the defendant in *Brown*, adopted a desegregation plan eight months before the decision, and the state's lawyer conceded at oral argument that the consequences of invalidating segregation in Kansas would not be serious. Even before *Brown II*, desegregation in Topeka was reported to be moving along "in fine shape."[2]

Border states, such as Delaware, Maryland, West Virginia, and Missouri, might have followed similar paths and desegregated even without Court intervention. Justice Stanley F. Reed's prediction that "segregation in the border states will disappear in 15 or 20 years" without judicial intervention was not absurd. *Brown* pushed against an open door in these states, where, as Jackson pointed out, segregation "lingers by a tenuous lease of life."[3]

Large cities in border states desegregated after *Brown* without waiting for follow-up litigation to coerce them. Baltimore, St. Louis, Wilmington, and Washington, D.C., began desegregating in the fall of 1954 or shortly thereafter, not even waiting for *Brown II*. Likewise, in Missouri, West Virginia, Arkansas, and West Texas, some counties with small black populations began desegregating shortly after *Brown I*. Some of these communities may have regarded *Brown* as a welcome "excuse to do what they wanted" but were not permitted to do under state law. A school superintendent in western Arkansas reported, "Segregation was a luxury we no longer could afford." Other counties may have preferred to maintain segregation but not so strongly that they were prepared to defy a Court ruling. Border state governors refused to join their colleagues in the South in condemning *Brown*. Governor Theodore R. McKeldin of Maryland called the idea of resistance "fantastic nonsense."[4]

Although these border states had not begun desegregating their schools before *Brown*, other racial practices had changed, which smoothed the way for peaceful school desegregation. Baltimore teachers had served on interracial committees and projects; the association of public school teachers was integrated, as were adult education classes; and in 1952, thirty-five blacks had begun attending the white Baltimore Polytechnic Institute because black high schools in the city offered no equivalent advanced engineering courses. Also in 1952–1953, theaters in downtown Baltimore ended segregation; the Baltimore Transit Company hired its first black employees; and some downtown department stores and drugstores desegregated their lunch counters. Given how far segregation barriers had already been breached, the readiness of city and state officials to comply with *Brown* is unsurprising.

Similarly, in St. Louis, black and white teachers already served together on committees; a citywide student council was integrated; and students competed in interracial sporting events. Most hotels had desegregated, as had some restaurants and theaters. The school superintendent in St. Louis pointed out that *Brown* "was consistent with rather than contrary to the pattern of thought and action which had characterized the progress of the city for a decade."[5]

In Wilmington, Delaware, Catholic schools, schools for the deaf and blind, adult education classes, and committees of public school teachers had been integrated for years by the time that public schools desegregated in 1954. Black and white students performed together in city choruses and orchestras, and they competed against one another on sports teams. Movie theaters, hospitals, and the Delaware National Guard had recently integrated. Thus, Wilmington was reported to be in a "state of acceptance and readiness" by the time of *Brown*.[6]

Brown easily desegregated schools in border state cities partly because most whites, even though opposed, were not intensely resistant. In 1954, these cities were less identifiably southern than they had been a decade or two earlier. Most border state politicians endorsed *Brown* or at least expressed a willingness to comply, as did many newspapers, religious organizations, labor unions, and teachers' associations. Blacks had substantial political power in these cities, as well as the money to bring desegregation lawsuits. Branches of the National Association for the Advancement of Colored People were strong, and violence against blacks seeking school desegregation was unlikely. Under such circumstances, *Brown* supplied the push that was necessary

to induce public officials to do what they would not have undertaken voluntarily but were not strongly resistant to doing.

Still, one should not overstate the ease with which border states complied with *Brown* or the amount of integration that occurred. In Baltimore, with roughly 60 percent of Maryland's black population, schools desegregated in the fall of 1954, but only 3 percent of black students chose to attend racially mixed schools under the city's open enrollment (freedom-of-choice) policy; this figure rose to 7.4 percent in 1955 and 13.8 percent in 1956. Desegregation came even more slowly elsewhere in the state. In southern Maryland and on the Eastern Shore, where blacks comprised roughly 25–50 percent of the population and the racial attitudes of whites were "more hostile than in Mississippi," essentially no desegregation occurred until the early 1960s, as whites pressured blacks not to exercise their transfer rights. Not until 1962 did the state board of education begin to pressure such counties to accelerate desegregation, and black attendance at formerly white schools there remained token until passage of the 1964 Civil Rights Act.[7]

Similar patterns prevailed throughout the border region. In the fall of 1954, Wilmington desegregated without incident, and other school districts in northern Delaware followed gradually thereafter. In southern Delaware, however, virtually no desegregation took place until nearly 1960, as polls showed that whites were almost unanimously opposed, and demonstrations by more than a thousand angry whites in Milford in 1954 convinced the school board to reverse its earlier decision to desegregate. Kansas City and St. Louis, where the vast majority of Missouri's blacks lived, desegregated with "extraordinary calm" in 1954–1955. But in the southeastern "boot-heel" counties along the Mississippi River, resistance was intense, and little desegregation occurred until the early 1960s. Most counties in Kentucky began desegregating in 1956, as did the state's largest city, Louisville, where peaceful desegregation earned national acclaim. But whites in Clay and Sturgis counties rioted against desegregation in 1956, and other rural counties held out against desegregation until the early 1960s. In both Oklahoma and West Virginia, most counties with small black populations desegregated with relative ease, but heavily black counties proved more intransigent, and desegregation came haltingly.[8]

Even in those border state cities where desegregation came quickly, the number of blacks attending racially mixed schools often remained small because of residential segregation. St. Louis easily desegregated its elementary schools in 1955, but because of segregated housing patterns, only twelve such schools had racially mixed student bodies, while ninety-eight remained single race. Desegregation in Oklahoma City placed only 15 percent of blacks in schools with whites; in Tulsa, where the school attendance zones were gerrymandered and a transfer option existed, the figure was just 3 percent.

Even that minimal amount of desegregation proved difficult to sustain over time, as mixed schools resegregated because of demographic shifts. Baltimore neighborhoods turned over so quickly, as the black population increased and whites fled to the suburbs, that by 1960 twenty-two formerly white Baltimore schools had student bodies that were majority black. In St. Louis, one high school that had been 74 percent white in 1955 was 99 percent black by 1963.

School segregation that resulted from a combination of residential segregation and neighborhood school policies was not obviously a violation of *Brown*, and the NAACP did not challenge such arrangements until the early 1960s. On the contrary, even civil rights advocates tended to regard border state desegregation as a success story in the 1950s.

The eleven states of the former Confederacy responded to *Brown* very differently from the border states. No desegregation at all occurred until 1957, other than in two school districts in Tennessee, five in Arkansas with few blacks, and roughly one hundred in West and South Texas, which contained about 1 percent of the state's black school children. In the spring of 1957, a black congressman conceded that the South had won "the first round in the battle for compliance" with *Brown*. That fall, just thirteen black students entered formerly white schools in Nashville. In Little Rock, there were nine. Three North Carolina cities accounted for that state's total of eleven.[9]

The Little Rock desegregation crisis, which culminated in President Dwight D. Eisenhower's use of federal troops, brought school desegregation nearly to a halt throughout the South. Other Arkansas districts that had planned to desegregate that fall now reconsidered. Texas passed a law that required cutting off state funds to districts that desegregated without conducting a referendum, and compliance with *Brown* then ground to a halt. No other southern state desegregated any schools until 1959, when Virginia ended its massive resistance by allowing twenty-one blacks into seven white schools in two cities, and Florida permitted Miami to desegregate two schools.

On *Brown*'s sixth anniversary in 1960, 98 of Arkansas's 104,000 black students attended desegregated schools; 34 of North Carolina's 302,000; 169 of Tennessee's 146,000; and 103 of Virginia's 203,000. In the five Deep South states, not one of the 1.4 million black school children attended a racially mixed school until the fall of 1960. This is probably not exactly what the justices had in mind by "all deliberate speed."

housing & neighborhood schools

Southern states

Little Rock — effects felt throughout the South

1960

The pace of desegregation increased in the early 1960s, as burgeoning direct-action protest made blacks more aggressive in demanding school desegregation, lawsuits proliferated, and federal judges grew less tolerant of delay. Louisiana and Georgia experienced their first desegregation in 1960 and 1961, respectively, as New Orleans and Atlanta schools desegregated under court order. Houston and Dallas also desegregated in 1960–1961, and desegregation in Florida spread beyond Miami, and the number of affected black students rose significantly. In North Carolina, Tennessee, and Virginia, the number of blacks attending desegregated schools doubled or tripled every year in the early 1960s. The largest increases in desegregation, in absolute numbers, came in Texas, where the state attorney general declared unconstitutional the 1957 law that required a referendum before desegregation, and in the border states of Maryland, Delaware, and Kentucky.

Although by 1963 the increased pace of desegregation was unmistakable, only 1.06 percent of southern black students yet attended desegregated schools. In the Deep South states of Georgia and Louisiana, desegregation had yet to expand beyond a few large cities. In Alabama, South Carolina, and East Texas, desegregation had just begun that fall and was also restricted to the largest cities. In Mississippi, it would not commence until the following year. Nowhere in the South had desegregation penetrated far into rural areas.

Justice Hugo L. Black had rightly predicted that "some counties won't have negroes and whites in the same school this generation." How could *Brown* have been so inefficacious for so long outside of the border states? The answer lies partly in the incentives of southern school boards and federal judges and partly in the constraints faced by southern blacks and the NAACP.[10]

Brown II explicitly noted that school boards would retain "primary responsibility" for placing students, subject to judicial oversight. Thus, the burden of implementing *Brown II* initially lay with school board members. Most of them undoubtedly thought that *Brown* was wrongheaded, as did most white southerners, so their inclinations were to delay and evade as much as possible. Because *Brown II* supplied no clear mandate for action, it seemed to invite evasion, which made voluntary compliance politically difficult.

For personal and political reasons, school board members resisted prompt and effective action toward desegregation. As we shall see in chapter 8, *Brown* radicalized southern politics, leading candidates for office to maneuver for the most extreme segregationist position and turning "moderation" into a derisive term. Board members were elected officials, who could ill afford to ignore public opinion. Those who did often lost their positions. School board members in Nashville, who were under intense local pressure to stall desegregation, defended a plan that a federal judge had already invalidated by noting that "we must represent the people." Board members were often caught in the crossfire between federal courts ordering desegregation and state politicians threatening to cut off funds or close schools if segregation laws were violated. School board members in Little Rock eventually resigned, having grown tired of being Governor Orval Faubus's "whipping boys."[11]

Such officials also had personal incentives to delay and evade compliance with *Brown*, as they had to live in communities that were staunchly opposed to desegregation. The school superintendent in Hoxie, Arkansas, and the high school principal in Clinton, Tennessee, resigned after desegregation riots resulted in ordeals for their families. Board members who desegregated schools received harassing letters in Greensboro, North Carolina; suffered economic reprisals in New Orleans; had crosses burned on their lawns in Macon County, Alabama; and were physically assaulted in Springer, Oklahoma.

They faced little pressure from the opposite direction. Until local litigation produced a desegregation order, they ran no risk of contempt sanctions for preserving segregation. Criminal prosecution and civil damages actions were also unlikely, as defendants in such suits, unlike those in injunction cases, have a right to a jury trial. In the 1950s, blacks were still rarely serving on southern juries, and white jurors would have been unlikely to convict public officials for resisting desegregation. Thus, the incentives of school board members were heavily skewed toward delay and evasion. Moreover, they possessed an ample array of legitimate excuses for postponing desegregation: administrative complications in reassigning large numbers of students, overcrowded schools, community resistance, and the lower achievement levels and alleged immorality of blacks.

School boards had strong reasons not to be the first in a state or region to desegregate, which would make them the focal point of segregationist pressure. The few boards that took or promised to take prompt steps toward good-faith compliance quickly reconsidered. The Chattanooga school board, believing that local opinion would support it, vowed after *Brown II* to comply with the Court's instruction to make a "prompt and reasonable start" toward desegregation. Under criticism for its "cowardly and disloyal" action, the board quickly recanted and announced early in 1956 that community sentiment would not permit desegregation for at least five years. The school board in Greensboro, North Carolina, announced the day after *Brown* that it would comply, which prompted harassing phone calls and threats to the school superintendent and the board chair. Not until three years later did Greensboro begin desegregation, and even then it was merely token.[12]

School boards that acted first also ran heightened risks of violence, as itinerant troublemakers, such as John Kasper, a New Jersey segregationist who openly advocated forcible resistance to *Brown*, would come to town to rally the opposition. Clinton and Nashville—the second and third school districts in Tennessee to desegregate—had to endure extended visits from Kasper, which were followed by school bombings.

Once a desegregation order had resulted in violence, school boards elsewhere became even more reluctant to end segregation. After a mob of angry whites closed a desegregated school in Milford, school boards elsewhere in southern Delaware refused to desegregate until compelled to do so by the courts. Facing hardening public reaction after Little Rock, most school boards chose the path of least resistance—delay and evasion—in order to avoid violence. Houston's school superintendent declared, "[T]he experiences of 1957 in some schools that tried integration show me that we are going to be slow to accept it." As late as 1961, one Tennessee school board was still rejecting desegregation because it was "alarmed at the instances of violence, bloodshed and willful destruction of property which took place when efforts were made to integrate other areas of the South."[13]

Few school boards ultimately desegregated until courts had ordered it or at least until parties had threatened to litigate. The Knoxville school board, desperately seeking political cover, beseeched Judge Robert L. Taylor to command, not merely instruct, it to submit a desegregation plan. Even a court order was sometimes insufficient to prompt school board action. In Milton, Delaware, board members who had agreed to desegregate under court order resigned in the face of massive white protests, and their replacements vowed to fight on. A school board member in Houston declared that she would rather go to jail than vote to desegregate. Because school boards would generally not desegregate without a court order, the implementation of *Brown* depended on the ability of black parents to bring suits and on the willingness of federal judges to order desegregation. Neither condition was easily satisfied.

Brown technically bound only school board defendants in five cases. Thus, litigation was necessary in every southern school district—of which there were thousands—in which resistant boards declined to voluntarily desegregate. President Eisenhower declined to request, and Congress would not have granted anyway, authority for the attorney general to file desegregation suits on behalf of black parents. Few blacks could afford the $10–15,000 necessary to litigate a case to the Supreme Court. They had little incentive to sue anyway, because litigation delays would probably prevent their children from reaping the benefits of a lawsuit. Only an organization that represented blacks as a group, such as the NAACP, could capture the benefits, and thus offset the costs, of desegregation litigation. Moreover, few white lawyers would have dared to take such cases.

Not surprisingly, then, virtually all desegregation litigation involved the NAACP. Comprehending this, southern whites declared war on the association. No sooner had the Miami branch filed a school desegregation suit in 1956 then the state legislature began investigating it for alleged communist infiltration and demanded its membership lists— which, if publicized, would have invited reprisals against members. In Clarendon County, South Carolina, the citizens' council circulated the names of NAACP members, who then promptly lost their jobs, credit, and suppliers. Virginia passed a law prohibiting organizations that lacked a pecuniary interest in litigation from soliciting suits for their lawyers—a measure that was clearly aimed at barring the NAACP from desegregation litigation, which would have effectively ended such suits.

Z. Alexander Looby and Arthur Shores, NAACP lawyers in Nashville and Birmingham who were responsible for school desegregation litigation, had their homes bombed. Alabama, Texas, and Louisiana temporarily shut down NAACP operations through litigation, thus severely hampering the organization's ability to bring desegregation suits. Even without this onslaught, the NAACP had limited resources and could not finance an infinite number of such suits. Further, the association remained weak in rural areas, where desegregation litigation rarely began until the mid-1960s.

Even when the NAACP could finance litigation, individual blacks still had to enlist as plaintiffs. The association desperately solicited litigants, but in the Deep South, few blacks volunteered, aware as they were that "the KKK tries your case long before it can get before the Supreme Court."[14]

Hundreds of blacks who signed school desegregation petitions in Deep South cities in 1954–1955 suffered swift and severe retribution. Newspapers published their names, which facilitated economic reprisals. Many of the petitioners had to relocate to find work. Some suffered violence, such as the president of the NAACP branch in Sulphur Springs, Texas, who had his home shot up and was driven out of the state.

Neither the association nor the petitioners had expected quite so ferocious a response, and it clearly deterred prospective litigants, who could guess what would be in store for them and their children. The Reverend J. A. De Laine, who had helped to organize the original school desegregation suit in Clarendon County, was fired from his job as a public school teacher, had his life threatened by the Ku Klux Klan, saw his church burned down, and then had to flee South Carolina after being charged with assault for defending himself against vigilantes who were attacking his home. When the Reverend Fred Shuttlesworth escorted his children to a white Birmingham school to desegregate it, he was badly beaten by members of a mob who wielded brass knuckles and baseball bats, and his church was bombed three times in retaliation for his desegregation activities.

Harassment of the NAACP and intimidation of prospective plaintiffs stymied desegregation litigation outside of the border states and the peripheral South. One of Justice Harold H. Burton's law clerks had noted that "this Court cannot do anything to Miss[issippi] if it chooses to continue segregation unless a Negro chooses to try to enforce his

Figure 5.1. The Reverend J. A. De Laine speaks at the NAACP Legal Defense Fund's annual meeting in 1974. Photo courtesy J. A. De Laine, Jr.

Figure 5.2. The Reverend Fred Shuttlesworth meets with the press after his release from the hospital after he was beaten by a mob while trying to desegregate a Birmingham high school in 1957. Birmingham Public Library, Department of Archives and Manuscripts, no. 829.1.1.61.

rights there." None did so at the grade school level until 1963. In Georgia, the first desegregation suit outside of Atlanta was not filed until 1962. In Alabama, the first suit outside of Birmingham was not filed until 1963. Martin Luther King, Jr., threatened a school desegregation suit in Montgomery in 1959, which prompted Governor John Patterson to go on statewide radio to warn blacks "that if you follow a man like Martin Luther King, it is only going to lead to chaos and disorder and violence and the destruction of our public school system." No desegregation suit was brought in Montgomery until 1964.[15]

Ironically, suits proliferated where desegregation was already furthest along. In 1956, the NAACP filed its eighth desegregation suit in Delaware and its ninth in West Virginia, while the first Deep South litigation was still years away. Desegregation litigation proved most feasible where resistance was the least intense and therefore litigation was least necessary, and vice versa.

Even so, litigation could only bring the issue before a judge, who would have to determine whether, when, and how schools would desegregate. Lower federal courts are the principal interpreters of Supreme Court opinions, and they would ultimately determine the meaning of *Brown II*.

federal judges

Justice Black had warned that "not one federal judge would favor [desegregation]"—a slight overstatement but not much of one. In 1954, all southern federal judges were white; the vast majority had been born and raised in the South; and their views on school desegregation did not deviate far from those of most white southerners. Many of them were openly disdainful of *Brown*, and almost none publicly endorsed it.[16]

Judge William H. Atwell of Dallas thought that segregation was "neither immoral nor unconstitutional," and he criticized *Brown* for its reliance on "modern psychological knowledge" rather than law. Judge T. Whitfield Davidson, born in East Texas though sitting on the bench in Dallas, insisted, "[T]he white man has a right to maintain his racial integrity and it can't be done so easily in integrated schools." Judge George Bell Timmerman of South Carolina believed that whites "still have the right to choose their own companions and associates, and to preserve the integrity of the race with which God Almighty has endowed them," and he insisted, "The judicial power of the United States . . . does not extend to the enforcement of Marxist socialism as interpreted by Myrdal, the Swedish Socialist." Judge R. Gordon West of Louisiana thought that *Brown* was "one of the truly regrettable decisions of all times." These were some of the judges who were charged with enforcing *Brown*.[17]

Even judges who profoundly disagreed with desegregation might have followed unambiguous Court orders to impose it, out of a sense of professional obligation. State and federal judges did nullify segregation laws after *Brown*, revealing a willingness to follow clear Court edicts, "distasteful as [they] might be," because they "had no right to reverse the rulings of the Supreme Court." Some of these judges protested that they were not "free agent[s]," and others volunteered their personal opinions that *Brown* was wrong—"most unfortunate, and . . . entirely unconstitutional," according to one—but they did their duty to enforce it by invalidating segregation laws. *Brown II*, however, was hardly an order to do anything. Its indeterminacy invited judges to delay and evade, which they were inclined to do anyway.[18]

attacks on judges

Lower court judges also faced political pressure not to order desegregation. Politicians attacked judges who seemed overly eager to desegregate, and judges could point to no order from above commanding desegregation at any particular time or in any particular manner. Senator Harry Byrd of Virginia accused Judge Walter E. Hoffman, who was the first judge to invalidate any of the state's massive resistance legislation, of "arrogance," "prejudice," and partisanship in his decisions. Governor George Wallace repeatedly assailed Judge Frank Johnson for his "integrating, scallawagging, carpetbagging" ways. One Louisiana legislator questioned Judge J. Skelly Wright's mental soundness, and another called for his arrest.[19]

Lifetime job tenure provided federal judges with some insulation from political attack but not from the disapprobation of friends and colleagues. Just like school board members, federal judges had to live in the communities that they were being asked to desegregate against the wishes of most whites. An aide to Governor Wallace suggested, "These federal judges should be scorned and they and their families and their friends ostracized by responsible Southerners."[20]

And so they were. Judges endured hate mail, harassing midnight phone calls, and occasional cross burnings. The grave of the son of Judge Richard Rives of the Fifth Circuit was desecrated. The home of the mother of Judge Frank Johnson of Montgomery was bombed. After Judge J. Waties Waring voted to desegregate schools in Clarendon County, South Carolina, shots were fired into his home. Soon thereafter, having tired of being "the lonesomest man in town," he retired from the bench and moved to New York.[21]

Lower court judges had little incentive to press desegregation where it was likely to produce school closures or violence. One federal judge, citing the violence in Milford and Little Rock, concluded that "total and immediate integration of the Delaware school system is out of the question." Judge Frank Hooper refused to order desegregation in Atlanta "so speedily that there will be violence." Judge Taylor, acknowledging his failure to foresee the "frightful lawlessness" and "terrorism" at Clinton, Tennessee, where he had ordered desegregation in 1956, justified a grade-a-year plan for Knoxville as necessary to avoid a repetition. Although *Brown II* instructed courts not to consider community resistance in fashioning desegregation orders, the justices had not taken that instruction seriously, and neither did most district judges, who thought that the size of the local black population, the intensity of white resistance, and the likelihood of violence were obviously relevant considerations.[22]

Personal and political incentives not to press desegregation, together with a legal standard that conferred broad discretion, led most federal judges to countenance delay. So long as school boards "studied" the problem, judges were generally satisfied for at least a couple of years after *Brown*. The first judicial desegregation orders generally required ending segregation with "all deliberate speed" but without imposing any deadline; such orders proved to be nearly worthless in practice. By the time that judges were ready to impose deadlines, southern political opinion had become so extreme that most of them were reluctant to order anything beyond token integration and some not even that.

In light of the indeterminate legal standard, it was predictable that a great deal would depend on the inclination of particular judges and on the environment in which they operated. Northern judges on the Eighth Circuit construed *Brown II* more stringently than did a southern judge in Little Rock, whose decisions they reviewed, and northern and southern judges on the Sixth Circuit had different opinions regarding desegregation in Tennessee. In the border state of Kentucky, some federal judges construed "all deliberate speed" to mean "now," and they imposed desegregation orders soon after *Brown II*. In upper South states, such as Arkansas, Tennessee, and Virginia, some judges issued desegregation orders with deadlines as early as 1956 or 1957.

But in recalcitrant districts, which were usually those with large black populations, judges were disinclined to impose early deadlines. Although each of his Virginia colleagues had already issued desegregation orders, in 1957 Judge Sterling Hutcheson refused to set a deadline for Prince Edward County, because the "present state of unrest and racial tension in the county" counseled "[p]atience, time and a sympathetic understanding." When the Fourth Circuit ordered him to set a deadline, Hutcheson chose 1965, which got him reversed again. In Dallas, protracted jousting between segregationist trial judges and an increasingly impatient Fifth Circuit, combined with years of legal uncertainty over the constitutionality of Texas's 1957 referendum requirement, delayed desegregation until 1961. In Louisiana, even the progressive-minded J. Skelly Wright, who issued a desegregation order without a deadline in 1956, permitted delays until 1960 in light of hostile opinion, which he conceded would not permit desegregation "overnight."[23]

When judges eventually ordered desegregation, the same incentives just noted inclined most of them to endorse gradualism and tokenism. In an early interpretation, Judge John Parker of the Fourth Circuit insisted that *Brown* "forbids the use of governmental power to enforce segregation"; it "does not require integration." In other words, the remedial obligation of school districts was to dismantle state-sponsored segregation, not to produce racial balance in the schools.[24]

Parker's interpretation may seem like a bad-faith distortion of *Brown*'s meaning, but he was no nullifier. Justice Burton had stated a similar view during *Brown II* deliberations: "The mere admission of colored children to white schools, or vice versa, is not in itself justifiable. The Constitution does not call for that." Lower court judges frequently cited Parker's dictum, which rapidly became the conventional interpretation. Even compliant judges thought that *Brown* "may well not necessitate such extensive changes in the school system as some anticipate."[25]

In the 1950s, most judges sustained proposals for even minimal desegregation, relieved to have avoided outright defiance and convinced that *Brown* had not authorized courts to substitute their judgment regarding pupil allocation for that of school boards. Courts upheld virtually every proposal for delay and evasion: grade-a-year, pupil placement, minority-to-majority transfer, and freedom of choice. *Brown II* had not plainly required more, and judges had powerful incentives not to push harder than the Court was mandating. With the justices indicating no disapproval, the evasive techniques of school boards were "confined more by the limits of personal ingenuity than by judicial restraint."[26]

Pupil placement and freedom of choice became the preferred methods of limiting desegregation. Placement laws, which were adopted by all southern states, authorized administrators to place students according to a long list of racially neutral factors, such as students' residence, psychological fitness, scholastic aptitude, health, and moral standards, the suitability of curriculums, and the availability of space and transportation. Although race was not an enumerated criterion, the purpose and effect of these plans was to enable administrators to maintain segregation, while insulating the system from legal challenge because of the difficulty of proving that a multifactor decision was racially motivated.

Such plans also delayed litigation in federal court, because parents who were dissatisfied with their children's placement could not sue until they had exhausted time-consuming and burdensome administrative appeals. Placement plans also presumptively maintained the segregationist status quo, as petitioners bore the burden of requesting placements other than to their current (segregated) schools. Finally, because the plans purported to extend individualized treatment, it was nearly impossible to bring class-action suits to challenge them, because plaintiffs could not demonstrate sufficient commonality of circumstance.

To avoid judicial invalidation, placement boards had to eventually permit some integration, but the numbers of blacks admitted were invariably token. In North Carolina, which pioneered pupil placement, twelve black students attended "desegregated" schools in three cities in 1957—enough race mixing to withstand an initial judicial challenge. Refusing to presume discriminatory administration, lower courts declined to invalidate pupil placement plans on their face, so long as they were disassociated from other legislation that mandated segregation or school closures, and the Supreme Court concurred.

School districts that eschewed pupil placement in favor of neighborhood schools generally offered liberal transfer options that curtailed desegregation. Broad transfer rights were consistent with Judge Parker's view that *Brown* required states to stop segregating but did not require them to integrate. Before 1954, southern whites had demanded compulsory segregation, but within a few years of *Brown*, they were treating freedom of association as a "God-given right."[27]

The vast majority of whites exercised minority-to-majority transfer options to leave desegregated schools to which they had been assigned. Most blacks who were eligible for desegregation opted out as well. In 1958 in Nashville, all but 4 percent did so. In Texas that year, only 1 black out of 1,229 who were eligible attended a desegregated school in Amarillo; 6 out of 2,111 in Lubbock; and 31 out of 1,100 in Austin. Counties on Maryland's Eastern Shore technically desegregated soon after *Brown*, but until the 1960s, most did not have a single black who exercised the right to transfer to a white school.

One NAACP leader thought it "disgraceful" that so few blacks took advantage of *Brown*. But black parents justifiably feared economic reprisals, mistreatment of their children, and even violence. In 1957, every black parent in Nashville who registered a child in a white school received a threatening call from the Klan. Black students who pioneered desegregation suffered taunting, threats, and physical abuse. Many of them ultimately capitulated to the pressure and returned to black schools, while those who endured often sacrificed good education in the service of integration.[28]

In the late 1950s, the Court did nothing to condemn this tokenism and was widely perceived to have endorsed it. The Eisenhower administration appeared to celebrate it, relieved at having avoided a repetition of Little Rock in Virginia in 1958–1959. Some school districts—mainly outside of the Deep South—that had been awaiting the resolution of school closure battles before beginning desegregation now implemented the tokenist measures that courts had validated.

The number of blacks admitted to white schools was minuscule, yet courts generally declined to interfere. State attorney general Malcolm Seawell told a congressional committee in 1959, when 40 of North Carolina's 300,000 black students were attending desegregated schools, that his state was gradually adjusting to *Brown*, and editors of the *New Republic* called the state a "Model for the South." The chair of the U.S. Civil Rights Commission thought that Nashville's progress was "very encouraging," even though only 44 of the district's 12,000 black students were attending desegregated schools in 1960.[29]

With good reason, Thurgood Marshall complained that massive resistance had given way to "token compliance," yet courts were acquiescing in the "unbelievably slow" pace. In 1961, he warned, "[A]n atmosphere has been created whereby pupil assignment and stairstep integration is becoming acceptable as a legitimate compromise for constitutional rights." Another civil rights leader worried that a "bored and disgusted nation might leave the South to handle the race problem in its own way." In the Deep South, aside from Atlanta and New Orleans, where nine and twelve black students, respectively, attended desegregated schools in the fall of 1961, nothing at all had happened.[30]

The pace of school desegregation accelerated primarily because of the civil rights movement. Beginning with sit-in demonstrations in 1960 and Freedom Rides in 1961, direct-action protest swept the South. In response, the NAACP began demanding more effective desegregation policies, more blacks brought suits, and some federal judges rejected tokenist strategies that had previously been deemed to be acceptable.

Soon after the sit-ins began, the NAACP's secretary reported, "Students who participated in protest demonstrations have been stimulated to move toward more desegregation in education." The association encouraged that development. In May 1960, an NAACP leader in Florida announced a mass campaign to enroll blacks in racially mixed schools. That summer and fall, both the number of blacks who petitioned for transfers to white schools under placement schemes and the number who declined to transfer out of racially mixed schools under neighborhood plans increased dramatically.[31]

This campaign expanded in 1961. Marshall made speeches across the South, denouncing token integration, which he called an insult to the intelligence of black people, and urging blacks to commence a massive assault on segregated schools. Civil rights rallies in Atlanta urged blacks to apply for transfers to white schools. The Florida NAACP called for an all-out campaign against school segregation, in which thousands of blacks would demand transfers under placement plans, which the association now denounced as subterfuges. The association organized several black families in Polk County, Florida, to seek admission to white schools after hundreds of blacks were arrested during direct-action protests.

In 1960, the annual race-relations report of the Tuskegee Institute observed that sit-in demonstrations had "encouraged a country-wide reexamination of the moral consequences of the continuing delays in implementing desegregation." Many judges also seemed to be reexamining their positions. In the summer of 1960, the Third Circuit rejected grade-a-year desegregation for Delaware, notwithstanding the justices' recent refusal to review the Sixth Circuit ruling sustaining that policy for Nashville. Shortly thereafter, Judge Albert V. Bryan threw out the grade-a-year plan of Fairfax County, Virginia, reasoning that Fairfax, with its 4 percent black population, could move more quickly than Nashville, with its 37 percent. In 1961–1962, several Tennessee judges rejected grade-a-year plans, ordering counties to desegregate several grades at once or, in some instances, all grades simultaneously.[32]

Late in 1960, the Fifth Circuit invalidated as discriminatory the minority-to-majority transfer option in the Dallas desegregation plan, disagreeing with the Sixth Circuit's resolution of that issue in the Nashville case. In 1962, the Fourth Circuit followed suit, and so did several district judges. Many courts now rejected certain features of pupil placement plans, such as the requirement for achievement tests, which applied only to blacks. Some judges went even further, ruling that placement schemes were inadequate as desegregation plans so long as they presumptively placed students in the same segregated schools—a clear departure from earlier decisions.

Even courts that still tolerated placement plans began to look more closely at their administration, found discrimination, and ordered large increases in the number of blacks assigned to desegregated schools. Early in 1961, the Eighth Circuit ruled discriminatory the Little Rock school board's administration of its pupil placement plan and demanded "affirmative action" to produce "integration on more than a token fashion." The number of blacks attending desegregated schools in Little Rock quadrupled the next year. In 1962, the Fourth Circuit began invalidating the discriminatory administration of placement plans in North Carolina and Virginia. That year, the school board in Charlotte-Mecklenburg, North Carolina, radically revised its placement policy to assign students primarily on the basis of geography rather than requiring blacks to petition for admittance to white schools; the number of blacks attending racially mixed schools promptly increased from 27 to 413.[33]

Desegregation also began to penetrate into new areas—eastern North Carolina, East Texas, the Florida panhandle—as some school boards saw the writing on the wall, and others were compelled by courts to act. Border states that had tolerated segregation in recalcitrant districts—rural Kentucky, Maryland's Eastern Shore, Missouri's boot-heel—began exerting pressure to eliminate it. Yet, some intensely resistant districts and segregationist judges still refused to accelerate the pace; they continued to practice and permit the discriminatory administration of placement plans, which yielded only token desegregation.

The altered social climate affected the politics of desegregation. In the fall of 1961, the U.S. Civil Rights Commission issued sweeping recommendations for accelerating desegregation, including requiring all districts to file desegregation plans with the federal government within six months and withholding 50 percent of federal education money from segregated districts. For the first time, the Kennedy administration threatened to litigate against, and to cut off funds for, segregated districts that received federal money to educate the children of military personnel. Southern officials expressed alarm at the prospect of losing millions of federal education dollars. The Justice Department filed the first such suits in 1962–1963, and many districts desegregated rather than run the risk of losing federal funds.

After the epic Birmingham street demonstrations in the spring of 1963 (described in chapter 9) and the administration's introduction of landmark civil rights legislation in response, the pace of school desegregation accelerated significantly. That summer, Attorney General Robert Kennedy told the Senate Judiciary Committee that desegregation must speed up, and the Justice Department intervened in an NAACP desegregation suit to tell the justices the same thing. The chair of the House Judiciary Committee, Emanuel Celler, warned that he was keeping "a watchful eye" on federal judges who were responsible for "unconscionable delay" in handling civil rights cases—a thinly veiled threat of impeachment. There were 161 school districts that desegregated in the fall of 1963, by far the largest number since 1956, and three and a half times the number of the preceding fall.[34]

The NAACP now demanded a "total end" to school segregation, and a few judges acquiesced in that demand. Pupil placement schemes were increasingly abandoned in favor of freedom-of-choice plans. Many districts announced the desegregation of all grades at once. For the first time, some judges barred school boards from making teacher assignments based on race. All of these developments occurred before the Supreme Court declared that the time for "deliberate speed" had expired.[35]

Notwithstanding this accelerated desegregation pace, when Congress passed the 1964 Civil Rights Act, only one black child in a hundred in the South attended a racially mixed school. The federal judiciary, acting without any congressional or much presidential backing, had proved powerless to accomplish more. Most of that 1 percent, moreover, had resulted from lower court decisions of the early 1960s, which had increased the pace of desegregation in response to broad social currents. Those decisions would not have happened without *Brown*, but they would also not have happened without the civil rights movement.

In supporting the 1964 act, Senator Paul Douglas of Illinois observed that desegregation would take one thousand years to complete in the Deep South if the current pace continued. Because of the statute, it did not. The attorney general exercised his newly granted authority to bring desegregation suits, and the Department of Health, Education, and Welfare (HEW) threatened to withhold federal education funds from districts that continued to segregate. The imposition by HEW of more stringent desegregation guidelines in 1966—rejecting freedom of choice in favor of actual integration—accelerated the process, especially as lower courts incorporated these guidelines into their desegregation decrees.

The percentage of southern black children in desegregated schools shot up from 1.18 percent in 1964, to 6.1 percent in 1966, 16.9 percent in 1967, 32 percent in 1969, and roughly 90 percent in 1973. (These figures do not distinguish between blacks attending schools with many whites and with few whites.) The 1964 Civil Rights Act, not *Brown*, was plainly the proximate cause of most school desegregation in the South. The following chapters investigate the linkage between the Court decision and the statute.

6

Brown's Indirect Effects

Counting the number of black children attending desegregated schools is only one way—and perhaps a rather poor one—of evaluating *Brown's* importance. Countless scholars have asserted *Brown's* broader significance, calling the decision "the most important political, social, and legal event in America's twentieth-century history" and "the foundation of our quest for equal justice in the United States." More specifically, observers have claimed that *Brown* "launched the public debate over racial equality," "raised black awareness," "stimulated black hope," and "awoke a new activism within the black community."[1]

This chapter considers several possible indirect effects of *Brown*: How much did the decision increase the salience of the segregation issue and thus force people to take a position? How much did the Court's moral authority educate people into condemning segregation? Did *Brown* inspire southern blacks to launch more aggressive legal challenges to Jim Crow? Did the decision motivate blacks to engage in alternative forms of protest, such as boycotts, sit-ins, Freedom Rides, and street demonstrations?

Did *Brown*, by cultivating faith in legal action, possibly *discourage* direct-action tactics? Did desegregation developments after *Brown*, by revealing the limits of litigation-induced social change, encourage a shift to direct-action tactics in the 1960s? Subsequent chapters consider the extent to which *Brown* mobilized southern white resistance, radicalized southern politics, and encouraged violence, which ultimately produced a national backlash in favor of civil rights legislation.

Unfortunately, the indirect effects of Supreme Court decisions cannot be measured with precision. History is not science; one cannot repeat experiments and control for particular variables. Still, one can make a plausible case that *Brown* mattered more in some of these ways than in others. Specifically, I shall argue that *Brown* was less directly responsible than is commonly supposed for the direct-action protests of the 1960s and more responsible for ensuring that those demonstrations would be brutally suppressed by southern law enforcement officers. That violence, when communicated through television to national audiences, transformed racial opinion in the North, leading to the enactment of landmark civil rights legislation.

Supreme Court rulings can direct public attention to previously ignored issues. Americans were not preoccupied with flag burning until the Court issued two controversial rulings on the subject in 1989–1990. Within six months of a 1990 decision on the right to die, a half million Americans drafted living wills.

Brown surely had this sort of impact. News coverage was extraordinary. Major newspapers heralded the decision in front-page banner headlines. The *New York Times* assigned fifty staff members to cover the story, and they produced seven published pages of information related to the ruling. A 1955 poll conducted in small towns in North Carolina and Georgia revealed that 60 percent of respondents had discussed *Brown* within the preceding week. Four days after *Brown*, a twelve-year-old girl from Brooklyn wrote to Justice William O. Douglas to praise the "wonderful" decision, which represented a "beginning for the negro people." Most Court decisions may escape the attention of most Americans, but *Brown* did not.[2]

Brown forced many people to take a position on school segregation. Before *Brown*, desegregation of the military and major league baseball had been salient issues; school segregation was not. In 1947, President Harry S Truman's civil rights committee took a position on nearly all salient race issues; school segregation was not among them.

Brown changed this. In 1952, neither the Democratic nor the Republican national party took a position on school segregation, but in

1956 both of them did. Civil rights generally, and school segregation particularly, played large roles at both parties' national conventions that year. During the presidential election campaign, all of the Democratic candidates for the nomination made several statements regarding school desegregation, and so did President Eisenhower and Vice President Richard Nixon. From the 1920s to the 1950s, civil rights bills in Congress had dealt with lynching, the poll tax, and job discrimination. School desegregation—in the context of the attorney general's authority to bring injunction suits—first became the subject of proposed legislation in 1956–1957.

Brown also dramatically increased the importance of race in southern politics. In the postwar years, populist politicians had won many victories throughout the South by supporting expanded public services and downplaying race. *Brown* rendered this strategy obsolete. By 1955–1956, school desegregation had become the dominant issue in most southern elections. Outside of politics, church groups, labor unions, and debating societies in the South resolved their support for *Brown* or, more frequently, their opposition to it.

That *Brown* forced people to take a position on school segregation is not to say that it influenced the position they took. Some endorsed it and others condemned it—and Eisenhower said that he would enforce it, while refusing to endorse or condemn it. Southern politicians, forced to take a position on an issue that many of them would have preferred to avoid, overwhelmingly denounced *Brown*. By contrast, northern liberals, who may not have had much previous occasion to consider school segregation, now condemned it as a moral evil. Most national religious organizations responded similarly. They had not previously expressed an opinion on school segregation, but once forced to do so, the only conceivable position they could take was to condemn it. Even the organizations of Southern Baptists and Methodists endorsed *Brown* as consistent with Christian principles, leading many of their local affiliates to violently dissent. In the mid-1950s, any serious Democratic presidential candidate had to endorse *Brown*.

Being forced to take a position in favor of *Brown* did not equate to being strongly committed to implementing the ruling. One could endorse *Brown* without supporting the use of federal troops to enforce it, or cutting off federal education funds to districts that defied it, or breaking a southern filibuster in the Senate over legislation to implement it. An early 1957 poll showed that 72 percent of Americans were opposed to cutting off federal education funds to districts that continued to segregate their schools. According to 1956 Gallup polls, more than

70 percent of whites outside of the South thought that *Brown* was right, but less than 6 percent considered civil rights to be the nation's most important issue. In the South, where over 40 percent thought that civil rights was the leading issue, only 16 percent of whites agreed with *Brown*. In the mid-1950s, the whites with the strongest feelings about *Brown* generally disagreed with it the most vehemently.

The passage of the 1957 Civil Rights Act illustrates these points about salience and relative intensity of preference. Without *Brown*, Congress most likely would not have enacted civil rights legislation when it did. No such bill had passed since 1875, and since the 1920s many proposed measures had succumbed to the threat or reality of Senate filibuster. After *Brown* raised the salience of race, many northerners — white and black — demanded civil rights legislation. Liberals in both parties endorsed the concept as the 1956 elections approached.

Although heightened attention to race after *Brown* made civil rights legislation possible, the relatively tepid preferences of northern whites ensured that any statute would be limited in scope and largely ineffectual. In an extraordinary display, Eisenhower publicly confessed that he "didn't completely understand" his administration's own bill. Title III, which would have authorized the attorney general to sue for injunctions over any civil rights violation, implicitly including school segregation, was stricken from the bill after the president appeared dismayed by Senator Richard Russell's charge that the measure would force desegregation with "[f]ederal bayonet[s]." The bill's scope was then restricted to voting rights, with liberal senators protesting that "the rug is [being] pulled from under our feet by the Administration."[3]

Yet even thus limited, the bill proved to be unacceptable to white southerners, who further sabotaged it with an amendment that guaranteed jury trials for those who were charged with criminal contempt for violating an injunction. Because few southern whites would convict public officials for disfranchising blacks, the jury trial provision essentially nullified the statute's impact. The crucial votes for narrowing its scope came from western Democrats, who traded their votes on civil rights legislation in exchange for southern support for federal water projects. Seven years later, when commitments to civil rights were stronger, even the longest filibuster in Senate history could not induce northern and western senators to abandon their support.

Brown increased the salience of the segregation issue, and in 1954 many Americans, if forced to take a position, could only be integrationists. Yet, endorsing a position and being strongly committed to it are very different things. Set against the intense preferences of southern whites for preserving segregation, the weak endorsement of *Brown* by many northerners was ineffectual.

Conventional wisdom holds that one of *Brown*'s most important consequences was to educate white Americans to condemn racial segregation. Yet, surprisingly little evidence supports this view. Americans have generally felt free to disagree with the Supreme Court and to make up their own minds about moral controversies. *Engel v. Vitale* (1962) ruled that the Constitution prohibits state-sponsored prayer in public schools, yet polls indicate that a solid majority of Americans still favor that practice today. Rather than educating people to oppose the death penalty, *Furman v. Georgia* (1972), which ruled capital punishment to be unconstitutional under certain circumstances, seems to have mobilized support for it. Opinion polls suggest that *Roe v. Wade* (1973), which invalidated most statutes criminalizing abortion, has not changed many minds on that subject. If none of these landmark decisions educated many people to agree with the Court, why should *Brown* have?

Of course, it is possible that *Brown* was simply different. The fact that other famous rulings have had little educational impact does not prove that *Brown* did not. The educational influence of *Brown* must be analyzed on its own. Yet one should not discount the possibility that most Americans ultimately agreed with *Brown* not because the Court influenced their thinking, but because other developments, such as the civil rights movement, did.

Opinion poll data suggest that *Brown* did not educate many southern whites. A 1959 Gallup poll showed that only 8 percent of southern whites supported *Brown*, down from 15 percent in earlier polls. Rather than persuading southern whites to support desegregation, *Brown* inspired them to ridicule the Court, to support curbs on its jurisdiction, to recommend impeaching its justices, and to propose investigating its members for communist influence. Southern whites were not educated by a decision that they believed ignored precedent, transgressed original intent, indulged in sociology, infringed on the reserved rights of states, and usurped Congress's authority. Newspaper editor James J. Kilpatrick stated a typical view:

> In May of 1954, that inept fraternity of politicians and professors known as the United States Supreme Court chose to throw away the established law. These nine men repudiated the Constitution, sp[a]t upon the tenth amendment, and rewrote the fundamental law of this land to suit their own gauzy concepts of sociology.

Another prominent southern journalist, John Temple Graves, wrote, "The Supreme Court . . . has tortured the Constitution. The South will torture the Supreme Court decision."[4]

Most northern whites did not ridicule *Brown* in this way, and many of them strongly endorsed it. Senator Hubert H. Humphrey of Minnesota called *Brown* "another step in the forward march of democracy," and Senator Herbert H. Lehman of New York said the decision was "news which all free men throughout the world must hail with joy." Yet to observe that most northerners applauded *Brown* is not necessarily to say that they were educated by it. Powerful political, economic, social, and ideological forces were impelling Americans toward more egalitarian racial views, quite independently of the Court's pronouncements. Revulsion against Nazi theories of Aryan supremacy and the Holocaust probably educated northern opinion at least as much as *Brown* did.[5]

Moreover, poll data reveal no large shift in northern attitudes toward school segregation in the years after *Brown*, as one might have expected if its educational influence were significant. One opinion poll showed that 5 percent more Americans agreed with *Brown* in 1959 than in 1954— an increase in antisegregation sentiment of 1 percent a year, which might easily have been attributable to extralegal forces as much as to the Court's ruling. *Brown* may have had a marginal impact on those who were undecided and thus most susceptible to the Court's influence, but it did not fundamentally transform the racial attitudes of most Americans.

Brown changed the minds of few southern whites, who generally ridiculed the decision rather than being educated by it. *Brown* may have had more influence on northern whites, but many of them condemned segregation independently of the Court, and many others would not do so until southern resistance to the civil rights movement in the 1960s dramatized for them the brutality of Jim Crow. Black Americans, of course, did not need the Court's moral instruction to convince them that racial segregation was evil.

Although *Brown* was unnecessary for educating blacks to condemn segregation, it unquestionably motivated them to challenge it. After both *Brown* rulings, the National Association for the Advancement of Colored People urged southern blacks to petition school boards for immediate desegregation on threat of litigation. Blacks filed such petitions in hundreds of southern localities, including in the Deep South. In a few cities, such as Baton Rouge, Louisiana, and Montgomery, Alabama, blacks even showed up in person to try to register their children at white schools.

In the mid-1950s, but for *Brown*, such challenges would have been inconceivable in the Deep South, where race relations had been least affected by broad forces for racial change. One might have predicted that a campaign for racial reform there would have begun with voting rights or the equalization of black schools, not with school desegregation, which was hardly the top priority of most blacks and was more likely to incite violent white resistance. Merely signing one's name to a school desegregation petition was an act of courage for blacks in the Deep South, and it frequently incited economic reprisals and occasionally physical violence. The petition campaign contributed significantly to the rise of white massive resistance in the mid-1950s; black efforts to implement *Brown* stimulated more resistance than did the decision itself. As the *Jackson Daily News* editorialized, "[T]here is only one way to meet the attack of the NAACP. Organized aggression must be met by organized resistance."[6]

Southern blacks took other, mostly litigation-based action as well "to strike while the iron is hot." Four days after *Brown*, Jo Ann Robinson, the president of the Women's Political Council in Montgomery, warned the mayor that blacks would boycott city buses if segregation did not end. In Columbia, South Carolina, blacks filed lawsuits challenging segregation in city parks and on city buses. In Birmingham, *Brown* inspired the Reverend Fred Shuttlesworth and his Alabama Christian Movement for Human Rights to seek out litigation opportunities, and suits were brought challenging segregation on city buses and in parks, the railroad terminal, and public employment. Mississippi blacks mounted voter registration campaigns in 1954–1955. Blacks in Greensboro, North Carolina, demanded desegregation of the public golf course and improvements in black schools.[7]

Brown motivated litigation, but what about direct-action protests? What is the connection between *Brown* and the Montgomery bus boycott or the 1960s sit-ins, Freedom Rides, and street demonstrations? Some have treated *Brown* as the "spiritual father" of direct-action protest, occasionally even suggesting that, without *Brown*, the 1960s civil rights movement would not have taken place when it did. Evidence for this causal connection is weak.[8]

There is no denying *Brown*'s symbolic importance to African Americans. One black newspaper stated a widely shared view: *Brown* was "the greatest victory for the Negro people since the Emancipation Proclamation." One black leader called *Brown* "a majestic break in the dark clouds," and another later recalled that blacks "literally got out and danced in the streets." A black journalist subsequently noted, "[I]t would be impossible for a white person to understand what happened within black breasts on that Monday."[9]

Blacks celebrated *Brown*'s anniversary, May 17, which attests to its symbolic importance. For the Court to have vindicated their cause, especially when few other important institutions were doing so, provided blacks with moral support. Because a principal obstacle for any social reform movement is convincing potential participants that success is feasible, *Brown* must have facilitated the mobilization of civil rights protests. Yet neither the symbolism of *Brown* nor the hopefulness it inspired were tantamount to putting black demonstrators on the streets. One cannot know for sure, but the evidence that *Brown* directly inspired such protests is thin.

What was the connection between *Brown* and the Montgomery bus boycott? The boycott began in December 1955 and lasted for an entire year. It was the first major direct-action protest of the modern civil rights era and demonstrated that tens of thousands of ordinary black southerners, united across class lines, were fed up with the racial status quo and were prepared to fight it, even at the cost of extreme personal hardship.

The boycott both fostered and featured black agency, as Montgomery blacks became convinced that, through collective action, they could transform social conditions. In the words of its organizers, the Montgomery movement marked "the passage of Southern Negroes from an attitude of servility and passivity to a spirit of solidarity, fearlessness and hope." The executive secretary of the NAACP, Roy Wilkins, thought that the boycott was important because it "demonstrates before all the world that Negroes have the capacity for sustained collective action."[10]

The skill, fortitude, and courage with which blacks organized and executed the boycott contravened southern white stereotypes of black ineptitude, laziness, and timidity. Montgomery whites had never seen blacks "organize and discipline themselves, to carry something out to a finish," and they were consequently "very much impressed by their determination and courage." Blacks, not immune from being influenced by white stereotypes, were impressed as well. Moreover, this obviously indigenous action flew in the face of southern white protestations that blacks were satisfied with the racial status quo and that "outside agitators," such as communists or the NAACP, were responsible for all racial discord in the South. Alabama whites could write off Autherine Lucy, who was attempting to desegregate the University of Alabama, as "just one unfortunate girl who doesn't know what she is doing, but in Montgomery it looks like all the niggers have gone crazy."[11]

The boycott also demonstrated the tactical value of nonviolent protest. The "quiet courage, dignity, and magnanimity" with which Montgomery blacks protested their racial oppression virtually ensured that white opponents, who used economic reprisals, trumped-up criminal charges, and even bombings, would face a "damning indictment" in the eyes of observers. The boycott attracted national and international attention. Thousands of dollars in financial support (as well as many shoes) poured in from around the country, and supporters participated in a national "deliverance day of prayer" to demonstrate solidarity with Montgomery blacks.[12]

The boycott also revealed the growing intransigence of southern whites toward even minimal black demands for reform, thus increasing the stakes of the burgeoning racial controversy in the South. Finally, Montgomery created and brought to national prominence a new black leader, Martin Luther King, Jr., who would play an instrumental role in the national civil rights movement.

Based on its timing—the boycott began just eighteen months after *Brown*—and a few statements by participants, some scholars have concluded that *Brown* was instrumental to the boycott. One cannot know for certain, but this seems unlikely. *Brown* may have induced Jo Ann Robinson of the Women's Political Council to complain about bus segregation to Montgomery's mayor, but it does not appear to have inspired tens of thousands of blacks to boycott the buses.

If *Brown* directly inspired the boycott, it is puzzling why protestors for the first two months did not include integration among their demands. Rather, they principally sought an end to the humiliating practices of white bus drivers, including verbal insults—"nigger," "black bastard"—physical abuse, and an enraging proclivity to drive off before black passengers, who had to pay the fare at the front of the bus, had boarded again at the rear. The boycott leaders also demanded the hiring of black drivers for predominantly black routes and seating practices that would fill buses on a first-come, first-served basis—whites from the front, blacks from the rear, and nobody forced to stand over empty seats or to relinquish her own.[13]

At the outset of the boycott, black leaders repeatedly stressed that they were not seeking an end to segregation, which would have been the logical goal had *Brown* been their primary inspiration. Indeed, the NAACP initially refused to support the boycott, because its leaders sought only "more polite segregation." The fact that boycott leaders did not originally contemplate litigation further weakens claims regarding *Brown*'s causal influence.[14]

[handwritten margin note: did not seek to end segregation]

A similar bus boycott had taken place the year before *Brown* in Baton Rouge, Louisiana, thus proving that direct-action protest did not require the inspiration of the Court. In June 1953, Baton Rouge blacks boycotted city buses for a week, after drivers had refused to comply with a new city ordinance that required that passengers be seated on a first-come, first-served basis. Several thousand blacks attended mass meetings; the boycott was nearly 100 percent effective; and the city council quickly offered a compromise that was accepted by black leaders. Montgomery's black ministers knew of the Baton Rouge boycott, were in touch with its leaders, and adopted some of its tactics.

Brown's most significant contribution to the events in Montgomery may have been its impact on whites rather than on blacks: Why did public officials in Baton Rouge capitulate to black protest, while those in Montgomery refused to accept the same seating practices that already prevailed in many Deep South cities? Rather than making some minimal concessions, Montgomery officials became intransigent, adopting a "get tough" policy, arresting boycott organizers on fabricated charges, joining the citizens' council, and failing to suppress violence against boycott leaders. The greater resistance of whites explains why the Montgomery boycott lasted a year, while the one in Baton Rouge was over in a week, and why the initially minimalist demands of Montgomery blacks turned into a federal court challenge to segregation.[15]

In the post-*Brown* South, whites tended to view all racial issues against the backdrop of school desegregation. Thus, Montgomery mayor W. A. Gayle thought that what blacks really wanted was "to destroy our whole social fabric," and another local segregationist called the bus demands "piddling stuff," as compared with the NAACP's real objectives: complete integration and interracial marriage. In such an environment, whites refused to make any concessions to black demands, no matter how reasonable. "If we granted the Negroes these demands," a white lawyer for the bus company privately explained, "they would go about boasting of a victory that they had won over the white people; and this we will not stand for." As public officials in Montgomery debated how to respond to the bus demands of blacks in January 1956, four southern governors were announcing that their states would defy *Brown* through interposition resolutions. Had it not been for the crystallization of southern white resistance that resulted from *Brown*, events in Montgomery might have taken a very different course.[16]

None of this is to deny that the Supreme Court's decision in *Gayle v. Browder* (1956), which extended *Brown* to invalidate bus segregation laws, was critical to desegregating Montgomery buses. The same day that *Gayle* was decided, November 13, 1956, city officials had secured a state court injunction against the carpools that blacks had organized to transport themselves while the buses were being boycotted; this ruling could have destroyed the boycott.

Yet to focus on *Gayle's* contribution to desegregating Montgomery buses is to risk fundamentally misunderstanding the significance of the boycott to the modern civil rights movement. The Montgomery bus boycott demonstrated black agency, resolve, courage, resourcefulness, and leadership. The boycott revealed the power of nonviolent protest, deprived southern whites of their illusions that blacks were satisfied with the racial status quo, challenged other southern blacks to match the efforts of those in Montgomery, and enlightened millions of whites around the nation and the world about Jim Crow. A less satisfactory outcome would have been disappointing to Montgomery blacks, but it hardly would have negated, or even greatly tarnished, the momentous accomplishments of the movement.

After Montgomery, surprisingly little direct-action protest took place in the South until 1960. The Montgomery Improvement Association undertook no further direct action. City parks and other public facilities, including schools, remained segregated. Blacks in a few other southern cities conducted bus boycotts that were patterned after Montgomery's— most notably, in Rock Hill, South Carolina, and in Tallahassee, Florida— but these proved to be less successful.

On *Brown's* third anniversary in 1957, Martin Luther King, Jr., led a prayer pilgrimage to Washington, D.C., in support of black voting rights, but the turnout was disappointing—only 15–25,000 people, as compared with the 50–60,000 that had been predicted. The prayer pilgrimage was part of the voter registration drive of the Southern Christian Leadership Conference (SCLC), the Crusade for Citizenship, which floundered in the late 1950s. In 1957–1958, blacks in Tuskegee, Alabama, protested the state legislature's gerrymandering them out of the city with an effective boycott of white merchants; mass rallies in support of the boycott attracted thousands. Blacks in Orangeburg, South Carolina, also conducted a boycott in response to the economic reprisals taken by whites against black parents who had signed school desegregation petitions. In 1958–1959, small sit-in demonstrations that protested lunch counter segregation took place in several cities in the southern and border states— Oklahoma City, Wichita, St. Louis, Miami, Nashville, and others—but they attracted little attention and generated no ripple effect. Thus, whether or not *Brown* inspired the Montgomery bus boycott, it produced no general outbreak of direct-action protests in the 1950s.

In 1960, however, the South exploded with direct-action protests against race discrimination. On February 1, four black college students sat-in at the segregated lunch counter in the Woolworth drugstore in Greensboro, North Carolina. Within days, similar demonstrations had spread to other cities in North Carolina; within weeks, to surrounding states; and within months, to much of the urban South. One NAACP official called the demonstrations "the most inspiring, and most dramatic appeals for citizenship of anything I've seen in all my 49 years."[17]

Those cynics who expected the demonstrations quickly to "fizzle out, panty-raid style" were disappointed. The sit-ins "caught the imagination of the entire nation," received extensive and generally favorable coverage in the national media, and were endorsed by many politicians of both parties. Supportive northerners raised funds to assist jailed southern protestors and conducted their own sympathy demonstrations in hundreds of cities.[18]

Over the next year, southern black youngsters, together with sympathetic whites, sat-in at restaurants, lunch counters, and libraries; "stood-in" at movie theaters; "kneeled-in" at churches; and "waded-in" at beaches. All told, an estimated 70,000 people participated in such demonstrations, and roughly 4,000 were arrested. More than a hundred southern localities desegregated some public accommodations as a result.

In the spring of 1961, black and white Freedom Riders traveled on buses through the South to enforce a Supreme Court decision forbidding segregation in interstate bus terminals. The initial demonstrators were severely beaten in Birmingham and Montgomery, Alabama, and their successors were incarcerated by the hundreds in Jackson, Mississippi. The Freedom Rides were a huge fundraising and public relations success for the Congress on Racial Equality (CORE), which sponsored them. Most northerners were appalled at the violence that was perpetrated upon peaceful demonstrators who were exercising federally guaranteed rights.

Beginning in late 1961, the SCLC commenced mass demonstrations against segregation in Albany, Georgia, which lasted for nearly a year. The Student Nonviolent Coordinating Committee (SNCC) began projects to register black voters in some of the most retrograde parts of Mississippi. In the spring of 1963, massive street demonstrations by blacks in Birmingham, Alabama, resulted in hundreds of arrests and produced televised scenes of violence by law enforcement officers against peaceful demonstrators that sickened northern audiences. In the months after Birmingham, spin-off demonstrations occurred in hundreds of southern cities and towns; more than 100,000 people participated, and nearly 15,000 were arrested.

What, if any, was the connection between *Brown* and the direct-action protests of the early 1960s? The nearly six-year gap between *Brown* and the Greensboro sit-ins suggests that any such connection must be indirect and convoluted. If *Brown* were a direct inspiration, why did the protests not begin until 1960?

The outbreak of direct-action protest can be explained independently of *Brown*. The background political, economic, social, and ideological forces had created conditions that were ripe for racial protest. As southern blacks moved from farms to cities, they became easier to organize as a result of superior urban communication and transportation facilities. The growth of black institutions in southern cities—social, political, civic, educational, and religious—provided the organizational framework from which a civil rights movement could emerge. Most notably, the black church provided leadership, funding, and a mass following, and black colleges produced aggressive young leaders and a corps of willing foot soldiers. The rising economic status of southern blacks enabled the financing of protest activities as well as boycotts to leverage social change. Greater black prosperity also highlighted the indignities of enforced social subordination. Better education for blacks created leaders who could direct social protest and college students who could participate in it.

Greater restraints on violence, especially in southern cities, also facilitated direct-action protest. Those restraints were both internal and external: Modern city dwellers in the South did not generally countenance violence, and businesspeople positively despaired of it, while by 1960, the federal government was less willing to permit southern whites to maim or kill blacks with impunity. The increasing political power of northern blacks made the national government more supportive of the civil rights protests of southern blacks. The growing political power of southern blacks made local officeholders more responsive to black concerns and less willing to countenance the brutal suppression of racial protest. The explosive growth of national media, especially television, ensured that news of black protest spread quickly to other southern communities, where it could be duplicated, and to the North, where sympathetic audiences rallied in support of its goals.

The ideology of racial equality that had flowed from World War II left in its wake fewer white Americans who were strongly committed to preserving Jim Crow. Black soldiers who served during and after the war were not easily intimidated by the threats of white supremacists, and they often found insufferable the incongruity between their former role as soldiers for democracy and their continuing racially subordinate status. Many of them became civil rights leaders.

That conditions for a mass racial protest movement were ripe does not explain why the explosion came in 1960 rather than, say, five years earlier. Two factors may help to explain the precise timing of the modern civil rights movement. The first has to do with the Cold War and McCarthyism.

The anxiety of Americans over spreading international communism and the threat it posed to national security had peaked in the early 1950s. Within the space of a year, beginning in 1949, the Soviets had detonated their first nuclear bomb; communists had won control over mainland China; and North Korea had invaded South Korea, which put the United States at war again. With the threat of nuclear holocaust looming on the horizon, the time was inopportune for a crusade for domestic racial reform.

Anxiety over domestic subversion peaked simultaneously, as Americans became transfixed by Senator Joseph McCarthy's allegations of communist infiltration of the State Department and by the trials of alleged Soviet spies, including Alger Hiss, Klaus Fuchs, and Julius and Ethel Rosenberg. Fear of communists was rampant, and any protest movement that challenged the established order was susceptible to charges of being communist inspired.

Integrationist groups such as the Southern Conference for Human Welfare, the Civil Rights Congress, the Southern Negro Youth Congress, and radical labor unions were devastated by the reactionary politics of McCarthyism. Southern segregationists deftly turned this dynamic to their advantage, charging that racial reformers were communist inspired. With liberal groups such as the NAACP devoting much of their time and energy in the early 1950s to purging left-wingers, it would have been difficult to launch large-scale direct-action protests.

By 1960, however, fear of domestic subversion had subsided—the issue played essentially no role in the presidential election that year—and the threat of nuclear holocaust had receded, if only slightly. Perhaps these developments opened space for the emergence of a mass racial protest movement. On this view, the civil rights revolution of the 1960s had little to do with *Brown* and much to do with the demise of McCarthyism and the slight easing of Cold War tensions, which had proven to be temporary impediments to a protest movement that was mainly spawned by World War II.

The decolonization of Africa may also have helped to trigger direct-action protest in 1960. In 1957, Ghana became the first black African nation to win its independence from colonial rule. Within a half dozen years, more than thirty other African countries had followed suit, seventeen of them in 1960 alone. American civil rights leaders identified the African independence movements as an important motivation for their own. They saw American civil rights protest as "part of the revolt of the colored peoples of the world against old ideas and practices of white supremacy."[19]

African freedom movements demonstrated to American blacks the feasibility of racial change through collective action, while heightening their frustration with the domestic status quo. As James Baldwin explained, American blacks who observed African independence movements lamented that "all of Africa will be free before we can get a lousy cup of coffee." In 1960, Roy Wilkins observed that Africans were electing prime ministers and sending delegates to the United Nations, while Mississippi blacks still could not vote.[20]

Conditions were ripe in the United States for a mass racial protest movement, and factors such as the decolonization of Africa and the demise of McCarthyism may have provided the spark that was necessary to detonate the explosion. Alternatively, the precise timing of the Greensboro sit-ins and the extraordinary spin-off responses they produced may simply be fortuitous. Compelling background circumstances did not dictate that the movement begin at a particular time and place. It is hard to know why the scattered sit-in demonstrations of 1958–1959 failed to produce the volcanic response of the Greensboro sit-ins in 1960. Once the latter attracted media attention, though, their repetition elsewhere was virtually guaranteed. And once sit-ins began to achieve some success at desegregating public accommodations, thus making racial reform seem feasible, new volunteers were certain to appear.

Brown was an important symbol to blacks, and it furthered a growing perception that fundamental racial reform was possible. Yet there is little evidence to directly connect *Brown* with the Montgomery bus boycott or with the direct-action protests of the early 1960s. Deep background forces set the stage for mass racial protest. *Brown* was not the spark that ignited it.

Indeed, in the short term, *Brown* may have *discouraged* direct-action protest. The NAACP's enormous Court victory encouraged blacks to litigate, not to protest in the streets. *Brown* also elevated the stature of the NAACP among blacks, and the association favored litigation and lobbying, not direct-action protest. How could anyone argue with the NAACP's litigation strategy after *Brown*? In 1955, the association reported a large increase in its income, which it attributed to *Brown* "and the hope and expectation that the Supreme Court decision had provided the basis for successful action through [the] courts."[21]

One cannot measure the extent to which *Brown* may have discouraged direct-action protest, so this claim is speculative. But it does have the virtue of explaining the relative absence of such protest in the mid-to late 1950s. Before World War II, sit-ins and street demonstrations were probably impractical in most of the South, because they would have incited brutal suppression. In such an environment, litigation was the most viable means of racial protest and possibly the only one.

The Montgomery bus boycott demonstrated that conditions had changed by the mid-1950s: Direct-action protest had become a viable alternative means of pursuing racial reform. Yet, even after Montgomery, little direct action occurred until 1960. After the NAACP's inspiring victory in *Brown*, perhaps most blacks were inclined to see what litigation could deliver. Many of the black activists who would participate in direct-action protests in the early 1960s were busy in the second half of the 1950s organizing black families to sign school desegregation petitions and to file lawsuits.

After Montgomery, a group of prominent black ministers in the South launched a direct-action organization, the SCLC, with which the NAACP had strained relations from the start. This tension was partly attributable to institutional jealousy. The NAACP saw itself as *the* civil rights organization, and it was not favorably disposed toward an upstart group that might compete for funding, membership, and headlines.

The two organizations also had different theories of how to achieve social reform. The Montgomery ministers who led the boycott had been slow to litigate in part because this was not their preferred method of pursuing social change. The extraordinary success of the boycott further convinced them of the virtues of direct-action protest. Though they did not denigrate the NAACP's past contributions, they believed that, after Montgomery, "a new stage ha[d] been set." Court decisions had to be implemented at the community level, and "direct action is our most potent political weapon."[22]

The NAACP drew a different lesson from Montgomery. The association was convinced that its victory in *Gayle* was "how the Montgomery buses *really* got desegregated," and it hoped that "some smart newspaperman will finally catch on." To NAACP leaders such as Thurgood Marshall, King was a "first-rate rabble-rouser." The association did not actively support the SCLC's prayer pilgrimage in 1957 or its other voter registration activities. When the SCLC tried to move into

Jackson, Mississippi, in 1958, with the NAACP under legal assault, the association's field secretary there "naturally discouraged" it.[23]

Montgomery notwithstanding, the NAACP remained committed to the same litigation tactics of the previous half century and discouraged direct action. By the late 1950s, some branches were suggesting that the "time-tested and eminently successful legal, legislative and educational approach of the NAACP be supplemented and supported by direct mass action." But the NAACP leadership would not budge. The association had a vested interest in discouraging alternative strategies of protest that it could not monopolize. Moreover, the NAACP was "composed of lawyers and they don't march in the streets."[24]

In the late 1950s, the association's national office tried to prevent the Oklahoma City youth council from conducting sit-in demonstrations. The national office also refused to support a direct-action challenge to segregation in the public library by the branch in Petersburg, Virginia. Thus, the chair of the NAACP branch in Greensboro, North Carolina, had good reason for turning to CORE, rather than to his own national office, when student sit-in demonstrators asked for his assistance in February 1960.

Into the 1960s, NAACP officials continued to question the value of direct-action protest. The association initially criticized the sit-in demonstrations. Only after those protests proved to be enormously popular and successful did the NAACP become eager to "identify the organization with this protest movement." The association hoped to respond to the "many ill-informed hints from outside that we may have outlived our usefulness" by demonstrating that it was not "purely a 'legal' agency," but rather "a multi-weapon action organization." NAACP officials, indulging in some creative historical revisionism, emphasized the association's involvement in sit-ins "since the very beginning," noting with pride that its youth branches in Oklahoma City and Wichita had first adopted the tactic in 1958 and that the four initial Greensboro demonstrators belonged to an NAACP youth chapter.[25]

Although the NAACP claimed, in relation to the "new spirit of protest," to be the "responsible generator, . . . the chief sustainer and guide, . . . and . . . the principal custodian of [its] working out," in fact the association continued to misunderstand the significance of direct action. While King was urging students to go to jail "to arouse the dozing conscience of our nation," the NAACP was telling them to take bail and trying to convert the sit-ins into "one or two" test cases. The association discouraged mass participation and arrests, because excessive bail obligations were causing an "unfortunate dissipation" of NAACP resources and because its leaders believed that litigation challenging the legality of arrests was equally effective regardless of the number of defendants.[26]

For the NAACP, then, the principal purpose of sit-in demonstrations was to test the constitutionality of laws that protected a shopkeeper's right to racially segregate his customers. The association failed to grasp the fundamental significance of sit-in demonstrations: They enhanced the agency of blacks through collective protest; they made it "absolutely clear that the Negro is not satisfied with segregation"; and they provoked vigilantes and law enforcement officers to use "Nazi-like tactics," including tear gas, police dogs, and fire hoses. Converting sit-in demonstrations into test cases, as the NAACP advocated, would have effectively nullified such contributions.[27]

In 1961, the association's opposition to direct action led it to discourage the Freedom Rides, which at the time Wilkins called "a big mistake." When CORE asked the NAACP's field secretary in Mississippi, Medgar Evers, to help organize a mass meeting around the bus demonstrators' arrival in Jackson, Evers demurred. The NAACP feared that the Freedom Rides would "possibly hamper some of [its] efforts already in progress" in Jackson. Only after these demonstrations proved to be enormously successful at exposing the "viciousness, crudity and disregard of law characteristic of Southern segregationists"—hardly a surprising accomplishment, given that this had been their purpose—did the NAACP change its tune and urge its college chapter members who were traveling home for the summer to insist on nonsegregated transportation.[28]

The NAACP officials were also slow to support other forms of direct-action protest in the early 1960s. As a result, the association increasingly had to compete with other organizations for the loyalty of its own members, who wished to partake in the spirit of the times. When the president of the Mississippi state conference of branches, Aaron Henry, evinced too much enthusiasm for cooperating with direct-action organizations, NAACP national officials took a dim view of his "belie[f] that whosoever frees him and his people should be used."[29]

The NAACP's predominant focus on litigation was myopic. In earlier decades, litigation had helped to mobilize black protest, build branches, raise funds, and educate northern whites about Jim Crow. But the capacity of litigation to transform race relations was limited. Litigation did not foster black agency—the belief among individual blacks that they could meaningfully contribute to racial change. Rather, it taught the lesson that individual blacks should sit back—as "passive

[margin note: NAACP did not grasp the significance of direct action protests]

[margin note: limits of litigation]

spectator[s]," in King's words—and allow elite lawyers and white judges to transform race relations for them.[30]

Litigation could not involve the black masses in the same way that boycotts, sit-ins, and street demonstrations could. Only direct-action protest could enable individuals to make personal, "daily rededication[s]" to changing their world and foster "community spirit through community sacrifice." Yet NAACP leaders continued to doubt the ability of ordinary black citizens to effect social change: "[H]owever much people are aroused over an issue, in the final analysis correction of the wrong must occur via the established agencies and procedures." Moreover, litigation was limited in its capacity to generate conflict and violence—conditions that proved to be indispensable to transforming northern opinion on race. By contrast, white supremacist vigilantes and law enforcement officers had difficulty restraining themselves when confronted with black street demonstrators.[31]

Finally, Court decisions such as *Brown* could significantly alter social practices only if lower courts aggressively implemented them, Congress and the president enforced them, and local officials could be prevented from nullifying them. Each of these conditions depended on educating public opinion, which direct action accomplished better than litigation could. As King stated, "Only when the people themselves begin to act are rights on paper given life blood." The accelerated pace of school desegregation that accompanied the outburst of direct-action protests in the early 1960s proves his point.[32]

Litigation and direct action can complement each other to a certain extent. For example, direct-action protests can enforce court decisions, as the Freedom Riders were attempting to do. Thus, an optimal allocation of resources within a broad social protest movement might distribute some to both litigation and direct action. King and the SCLC tended to emphasize ways in which direct action complemented litigation, perhaps seeking to defuse the NAACP's visceral defensiveness toward potential competitors.

But the civil rights movement had no unitary oversight board to allocate scarce resources to their optimal uses. Rather, the NAACP and direct-action organizations competed for limited money and personnel. In the late 1950s, the NAACP's greater prestige, which was only enhanced by *Brown*, probably attracted more resources to litigation than was desirable from the perspective of those seeking to promote progressive racial change.

Brown may have indirectly discouraged direct-action protest for another reason. The extraordinary violence that *Brown* unleashed in the

South made direct action dangerous. Mississippi blacks were killed for voting in 1955, which they had not been in the late 1940s. One reason that SCLC founders initially shied away from further direct action after Montgomery was their fear of eliciting violence; the bus boycott itself had incited numerous bombings and shootings.

Summary conclusions re Effects of Brown

Thus, although *Brown* probably contributed to the belief among blacks that Jim Crow was vulnerable, it did not foster the view that they could personally help to end it. Rather, the high court's ruling encouraged additional investment in litigation, as elite NAACP lawyers tried to convince white judges to end segregation. *Brown* possibly discouraged direct-action tactics, which had the capacity to enhance individual agency and to generate transformative conflict. Further, by elevating the NAACP's stature, *Brown* solidified control over the civil rights agenda by an organization that was profoundly skeptical of direct-action protest.

In the short term, *Brown* may have delayed direct action by encouraging litigation. But this aspect of the decision was self-correcting, as *Brown* either would or would not produce school desegregation. Within a few years, it had become clear that litigation without a social movement to support it could not produce significant social change. Thus, over the long term, *Brown* may have encouraged direct action by raising hopes and expectations, which litigation then proved incapable of fulfilling. Alternative forms of protest arose to fill the gap.

Generalizing about what most blacks expected to happen after *Brown* is difficult. Some predicted that implementation would be a "long and laborious process" and that "the months that lie ahead will be ones that will try our very souls." But others were optimistic about enforcement, and few could have predicted the nearly complete nullification that took place in the South over the next half decade. White southerners had earlier warned that desegregation of higher education could not happen without bloodshed, yet it had, leading many blacks to discount the threats of violence and school closures made by southern whites after *Brown*.[33]

In 1955, NAACP officials insisted that their goal was school desegregation "in most areas of the South by not later than September 1956," and they predicted that all forms of segregation would be eliminated by 1963 (whereas, in fact, three Deep South states had yet to desegregate a single grade school by then). They may have privately been less confident, but NAACP officials seem to have believed that rapid desegregation of urban schools, even in the Deep South, was feasible. Such expectations were not completely naive, as one would have had difficulty predicting the ferocity of resistance among southern whites or the tepid commitment to enforcement of the Eisenhower administration.[34]

That litigation alone could not desegregate schools was clear by 1960, if not earlier. Through a campaign of massive defiance, fraud, and evasion, southern states almost completely nullified *Brown*. One cannot precisely measure the connection between black frustration over the pace of court-ordered desegregation and the explosion of direct-action protests, but many contemporaries explicitly identified such a linkage.

King attributed direct-action protest to black "disappoint[ment] over the slow pace of school desegregation." The NAACP's 1960 convention declared the youth protests to be "symptomatic of the growing impatience of Negro Americans with the injustices of segregation and snail-like pace of desegregation." Roy Wilkins thought that blacks were tired of "this foolishness"—the white South's nullification of *Brown*—and were "in a hurry for their rights." They were no longer "so particular" about whether to use "mass demonstration" or litigation. James Farmer of CORE defended the Freedom Rides on the ground that "we've had test cases and we've won them all and the status remains quo."[35]

blacks had become impatient [handwritten margin note]

By the early 1960s, many blacks were seeking not only faster methods of change but also extralegal ones. White southerners' nullification of *Brown* through legal machinations, economic reprisals, and extralegal violence had disillusioned many blacks about the capacity of law to secure racial justice. Some southern officials and judges had proved willing to lie in their efforts to evade *Brown*. In response to desegregation suits, a Birmingham school board member denied that city schools were segregated, and the chancellor of the University of Mississippi insisted that the exclusion of James Meredith had nothing to do with his "being a Negro." Astonishingly, federal district judge Sidney Mize agreed, dismissing Meredith's suit on the ground that Ole Miss "is not a racially segregated institution"—news that "may startle some people in Mississippi," Judge John Minor Wisdom pointed out in reversing Mize's judgment.[36]

State judges were sometimes even worse. One ran for reelection declaring, "I speak for the white race," and he promised to deal the NAACP "a blow from which [it] shall never recover." The chief justice of the Alabama Supreme Court volunteered that he "would close every school from the highest to the lowest before I would go to school with colored people." A few state jurists actually declared the Fourteenth Amendment to be unconstitutional. Others engaged in extraordinary chicanery to evade desegregation or otherwise deny justice to blacks.[37]

Thus, direct action had the virtue not only of being quicker but also of being extralegal while remaining nonviolent. Those blacks who were even more profoundly disillusioned by massive resistance abandoned the hope of peaceful change and the goal of racial integration, and they turned instead to black nationalism and violence as methods of racial betterment. The rapid growth of the Black Muslims in the 1960s was the most extreme manifestation of the black revolt against litigation as a method of social reform.

Brown contributed to direct-action protest in another way as well. As southern states moved to suppress the NAACP, southern blacks had no choice but to support alternative protest organizations.

Before *Brown*, most white southerners thought the NAACP "at worst was a bunch of Republicans." But afterward, it "became an object of consuming hatred." According to four black ministers in South Carolina, "The business of fighting the NAACP is to many Southern white men today as necessary as breathing." Because many white southerners thought that "integration is the southern expression of communism," they saw the NAACP as a communist agent or stooge. The South Carolina legislature asked the U.S. attorney general to list the association as subversive, and the attorney general of Georgia alleged that "two-thirds of the officers of the NAACP have subversive or Communist backgrounds."[38]

Southern states proved enormously creative at translating white hatred of the NAACP into legal mechanisms for shutting it down. The most popular initiative sought to obtain association membership lists, which could be publicized and used to persecute members. States sought to compel disclosure of membership lists via corporate-registration statutes, tax ordinances, legislative antisubversion investigations, and laws that required public school teachers to list their organizational memberships. Another popular anti-NAACP measure barred members from public employment, especially as schoolteachers, on the ground that affiliation was incompatible with the peace and tranquility of the community.

Many states harassed the NAACP and its lawyers with criminal prosecutions and bar association disciplinary proceedings, charging offenses such as stirring up lawsuits, financially supporting litigation, taking control of litigation, and the unauthorized practice of law. Citizens' councils used economic pressure against NAACP members, denying them jobs, credit, and access to goods and services. Where legal methods failed, violence sometimes succeeded. Whites in Belzoni, Mississippi, shot Gus Courts, the president of the local

NAACP branch, for his voter registration activity. The home of Daisy Bates, the head of the NAACP in Arkansas, was the target of repeated cross burnings, shootings, and bombings. The NAACP saw itself as engaged in a "bitter cold war," where "no holds are barred."[39]

This anti-NAACP crusade took its toll on the organization. Alabama shut down local operations for eight years (1956–1964), and Louisiana and Texas did so for briefer periods. In 1957, Wilkins reported that "the future operation of the NAACP in the Southern states" was at risk. Southern membership fell from 128,000 in 1955 to 80,000 in 1957, and nearly 250 branches shut down. Most of the losses came in the Deep South, where the assault was sharpest. Membership in Louisiana fell from more than 13,000 to 1,700 and in South Carolina from 8,200 to 2,200. Mississippi field secretary Medgar Evers reported that "economic pressures and violence" were so prevalent that only the "pure in heart" were sticking with the association.[40]

To fend off this attack, the NAACP had to divert scarce resources from challenging school segregation. Association members also suffered psychologically. The national director of branches reported an "atmosphere of gloom . . . pervading" the annual Texas meeting, as injunction proceedings "succeed in arresting our activities and have a traumatic effect on our leadership." Something had to be done "to regain the confidence of

Figure 6.1. Gus Courts recovers in the hospital after he was shot, 1955. Library of Congress, Prints and Photographs Division, Visual Materials from the NAACP Records.

the Negroes in the southern branches." Even though courts eventually invalidated most of the anti-NAACP legal measures, the litigation dragged on for years. While such suits were pending, membership fell, spirits sagged, and resources were diverted.[41]

As the NAACP struggled to survive in the South, blacks turned elsewhere for leadership. Black ministers, many of whom held prominent positions in NAACP branches, formed new organizations, such as the Alabama Christian Movement for Human Rights in Birmingham, the United Christian Movement in Shreveport, the Inter-Civic Council in Tallahassee, and the SCLC. The leadership vacuum created by the anti-NAACP assault also facilitated the expansion into the South of an older organization, CORE. These other groups used the NAACP's base of supporters, but they deployed their resources differently. By inciting massive retaliation against the NAACP, *Brown* ironically fostered new organizations that lacked the association's institutional and philosophical biases against direct action.

With school desegregation litigation achieving paltry results and the chief litigators under withering assault, southern blacks had little choice but to explore alternative methods and organizations of social protest. By revealing the limits of litigation as an engine of social change and by provoking massive retaliation against the NAACP, *Brown* may have indirectly accelerated the transition to direct action.

7

Brown's Backlash

Whatever its connection to *Brown*, a powerful direct-action protest movement had exploded in the South by the early 1960s. Sit-ins, Freedom Rides, and street demonstrations became a regular feature of southern life. When law enforcement officers responded to such protests with restraint and (even unlawful) arrests, media attention quickly waned, and demonstrators usually failed to accomplish their objectives. This is how Sheriff Laurie Pritchett defeated mass demonstrations in Albany, Georgia, in 1961–1962 and how Mississippi officials defused the Freedom Rides in the summer of 1961. By contrast, when southern sheriffs violently suppressed demonstrations with beatings, police dogs, and fire hoses, media attention escalated, and northerners reacted with horror and outrage. It was the brutality of southern whites resisting desegregation that ultimately rallied national opinion behind the enforcement of *Brown* and the enactment of civil rights legislation. *Brown* helped to bring that violence about.

In the years immediately preceding *Brown*, racial moderates generally controlled southern politics: Big Jim Folsom, John Sparkman, and Lister Hill in Alabama; Lyndon Johnson in Texas; Earl Long in Louisiana; Kerr Scott in North Carolina; Sid McMath, William Fulbright, and the early Orval Faubus in Arkansas; and Albert Gore (the future vice president's father), Estes Kefauver, and Frank Clement in Tennessee. These politicians were economically populist and, although segregationist, they downplayed race while accommodating gradual racial reform. Coalitions composed of less affluent whites and the growing number of enfranchised blacks elected candidates who supported increased government spending on education, roads, public health, and old-age pensions. Many of these politicians defeated opponents who warned that white supremacy was in danger.

Big Jim Folsom was perhaps the leading exemplar of this phenomenon. In 1946 and 1954, he won gubernatorial elections in Alabama, running on populist platforms of expanded public services, abolition of the poll tax, and reapportionment of the legislature. With regard to race, Folsom stated that "all men are just alike"; he urged "fellowship and brotherly love"; and he declared that blacks were entitled to their fair share of Alabama's wealth. Folsom appointed registrars who were committed to the nondiscriminatory administration of voting registration requirements, favored equalizing the salaries of black teachers, and supported the creation of more state parks for blacks. When pressed during the 1954 campaign for his views on *Brown*, which had just been decided, Folsom joked, "I don't intend to make the good colored people of Alabama . . . go to school with us white folks." That year, he easily defeated candidates who emphasized the looming threat to white supremacy—a striking contrast with the racial fanaticism that would soon characterize Alabama politics.[1]

Exceptions do exist to this general rule that racial moderates prospered in southern politics between World War II and *Brown*. The most obvious one is the Dixiecrat revolt against the Democratic party in 1948. But Dixiecrats carried only four states—those with the largest percentages of black residents—and even those victories depended on having secured control of the Democratic party machinery, which enabled Dixiecrats to capitalize on the traditional party loyalties of southern voters by running slates of electors pledged to presidential candidate Strom Thurmond and vice presidential candidate Fielding Wright under the Democratic label. Thus, in the one Deep South state where Dixiecrats were kept off the Democratic ticket—Georgia—they won only 20.3 percent of the vote, as compared with 79.8 percent and 72 percent in neighboring Alabama and South Carolina.

Figure 7.1. Big Jim Folsom towers over the crowd at a campaign rally. Birmingham Public Library, Department of Archives and Manuscripts, no. 98.45 H.

Outside of the Deep South, the New Deal/Fair Deal coalition held up well for President Harry S Truman, and Thurmond usually ran third, trailing the Republican candidate, Thomas Dewey, as well. In Arkansas and Virginia, states that would lead massive resistance in the mid-1950s, Dixiecrats won only 16.5 percent and 10.3 percent of the vote, respectively. In 1950, Dixiecrats suffered additional defeats at the polls, most notably Thurmond's loss to Olin Johnston in South Carolina's Senate race. Rather than viewing the Dixiecrat revolt as evidence of a powerful pre-*Brown* racial backlash, a contemporary political scientist concluded from its defeat that the "great masses of southerners would no longer be bamboozled by racist appeals."[2]

Victories by the race-baiting Talmadges, father Eugene and son Herman, in Georgia gubernatorial elections in 1946, 1948, and 1950 confirm that politicians could manipulate the race issue to their advantage even before *Brown* had increased its salience. But the lesson should not be overdrawn. Georgia's unique county-unit system for electing statewide officials inflated the voting power of rural whites, who were the most committed to preserving white supremacy. This is why Georgia consistently produced some of the region's most demagogic governors. Moreover, both Talmadges used recent Court decisions—*Smith v. Allwright* in the

1946 election, *Sweatt v. Painter* in 1950—to exaggerate the threat being posed to white supremacy.

The famous defeats in the 1950 primaries of Senators Frank Porter Graham in North Carolina and Claude Pepper in Florida are also weaker evidence of the existence of a pre-*Brown* racial backlash than is often supposed. Both incumbents were "soft" on race, but the defeat of neither should be seen as a referendum victory for racial reaction. Pepper's opponent, George Smathers, focused his attack less on the senator's racial liberalism and more on his support for New Deal/Fair Deal redistributive policies, his close labor union ties, and his moderate stance toward the Soviet Union (labeling the senator "Red Pepper").[3]

Similarly, in the initial North Carolina primary that year, Willis Smith mainly criticized Graham's past affiliations with allegedly subversive organizations (calling him "Frank the Front") and his present support for the allegedly socialist policies of Truman's Fair Deal, such as national health insurance and repeal of the Taft-Hartley labor law. Such tactics duplicated those of Republicans throughout the nation in 1950: antisocialism attacks on Truman's domestic policies and McCarthyite challenges to his alleged softness on communism, foreign and domestic. The defeats of these racial moderates had more to do with Truman's unpopularity and the potency of McCarthyism as an electoral weapon than with any incipient racial backlash in the South.[4]

Race was more important to Graham's defeat in the runoff primary, though even here the lesson is uncertain. Graham was probably more exposed on the race issue than any other southern politician. Widely identified as his generation's foremost southern liberal, Graham was a member of Truman's civil rights committee, the first president of the interracial and integrationist Southern Conference for Human Welfare, and one of only three southern senators to oppose the filibuster against fair employment practices legislation. Graham was almost unique among southern officeholders in endorsing the eventual abolition of racial segregation.

Thus, rather than treating his defeat as evidence of a pre-*Brown* racial backlash, perhaps one should be struck that a southern politician who was this liberal on race nearly won the first primary—earning 48.9 percent of the vote—and barely lost the runoff with 48 percent. Graham could not possibly have done this well in the racial hysteria that characterized southern politics after *Brown*. Moreover, only the intervention of the Supreme Court's 1950 decisions, which invalidated segregation in graduate and professional schools, enabled Smith to make race the dominant issue in the runoff, thus demonstrating the backlash potential of the Court's race rulings.

In sum, neither the Dixiecrat revolt, nor the defeats of Senators Graham and Pepper, nor the Talmadges' gubernatorial victories are convincing evidence of a pre-*Brown* racial backlash. On the contrary, populist southern politicians who supported expanded public services while downplaying race prospered between World War II and *Brown*. In such a political environment, gradual racial reform could be accomplished without inciting a white backlash.

Black voter registration in Mississippi and Alabama increased tenfold in the decade following World War II, and in Louisiana it increased more than twentyfold. Dozens of urban police forces in the South hired their first black officers. Minor league baseball teams, even in places such as Montgomery and Birmingham, Alabama, signed their first black players. Most southern states peacefully desegregated their graduate and professional schools under court order. Blacks began serving again on southern juries, even in places such as Natchez and Greenville, Mississippi. In most states outside of the Deep South, the first blacks since Reconstruction were elected to urban political offices, and the walls of segregation were occasionally breached in public facilities and public accommodations. These racial changes generated no significant white backlash.

[margin handwritten: pre-Brown signs of progress]

None of this is to suggest that the South was moving gradually but inexorably toward peaceful school desegregation. In the absence of *Brown*, southern states almost certainly would *not* have desegregated their schools within a decade or two. Southern whites were much more intensely resistant to school desegregation than to allowing blacks to vote, to become police officers, or to play on integrated baseball teams. Moreover, most southern blacks were more interested in improving black education, reducing police brutality, and securing access to decent jobs than in desegregating grade schools. Yet, before *Brown* focused attention on school desegregation, southern politics was generally controlled by moderates, who downplayed race while accommodating gradual racial change. *Brown* turned that political world upside down.

[margin handwritten: priorities]

Politicians outside of the Deep South initially reacted to *Brown I* with restraint, even in states that would quickly become leaders of massive resistance. Governor Francis Cherry of Arkansas promised that his state would "obey the law. It always has." The governor of Virginia, Thomas B. Stanley, guaranteed a "calm" and "dispassionate" response to *Brown*. Governor Frank Clement of Tennessee observed that the ruling was "handed down by a judicial body which we, the American people, . . . recognize as supreme."[5]

[margin handwritten: upper south & border states]

That spring and summer, *Brown* attracted little attention in Democratic primaries in Arkansas, Alabama, Florida, and Texas. Most southern newspaper editors urged calm and avoided talk of defiance. The *Nashville Tennessean* declared that southerners "have learned to live with change. They can learn to live with this one." Ralph McGill of the *Atlanta Constitution* was reported to have said, "Segregation is on the way out . . . and he who tries to tell the people otherwise does them great disservice." The day after *Brown*, the school board of Greensboro, North Carolina, voted to instruct the superintendent to study means of compliance, and within a week the Little Rock school board had followed suit.[6]

Political reaction in the Deep South was sometimes more defiant. The Louisiana legislature, in session when *Brown* was decided, overwhelmingly resolved to censure the Court's "usurpation of power" and invoked its police power to adopt a new school segregation law. Governor Herman Talmadge declared, "Georgia is going to resist mixing the races in the schools if it is the sole state of the nation to do so," and eight of the nine candidates competing in Georgia's pending gubernatorial primary favored preserving school segregation. Senator James Eastland of Mississippi announced, "The South will not abide by or obey this legislative decision by a political court," and Mississippi officials warned that they would abolish public education before integrating.[7]

By the fall of 1954, statements from some Deep South politicians had become even shriller. Talmadge declared, "[N]o amount of force whatever can compel desegregation of white and Negro schools," while Governor-elect Marvin Griffin announced, "[C]ome hell or high water, races will not be mixed in Georgia schools." Voters in Georgia and Mississippi passed constitutional amendments that authorized legislatures to close schools rather than desegregate them.[8]

Would the rest of the region fall in line behind the defiant proclamations of the Deep South? The answer became apparent over the next eighteen months, as white opinion throughout the South grew more extreme. Citizens' councils, new organizations that were committed to preserving white supremacy by all means short of violence—the "uptown" Klan, according to critics—began forming in Mississippi in the summer of 1954, quickly spread to Alabama, and then expanded across the South, achieving a maximum membership of perhaps 250,000. Whites flocked to the councils as southern blacks began filing desegregation petitions with school boards, many of them reasoning that "[w]e must make certain that Negroes are not allowed to force their demands on us."[9]

When lower courts began ordering desegregation, violence erupted, which further radicalized white opinion. The admission of Autherine

Lucy to the University of Alabama in February 1956 produced a race riot, and Alabama whites, already riled over the Montgomery bus boycott, now joined citizens' councils in droves. That month, a segregationist rally in Montgomery drew 10,000 people.

Several state legislatures in the South adopted interposition resolutions that purported to nullify *Brown*. They also passed dozens of laws designed to avoid desegregation—measures that authorized school closures, repealed compulsory attendance requirements, cut off public funding for integrated schools, and provided public money for private schools. In March 1956, most southern congressional representatives signed the Southern Manifesto, which assailed the Court's "clear abuse of judicial power" and pledged all "lawful means" of resistance.[10]

Political contests in southern states quickly assumed a common pattern: Candidates maneuvered to occupy the most extreme position on the segregationist spectrum. "Moderation" became a term of derision, as the political center collapsed, leaving only "those who want to maintain the Southern way of life or those who want to mix the races." Moderate critics of massive resistance were labeled "double crossers," "sugar-coated integrationists," "cowards," and "traitors." Most moderates either joined the segregationist bandwagon or they were retired from service. A Virginia politician observed that it "would be suicide to run on any other platform [than segregation]." A liberal southern editor explained, "[I]t takes guts not to come out for segregation every day."[11]

Brown radicalized southern politics, whereas earlier racial changes had not, for three principal reasons. First, *Brown* was harder to ignore than earlier changes. Most white southerners did not see black jurors or black police officers, who patrolled black neighborhoods only, and they would have been largely unaware of the dramatic increases in black voter registration. Even some instances of integration—such as on city buses or golf courses—would have gone unnoticed by many white southerners.

But they could not miss *Brown*, which received front-page coverage in virtually every newspaper in the country and was a constant topic of southern conversations. A northern white visitor found after *Brown* that segregation "is the foremost preoccupation of the Southern mind. . . . [It] intrudes into almost every conversation. It nags, it bothers and it will not be ignored." A citizens' council leader credited the Court with "awaken[ing] us from a slumber of about 30 years," and an Alabama official noted that white southerners owed the justices a "debt of gratitude" for "caus[ing] us to become organized and unified."[12]

Second, *Brown* represented federal interference in southern race relations—something that white southerners, who harbored deep resentment at historical memories of Reconstruction, could not tolerate. Some earlier racial changes—such as the hiring of black police officers or the desegregation of minor league baseball teams—flowed from choices made by white southerners. Other changes—such as the increased public funding of black education and the growing number of blacks registered to vote—had been influenced by federal court decisions, but they still depended on choices made by southern whites. *Brown* was different; it left southern whites no choice but to desegregate their schools. Accordingly, *Brown* was "viewed by many white Southerners as federal intervention designed to destroy their way of life."[13]

Third and perhaps most important, *Brown* commanded that racial change take place in a different order than might otherwise have occurred. By the early 1950s, many southern cities had relaxed Jim Crow in public transportation, police department employment, athletic competitions, and voter registration. White southerners were more intensely committed to preserving grade school segregation, which lay near the top of the white supremacist hierarchy of preferences. Blacks, conversely, were often more interested in voting, ending police brutality, securing decent jobs, and receiving a fair share of public education funds than in desegregating grade schools.

These partially inverse hierarchies of preference among whites and blacks opened space for political negotiation—to the extent that blacks had the power to compel whites to bargain. *Brown* mandated change in an area where whites were most resistant, thus virtually ensuring a backlash. Had the Court first decided a case such as *Gayle v. Browder*, desegregating local bus transportation, the reaction of white southerners would probably have been more restrained.

For these reasons, *Brown* provoked greater white resistance than did earlier racial changes. This is not a criticism of *Brown*. The justices were neither bound by the hierarchy of preferences of white supremacists, nor were they required to accommodate the visceral resistance of white southerners to externally coerced change. Explaining the reasons that *Brown* radicalized southern politics does not entail endorsing an alternative path to racial reform as preferable.

The post-*Brown* backlash in the South was manifested in at least two different ways. First, there were clear instances of racial retrogression—reversal of racial reforms that had occurred before *Brown*. Second, politics in every southern state moved dramatically to the right.

One striking racial retrogression in the post-*Brown* South was the resurgence of the Ku Klux Klan, which had earlier seemed destined for extinction. Another was the legal assault on the National Association for the Advancement of Colored People. For decades, southern whites had grudgingly tolerated the association, but after *Brown*, they declared war on it. The association's southern membership, which had been steadily rising after the war, plummeted in the wake of *Brown* as affiliation became too dangerous.

With school desegregation lurking in the background, whites in the Deep South suddenly could no longer tolerate blacks voting. Dramatic postwar expansions of black suffrage were halted and then reversed. Late in 1954, Mississippi voters adopted by a 5–1 margin a more stringent literacy test, which they had rejected just two years earlier. Registrars in Mississippi and Louisiana purged thousands of blacks from the voter rolls under laws that granted them discretion to expunge names for technical registration flaws. Black voter registration in Mississippi declined from 22,000 in 1954 to 8,000 in 1956.

black suffrage declined

Alabama, Georgia, and Virginia passed new laws making voter registration more difficult. A regional trend toward eliminating the poll tax abruptly ended with *Brown*. In 1955, two Mississippi blacks, the Reverend George Lee and Lamar Smith, were murdered for encouraging blacks to vote. Mississippi whites had beaten and threatened blacks who tried to vote in the late 1940s, but they had not killed anybody.

Brown also retarded progress in university desegregation. In the early 1950s, most southern states had peacefully desegregated graduate and professional schools under lower court orders that enforced *Sweatt v. Painter*. By 1955, roughly 2,000 blacks attended desegregated universities in southern and border states—a "quiet revolution" from 1950. Even in the Deep South, four of Louisiana's seven public universities had desegregated. One might have predicted that other Deep South universities would soon follow. Indeed, in 1953, the president of the University of South Carolina confided to a colleague that he expected to desegregate within two or three years.[14]

Brown changed all of that. The University of Texas quickly reversed a decision to extend desegregation to undergraduates. Universities in the Deep South used extraordinary legal maneuvers to resist desegregation, sometimes dragging out litigation for nearly a decade. After court orders finally compelled desegregation, race riots erupted at the University of Alabama in 1956, the University of Georgia in 1961, and Ole Miss in 1962. Most public universities in the Deep South did not ultimately desegregate until more than a decade after *Sweatt*. Meanwhile, the Louisiana legislature tried to undo the university desegregation that had occurred in that state before *Brown*. State legislators passed a measure that was designed to exclude blacks from formerly white universities by requiring all applicants to produce "good character" certificates from their high school principals, who could be fired for providing them for blacks under another state law, which prohibited promoting integration. Segregationists then insisted that the law be applied retroactively to blacks who were already attending integrated universities. In 1956, Louisiana blacks largely ceased applying to such institutions. Federal courts quickly enjoined the enforcement of these statutes, but black enrollment at Louisiana's desegregated universities nonetheless declined from 650 to fewer than 200.

The post-*Brown* backlash also reversed progress that had been made in desegregating sports. Early in 1954, the Birmingham City Commission, eager to encourage a spring-training visit from Jackie Robinson and the Brooklyn Dodgers, repealed the city's ban on interracial sporting competitions. Within two weeks of *Brown*, voters in a referendum reversed that decision by a 3–1 margin. A couple of years later, Montgomery likewise abandoned its policy of permitting integrated minor league baseball games.

Deep South states also reversed a trend toward allowing college basketball and football teams to compete against integrated squads in games played outside of the South. In 1955, a college football team from Mississippi squared off against a school with black players in the Little Rose Bowl, but legislative threats to cut off funding induced state football and basketball teams to decline similar invitations the next year. As late as 1962, the Mississippi State basketball team had to reject an invitation to the National Collegiate Athletic Association (NCAA) tournament because of the state's informal ban on interracial sporting competitions.

In the early 1950s, the University of Georgia football team competed several times against squads with black players, but in 1956 Governor Griffin asked the university board of regents to bar Georgia Tech from playing in the Sugar Bowl because its scheduled opponent had a black player. Griffin reasoned that competing against blacks on the gridiron was no different from attending school with them. The regents rebuffed Griffin after 2,500 Tech students marched on the state capital, but they insisted that no integrated collegiate sporting events take place within the state.

Even minor interracial courtesies and interactions that were uncontroversial before 1954 often had to be suspended in the post-*Brown* racial hysteria. In 1959, Governor John Patterson of Alabama barred black marching bands from the inaugural parade, where they had previously been warmly received. Since its founding in 1942, Koinonia Farm, an interracial religious cooperative in Americus, Georgia, had experienced little harassment, but after *Brown*, its products were boycotted and its roadside produce stands were shot at. Interracial unions that had thrived in the South for years self-destructed after *Brown*. Many whites stopped contributing to the Urban League, which was not even involved with school desegregation, and many white audiences ceased inviting singing groups from black colleges to perform.

Brown's backlash was also evident in the rightward shift in southern political opinion in the mid-1950s. In 1954, Arkansans had elected Orval Faubus as governor on a populist platform of increased spending on public education and old-age pensions; neither Faubus nor his opponent highlighted race. In his inaugural address, Faubus again ignored race, and in 1955 he became the first Arkansas governor to appoint blacks to the state Democratic Central Committee. In the year after *Brown I*, three Arkansas school districts with small black populations desegregated without interference from Faubus, who disclaimed authority to intervene in local school matters. Meanwhile, school boards in the state's largest cities, such as Little Rock, were considering early implementation of desegregation plans.

By 1956, though, polls registered a rightward shift in public opinion, and Faubus's principal opponent for reelection was Jim Johnson, chief organizer of the state's citizens' councils. With Johnson calling him "pussy-footing" and demanding a special legislative session to consider resistance measures, Faubus became more extreme, endorsing an interposition resolution. Though Johnson proposed closing schools that had already desegregated, Faubus won an easy victory by promising that no school district would have to integrate against its will.[15]

The following year, under increasing segregationist pressure, Faubus reconsidered his position on local control. In the summer of 1957, with the Little Rock citizens' council pressuring him to intervene against court-ordered desegregation, Faubus declared that no city with as large a black population as Little Rock's was ready for even token integration. Faubus testified before a state judge that he had evidence that racial mixing would produce violence, and the court enjoined desegregation, only to be quickly overturned by a federal judge.

Invoking the need to protect lives and property, Faubus then used the state militia to block desegregation. He withdrew the state troops after being threatened with contempt sanctions, leaving in their place only an inadequate city police force to fend off an angry white mob that surrounded Central High School. President Dwight D. Eisenhower then dispatched federal troops to protect the black students. Faubus's motives in the Little Rock crisis are uncertain: Did he deliberately foment a riot to bolster his candidacy for a third term as governor, or did he stumble into a situation that he proved unable to control? Whatever his intentions, there is no denying that Faubus's position on desegregation had become much more extreme since 1955.

White opinion in Virginia also radicalized after 1954. Public officials had counseled restraint after *Brown*, and a "general air of calm resignation" existed in the state's largest cities. As late as November 1955, the Gray Commission, appointed by the governor to recommend desegregation policy, endorsed local option, which would permit desegregation in willing communities, and public tuition grants for students who wished to attend private, segregated schools. Governor Stanley seemed to support the plan.[16]

But James J. Kilpatrick, editor of the *Richmond News Leader*, launched a campaign to have southern state legislatures nullify *Brown*, and Senator Harry Byrd organized regionwide massive resistance. The Virginia legislature then rejected local option and instructed the Gray Commission to consider other proposals. In the summer of 1956, as federal district courts ordered desegregation in Charlottesville and Norfolk, the governor endorsed massive resistance and called the legislature into special session to implement it. In August, the Gray Commission also approved massive resistance. The special legislative session enacted laws that provided for state pupil placement (thus rejecting local option) and the closing of desegregated schools.

In Florida, Governor LeRoy Collins tried to pursue a moderate course, warning that the state "cannot afford an orgy of race conflict and discord," avoiding defiant talk, and criticizing interposition as serving "no useful purpose." But in 1956, extremist Sumter Lowry challenged Collins for the governorship, insisting that "segregation is the only issue." Collins and other candidates were forced "to hop on the segregation train." Previous pleas by Collins for "moderation" and "understanding" now became promises to preserve segregation by "every lawful means." Richard Ervin, the state attorney general, previously known as "one of the most level-headed and far-sighted" politicians in the state, likewise adopted in his reelection bid most of his opponent's extreme segregationist views.[17]

Two months into the spring electioneering, one state official reported "a great deterioration of race relations all over the state." During the campaign, Florida's only black assistant state attorney lost his job for being "too outspoken" on segregation; he had stated in a radio interview that his work was "not necessarily confined to Negro cases." Collins won a decisive victory in the gubernatorial primary, which moderates portrayed as a "crashing rebuke to the criers of race hatred," but in fact Florida's racial politics had become much more extreme.[18]

The most stunning defeat for moderation came in Alabama, where Big Jim Folsom was destroyed by the post-*Brown* racial hysteria. Folsom had refused to join other southern governors in a statement condemning *Brown*, vetoed several pieces of massive resistance legislation, ridiculed a nullification resolution as "just a bunch of hogwash," lambasted the citizens' councils as "haters and baiters," and invited the black congressman from Harlem, Adam Clayton Powell, to the governor's mansion for a drink, which was later described as "the most expensive scotch and soda in the history of Alabama politics." By the fall of 1955, some legislators and the citizens' councils were denouncing the governor.[19]

Early in 1956, Folsom began to move to the right, as the race riot resulting from the admission of Autherine Lucy to the University of Alabama crystallized extremist sentiment in the state. With citizens' council rallies drawing mass participation, for the first time Folsom declared his support for preserving segregation, and he signed several bills designed to do so. As he traveled around the state in his campaign to become a Democratic National Committee member, Folsom defended himself from charges of moderation. His opponent was a little known state representative, Charles McKay, who had authored the legislature's nullification resolution and now accused Folsom of being one of the "foremost supporters of the NAACP." Political commentators treated the contest as a bellwether of public opinion on race in Alabama. Folsom was annihilated, losing by a margin of 3–1.[20]

After his defeat, he moved even further in the extremists' direction, promising that schools would not integrate so long as he was governor and promoting segregationist legislation. By the summer of 1957, he was signing a nullification resolution and denying that he had ever opposed the concept. But Folsom's change of heart came too late. In the 1958 gubernatorial election, all leading candidates distanced themselves from the governor's "moderate" racial views, and the most extreme segregationist, John Patterson, won.

In 1955–1956, political opinion also became more extreme in North Carolina, Tennessee, and Texas. Running for reelection in 1956, the governor of North Carolina, Luther Hodges, was attacked for his "very lukewarm stand" on segregation. In response, he called the legislature into special session to enact segregationist measures, such as proposed constitutional amendments that would authorize local referendums on school closures and public tuition grants to attend private schools— measures that he had opposed just a year earlier. Two of the three North Carolina congressional representatives who refused to sign the Southern Manifesto early in 1956 were defeated for reelection that spring. The manifesto issue clearly caused the lopsided defeat of Representative Charles B. Deane, as he had not even faced competition in the previous two elections, and no opponent had come forward in 1956 until Deane took his rebellious stand.[21]

TN

Also in the spring of 1956, two Tennessee education boards made "rather sudden and unexpected reversals of desegregation policies." The University of Tennessee's board of trustees, which had approved a gradual desegregation plan for undergraduates, now decided to indefinitely postpone its implementation. The Chattanooga board of education, which had agreed to comply with *Brown*, now opposed desegregation for at least five more years. One newspaper reported that recent developments made it "increasingly difficult for Tennessee's politicians to steer a middle course on the subject of desegregation." Governor Frank Clement, who had previously resisted legislative action on this issue, now proposed several segregationist measures.[22]

TX

In Texas, the policy of local option had enabled more than one hundred districts, mostly in western counties with minuscule black populations, to desegregate after *Brown*. Governor Allan Shivers had voiced no opposition to communities choosing for themselves to desegregate. But in 1956, Texas opinion polls registered growing public opposition to desegregation, and voters overwhelmingly approved an interposition resolution and stronger segregationist measures. In the summer of 1956, the governor twice used state troops to block court-ordered desegregation, and in 1957 the legislature cut off funds to school districts that desegregated without first conducting a referendum. Desegregation in Texas ground to a halt.

That Mississippi, Louisiana, South Carolina, and Georgia would massively resist *Brown* was never seriously in doubt. That the border states would desegregate with relative ease was equally certain. How the rest of the South would respond was unclear. Until *Brown II*, and in some cases for months afterward, these states pursued a wait-and-see strategy. Massive resistance would have played out very differently had they decided not to follow the Deep South's lead. But by early 1956, the South was "marching in close order along the same resistance road."[23]

Deep South took the lead

Little Rock

The Little Rock crisis of September 1957 further radicalized southern politics. Even moderate opponents of massive resistance criticized the use of federal troops to enforce desegregation orders. In North Carolina, Governor Hodges called the use of troops "a tragic mistake" and declared, "I have to associate myself with the people of my section," while Senator W. Kerr Scott compared Little Rock to the carpetbagger invasion of Reconstruction and deplored this "blow at the sovereignty of the states." Southern state legislatures called on Congress to censure the president, and they enacted "Little Rock" laws, which required the automatic closure of schools that were forced to integrate by federal troops. Governor Faubus became a regional hero, and other southern politicians drew the lesson that aggressive defiance of federal authority translated into political gain.[24]

The 1957 gubernatorial election in Virginia, which took place just one month after federal troops entered Little Rock, was a bellwether of southern political opinion. Virginia was one of the few southern states with a significant Republican presence. In 1953, the GOP's gubernatorial candidate, Theodore Dalton, won roughly 45 percent of the vote on a platform of increased state services and poll tax repeal. *Brown* weakened Virginia Republicans, as the Democratic Byrd machine championed white supremacy and minimized the significance of other issues.

VA backlash

Even before Little Rock, school segregation dominated the 1957 gubernatorial race. Democrat J. Lindsay Almond endorsed massive resistance, while Dalton favored token integration through pupil placement. Little Rock destroyed whatever slim chance Dalton may have had. White Virginians who were angry with Eisenhower for using federal troops to coerce desegregation delivered a message to the president by rejecting Dalton, whose share of the vote fell by nearly ten percentage points from 1953.

Commentators agreed that Little Rock was devastating to southern Republicans. Dalton concluded, "Little Rock knocked me down to nothing. It wasn't a little rock, it was a big rock." Republican congressman Joel T. Broyhill of Virginia declared, "[A]ny Republican in the South who supports integration is a dead duck."[25]

Faubus parlayed his defiance of federal authority into a landslide victory in his quest for a third term as governor in a state with a tradition of two-term chief executives. During the summer and fall of 1958, political opinion in Arkansas became even more extreme, as the Supreme Court rejected the Little Rock school board's request to postpone desegregation, and Faubus then closed the city's high schools—a decision that was promptly vindicated by Little Rock voters in a referendum. That fall, Faubus's political clout peaked when his opposition to the reelection of Congressman Brooks Hays enabled a politically unknown opponent, who conducted an eight-day write-in campaign attacking Hays's racial moderation, to defeat this nationally prominent, eight-term representative.

Faubus subsequently won three more consecutive gubernatorial elections for a grand total of six. Throughout the South, huge and wildly enthusiastic crowds attended Faubus's speeches. In 1960, the States'

Faubus' 6 terms as governor

Rights party ran him as their presidential candidate. A national Gallup poll, registering the view of white southerners, identified him as one of the world's ten most admired statesmen, along with Eisenhower, Truman, and Winston Churchill.

Elsewhere in the South, post–Little Rock political contests featured militant segregationists competing for the most extreme positions and bragging of their willingness to defy federal authority. In Alabama's 1958 gubernatorial primary, all of the candidates repudiated Folsom's racial moderation and touted their segregationist credentials. George Wallace, who was tainted by his past affiliations with Folsom and an early reputation for "softness" on race, bragged of his own defiance of federal authority. In 1956, as circuit judge in Barbour County, Wallace had threatened to arrest FBI agents if they came into his county seeking access to jury selection records to verify charges of race discrimination.

Now, in his 1958 gubernatorial campaign, Wallace promised to close schools rather than see them integrated by federal troops. His principal opponent was the state attorney general, John Patterson, who bragged of having shut down NAACP operations in the state. The Klan endorsed Patterson, whom Wallace criticized for not repudiating the endorsement. Patterson was so extreme that Wallace unwittingly became the candidate of moderation and won heavy black support. Patterson easily won the runoff primary, leading Wallace to vow that "no other son-of-a-bitch will ever out-nigger me again."[26]

Other election contests in the Deep South that year were similar. In Georgia, Lieutenant Governor Ernest Vandiver, who was running for governor, declared, "There is not enough money in the federal treasury to force us to mix the races in the classrooms of our schools," and he promised to use the National Guard to block integration. In response, his opponent called Vandiver "weak" on segregation and accused him of being the NAACP's candidate. In Florida, the more extreme candidate won the Senate race over an opponent who emphasized his "two Confederate grandfathers," and the only state legislator to oppose segregation bills in the past lost his congressional reelection bid in a campaign in which he was portrayed as a "member and tool of the NAACP."[27]

The radicalizing political effect of Little Rock was ironic. Eisenhower's use of troops should have demonstrated the futility of massive resistance, but instead it undermined moderates and bolstered extremists. The only way to maintain segregation after Little Rock was to close schools that had been ordered integrated. Governors Almond and Faubus did this in 1958, thus altering the calculus of segregationist politics. Before school closures, most whites were prepared to experiment with massive resistance. Afterward, they had to compare the costs and benefits of school closures against those of token integration.

Different states resolved this trade-off differently. In 1959, Virginia and Arkansas ended their massive resistance, and Texas, Tennessee, and Florida also charted courses toward token compliance, following the path chosen by North Carolina from the outset. In the Deep South, however, massive resisters continued to dominate politics for several more years.

Virginia's massive resistance ended abruptly. On January 19, 1959, federal and state courts invalidated key components of the state's massive resistance legislation. Governor Almond, after one final defiant outburst, did a volte-face, condemned further resistance as futile, and called for legislative changes that would permit token desegregation. Two weeks later, twenty-one black students entered seven formerly white schools. In April, the general assembly, by the margin of a single vote in the senate, substituted local option for massive resistance. Popular and legislative support for defiance steadily declined thereafter. By 1961, both leading gubernatorial candidates preferred freedom of choice to massive resistance.

Arkansas likewise changed direction in 1959. The legislature denied Governor Faubus's request to expand the size of the Little Rock school board, which would have enabled him to pack it with segregationists. That spring, moderates regained control of the board, as voters rejected Faubus's entreaties and evicted segregationist board members who had attempted to purge scores of moderate teachers and administrators. In June, a federal court invalidated the state's school-closing legislation, and later that summer, Little Rock high schools reopened for the first time in a year.

In an effort to save face, Faubus continued to condemn the Court, criticize integration, and predict violence, but he ceased interfering with school desegregation, and he urged segregationists to fight their battles at the polls, not on the streets. Voters continued to reward Faubus politically for his past defiance of federal authority, but a majority no longer supported his massive resistance policies. Over the following year, desegregation of Little Rock schools expanded without incident, and by 1960 even the eastern Arkansas "Black Belt" was beginning to peacefully desegregate, as citizens' councils decided to abandon forcible resistance. That year, Arkansas voters overwhelmingly rejected a state constitutional amendment that would have authorized local school closures.

Florida, Texas, and Tennessee, states that had never fully embraced massive resistance, further distanced themselves from it in 1958–1959.

The month after massive resistance ended in Virginia, the school board in Dade County, Florida, became the first in the Deep South to announce that it would desegregate a grade school, in the fall of 1959. Governor Collins endorsed the move, though many legislative leaders denounced it as "outrageous." For the rest of the year, the governor battled with segregationist legislators over anti-integration proposals, but the legislature eventually authorized pupil placement, and in September, Dade County desegregated two schools without incident. In 1960, the victor in the governor's race was an opponent of school closures.[28]

The governor of Tennessee, Buford Ellington, who had won a typical post–Little Rock contest in 1958 by calling himself an "old-fashioned segregationist" and promising to close schools if necessary to avoid integration, declared in February 1959 that he was no smarter than Governor Almond, who "threw in the towel" in Virginia. The following year, Senator Kefauver won a sweeping victory over an opponent who assailed his racial moderation and his refusal to sign the Southern Manifesto. The segregation issue was essentially dead in Tennessee politics.[29]

Texas seems to have avoided the Little Rock effect entirely. In 1958, racial moderates won gubernatorial and Senate races, and that fall an opinion poll showed that two-thirds of Texans believed that segregation in the state would be abolished. By 1960, the issue had largely disappeared from state politics, and an opinion poll revealed that 54 percent of Texans favored some integration, and only 31 percent endorsed defiance or evasion to maintain complete segregation.

In the Deep South, however, massive resisters continued to dominate politics. In the months following *Cooper v. Aaron*, the Little Rock case, politicians from that region declared that the South would never "surrender" and that "if we stand determined and united, there is no power on earth that can force us to mix the races in our schools." At the end of 1959, one newspaper publisher concluded, "Deep South convictions . . . are unchanged by recent developments," and another thought that it would be "many, many years before we have integration even on a limited scale."[30]

The 1959 gubernatorial primary in Mississippi featured four candidates, all of whom agreed on banning the NAACP and maintaining complete segregation. Representative John Bell Williams, who contemplated entering the race, had declared that Mississippi's next governor must be prepared "to rot in a federal prison for contempt of a court order . . . forcing integration." Lieutenant Governor Carroll Gartin promised "never [to] weaken in my stand for total and complete segregation," and another candidate declared that "the will of the people, and not the decisions of the United States Supreme Court, is the law of the land."[31]

Ross Barnett, the extremist in the field, sought to tie Gartin to the relatively moderate racial policies of Governor James Coleman, who had criticized nullification as "foolish" and "legal poppycock" and had promised to maintain segregation without "keep[ing] ourselves in a daily uproar over it." By contrast, Barnett assailed moderation as "the foot in the door for integration," bragged of his membership in a citizens' council, attributed the downfall of Egyptian culture to the "mongrelization" of the races, and proclaimed, "The good Lord was the original segregationist." In a landslide, Mississippi whites preferred Barnett's extremism to Gartin's "sane and sensible" approach to maintaining segregation. In his inaugural address, Barnett reiterated, "[O]ur schools at all levels must be kept segregated at all costs."[32]

Louisiana's gubernatorial primary in 1959–1960 confirmed that much of the Deep South was oblivious to the end of massive resistance elsewhere. The racial hysteria that swept Louisiana after Little Rock destroyed the Long machine's coalition of poor whites and blacks. Governor Long had previously criticized citizens' council members as "hotheads," declined to lead the legislative drive toward massive resistance, and opposed the purges of black voters. On the defensive after Little Rock, Long now insisted that he was "1,000 percent for segregation," while he continued to criticize the dean of Louisiana segregationists, Willie Rainach, for "scar[ing] everybody in the state to death . . . [e]very time you say Nigger." All eleven Democratic candidates for governor affirmed their commitment to preserving segregation.[33]

For the first time in a generation, no Long candidate made the runoff. The winner, Jimmie Davis, promised "no retreat, no compromise." Several months after the election, a poll showed that parents of white school children in New Orleans—almost certainly the most moderate whites in the state—favored school closures over token integration by more than 4–1. Political leaders remained united behind the policy of maintaining complete segregation, and that fall, the legislature went to war against Judge J. Skelly Wright, as it fought to block the desegregation of New Orleans schools.[34]

Georgia, South Carolina, and Alabama showed few signs of retreat either. In his inaugural address in January 1959, Georgia governor Vandiver proclaimed, "[W]e have only just begun to fight," and he sharply criticized token integrationists as "fomenters of division and discord." Admitting that the defeat of massive resistance in Virginia was a "blow to our cause," Vandiver reiterated his commitment to maintaining complete segregation. Early in 1959, he proposed and received legislation that authorized the governor to close a single school within a system if it was ordered to be integrated—a response to the pending desegregation suit in Atlanta. In his state-of-the-state address in 1960, Vandiver promised that Georgia would resist "again and again and again" and use every lawful means to preserve segregation.[35]

SC

In his 1959 inaugural address, the governor of South Carolina, Ernest Hollings, similarly vowed to maintain school segregation, and he later criticized Governor Almond for abandoning massive resistance in Virginia. Lieutenant Governor Burnet R. Maybank promised that South Carolina would not "yield one inch," and a leading newspaper in the state urged citizens to begin seriously considering private education.[36]

AL

Alabama, which had reacted to *Brown* with restraint under Folsom, now became the most defiant southern state under Governor Patterson. In his 1959 inaugural address, Patterson denounced the notion of "a little integration" and promised to use "every ounce of energy" to block desegregation. When Virginia's massive resistance legislation was invalidated on the same day as Patterson's inaugural, he warned that Alabama might have to abandon public education altogether. The *Montgomery Advertiser* thought that school closures were inevitable. Over the next year, Patterson reiterated his promise to close integrated schools, denounced token integration as a "sign of weakness," and predicted violence if integration occurred.[37]

The Deep South's desegregation crisis loomed near, as federal courts in the summer of 1959 ordered school boards in New Orleans and Atlanta to present desegregation plans with an eye toward action in the fall of 1960. In both states, rural-dominated legislatures seemed inclined to close schools rather than to desegregate them. But in both cities, groups of parents and businesspeople, and in New Orleans leaders of the Catholic church as well, began mobilizing behind open schools and token desegregation. Such groups were stronger and quicker to act in Georgia, and the New Orleans crisis culminated first, which allowed Georgia to learn from it.

urban movements for desegregation

New Orleans

The desegregation crisis in New Orleans in the fall of 1960 illustrates how fanatical Deep South politics had become. The earlier Little Rock episode had clearly established that court orders could not be defied indefinitely and that efforts to do so entailed potentially enormous costs, including school closures, an end to business relocations, and the tarnishing of a city's national image. Under heavy political pressure in the summer of 1960, the Orleans Parish school board asked the governor to block Judge Wright's desegregation order. But if schools could

not be kept open and segregated, a majority of the board members preferred token integration to school closures.

However, the rural-dominated legislature and a governor elected on a
platform of diehard resistance would not permit New Orleans to desegregate without a fight. In August, Governor Davis seized control of the
schools but was quickly enjoined by a federal court, which invalidated laws
enabling the governor and the legislature to maintain segregated schools
and restored control over New Orleans schools to the parish school board.
Governor Davis then called the legislature into special session, where it
enacted more than twenty segregation measures, including statutes that
authorized the legislature to take over New Orleans schools and the governor to close them and an interposition law that directed the arrest of any
federal judge or marshal who implemented desegregation orders.

Judge Wright promptly enjoined all of these measures and then
issued a restraining order against the governor, the legislature, and hundreds of other state and local officials. In November, four black first-
graders integrated two schools, which prompted nearly all whites to
boycott them. For months, segregationist legislators continued to med-
dle in the city's educational affairs, but within a year of this "Second
Battle of New Orleans," state officials had retreated from massive resistance and substituted local option, pupil placement, and public tuition
grants to attend private schools.

With court-ordered desegregation in Atlanta set for the fall, early in
1960 the Georgia legislature appointed the Sibley Commission to can-
vass public opinion and to recommend whether to abandon massive
resistance in favor of local option. The dominant opinion in Atlanta
favored keeping schools open, and had the state legislature not been so
malapportioned, massive resistance might have died more easily. Atlanta
businesspeople, ministers, politicians, and a parents' group, Help Our
Public Education, worked furiously to shift opinion in favor of open
schools. Former governor Ellis Arnall entered the 1962 gubernatorial
race early, on a platform of open schools, and former governor M. E.
Thompson declared, "[I]t is absurd to close all state schools just to keep
one Negro from going to school with white pupils in Atlanta." Other
politicians, however, pledged resistance to the bitter end.[38]

In April, the Sibley Commission submitted a sharply divided report:
A slender majority had approved local option, pupil placement, and a liberal transfer policy. Whether the legislature would approve this recom-
mendation was far from clear. Federal judge Frank Hooper now extended
the desegregation deadline by a year to give legislators a final opportunity
to repeal massive resistance laws, which he urged them to do. Hooper also

[margin notes: resistance / governor / vs. / fed. judge— Skelly Wright / G.A. / public opinion moving toward moderation / Frank Hooper]

made it clear that if schools closed in Atlanta, they would have to shut down in the rest of the state as well to avoid an equal protection violation.

Two intervening events helped to tilt the balance in favor of keeping Atlanta schools open. First, New Orleans exploded in violence as two schools desegregated there in November 1960. Atlanta businesspeople and politicians cringed at the thought of such violence being replicated in the "city too busy to hate."

Second, time ran out on the University of Georgia before Judge Hooper's deadline for Atlanta expired. In January 1961, Judge William A. Bootle ordered two blacks admitted to the Athens campus, and when the Fifth Circuit overturned his stay, they entered immediately. After rioting by whites led to the black students being suspended for their own safety, Judge Bootle ordered them reinstated and the university complied, bringing Georgia its first desegregation at any educational level. Most legislators preferred admitting two black students to closing the university, which was the alma mater of many of them.

Governor Vandiver then quickly abandoned massive resistance, calling for legislation to enable him to keep desegregated schools open. Diehards such as Roy Harris and Marvin Griffin criticized the governor's capitulation, but the legislature replaced mandatory school closures with local option, pupil placement, and public tuition grants to attend private schools. The desegregation of the University of Georgia thus paved the way for Atlanta's school desegregation that fall, which took place without incident.

With token grade school desegregation accomplished in New Orleans and Atlanta, the collapse of massive resistance elsewhere seemed inevitable. Only South Carolina, Mississippi, and Alabama remained completely segregated, and their ability to hold out much longer was doubtful. Opinion polls revealed that most southerners now regarded desegregation as inevitable: 76 percent in 1961, compared with only 43 percent in 1957. One former diehard segregationist explained, "I was for segregation as long as it had a chance to win, but there's no use beating a dead cat."[39]

With Atlanta schools desegregated, Georgia voters in 1962 faced a choice in the gubernatorial race between the moderate Carl Sanders—"moderate means that I am a segregationist but not a damned fool"—and the rabid segregationist former governor Griffin. During the campaign, Griffin urged that words such as "compromise" and "inevitable" be stricken from southerners' vocabulary, attacked Sanders as Martin Luther King, Jr.'s candidate, and issued a joint call with George Wallace for Deep South unity against integration. Sanders, who criticized both King and Wallace, promised that Georgia would not close its schools.[40]

With the aid of a federal court decision invalidating the county-unit
system, which vastly overrepresented rural voters in statewide elections,
Sanders won handily, leading political observers to note the end of an era
in Georgia. Even the diehard segregationist attorney general, Eugene
Cook, now proclaimed that "99 percent of the people of Georgia have
abandoned the feeling that we should close every school in the state rather
than admit one Negro." That same year, the first black elected to the state
legislature since Reconstruction, Leroy Johnson, reported, "[T]here's a
new look in Georgia."[41]

There was still a distinctively old look to Alabama and Mississippi,
where politicians seemed to prefer embracing "embattled martyrdom" to
acknowledging the inevitability of desegregation. Candidates seeking to
succeed John Patterson as governor of Alabama in 1962 vied for the most
extreme segregationist position. Reflecting the tenor of the times, former
governor Folsom abandoned the moderation of his earlier campaigns,
promised to preserve school segregation during his constituents' lifetimes,
criticized Patterson for not jailing the Freedom Riders, and frequently
used the word "nigger" in his speeches, which political observers could
not recall his ever before doing. Bull Connor attacked "weak-kneed" integrationists and ran for governor on the record of diehard resistance to
racial change that he had compiled as Birmingham's police commissioner. State senator Albert Boutwell emphasized his sponsorship of massive resistance legislation. Attorney General MacDonald Gallion touted
his success at keeping the NAACP out of business.[42]

The frontrunner in the field, George Wallace, denied that desegregation was inevitable and campaigned mainly against federal judicial
tyranny, bragging that he had defied a 1958 court order to turn over voting records to the U.S. Civil Rights Commission. Wallace also promised
to defy any integration order, "even to the point of standing at the
school house door in person." His opponent in the runoff primary, state
senator Ryan deGraffenried, criticized as irresponsible Wallace's "running around, daring the federal government to throw him in jail," but
Alabama voters apparently preferred Wallace's extremism, awarding
him an easy victory.[43]

At least Wallace's defiant threats subjected him to criticism. In
Mississippi, where whites simply hoped "to put [up] a good fight before
losing," political extremism went mostly unchallenged. The legislature
continued to pass massive resistance measures after other states had
stopped doing so. The state attorney general, Joe T. Patterson, instructed
state officers to enforce segregation laws, notwithstanding contrary federal
authority. As a crisis loomed over court-ordered desegregation of Ole Miss

in September 1962, Governor Barnett reiterated, "[N]o school will be integrated in Mississippi while I am your governor," and he announced that all officeholders should resign unless they were prepared to go to jail. Business and professional leaders remained silent until it was too late.[44]

The race riot at Ole Miss, which brought federal troops back into the South, turned the massive resistance tide in South Carolina. Even before Ole Miss, public officials in South Carolina began hinting that flexibility could preserve the most segregation, and Governor Ernest Hollings declined to criticize such statements, noting that South Carolina had a "firm policy of flexibility." In August, a well-connected journalist wrote that politicians realized the state would have to integrate soon, though they would not publicly admit it.[45]

The Ole Miss crisis produced a "very significant change of mood," as South Carolina's "vicarious suffering" yielded a conviction that "it must not happen here." With a court order to integrate Clemson University looming late in 1962, the departing governor, Hollings, promised that South Carolina would not duplicate Little Rock or Ole Miss and implicitly criticized Barnett and Wallace for their last-ditch stands. Even the strongly segregationist Columbia *State* conceded, "[T]he issue is no longer one of whether there shall be integration, but of how reasonably it will be brought about."[46]

Clemson alumni, many of whom held powerful political positions, insisted that they "had too much sense" to close the university to prevent integration, and they promised to avoid "any tragedy like Mississippi." Business leaders closed ranks behind a call to preserve law and order even in the face of a judicial command to integrate. When black student Harvey Gantt (who later became mayor of Charlotte, North Carolina, and a candidate for the U.S. Senate) entered Clemson in January 1963 — the first desegregation at any educational level in South Carolina since Reconstruction—a formidable law enforcement presence ensured that no disturbances occurred.[47]

Alabama politicians were more divided over what lesson to learn from Ole Miss. Governor Patterson telegrammed his support to Governor Barnett and criticized the "tyrannical" use of troops, which would "mark the end of our existence as a democratic republic." The state's entire congressional delegation also supported Barnett, declaring, "Mississippi's fight is Alabama's fight." Governor-elect Wallace dared the federal government to throw Barnett in jail and continued his railing against "lousy, no-account judges."[48]

Yet dissenting voices were now heard in Alabama. Prominent business, civic, and political leaders condemned Wallace's "bravado," urged against school closures, and insisted that "another Oxford [Mississippi]" must be avoided at all costs. But Wallace would have none of it, refusing to "take back one single utterance," and he informed those who passed resolutions urging him to stand down that they were "wasting paper." In his inaugural address in January 1963, Wallace reaffirmed his defiant stand: "In the name of the greatest people that have ever trod this earth, I draw the line in the dust and toss the gauntlet before the feet of tyranny and I say segregation now, segregation tomorrow, segregation forever."[49]

By contrast, Attorney General Richmond Flowers, in his inaugural statement, urged Alabamans to distinguish between "a fighting chance and a chance to fight" and warned that defiance of federal court orders "can only bring disgrace to our state." Business leaders criticized "indecent and irresponsible" political elements for creating a national image of Alabama as a place of "reaction, rebellion and riots, of bigotry, bias and backwardness."[50]

In April 1963, Attorney General Robert Kennedy met with Wallace in Montgomery but was unable to budge him, as Wallace reaffirmed his pledge to maintain segregation forever. In June, in a carefully orchestrated charade, Wallace physically blocked desegregation of the University of Alabama, before standing down in the face of superior federal force. That fall, he obstructed court-ordered desegregation of grade schools in several Alabama cities before capitulating there as well.

Although Deep South politicians continued to fulminate against integration, massive resistance came to an end. In Louisiana, parochial schools desegregated in 1962, and by the following year, citizens' councils were largely a spent force. In the gubernatorial primary of 1963–1964, race continued to dominate, but the loser, deLesseps S. Morrison, referred to himself as a segregationist "within the rule of reason," and the more avidly segregationist victor, John McKeithen, pointedly rejected school closures.[51]

In Mississippi's 1963 gubernatorial race, school segregation dominated, and Lieutenant Governor Paul Johnson emphasized his role in physically blocking James Meredith's admission to Ole Miss—"Stand Tall with Paul"—while promising, if necessary, to again interpose his body between the forces of federal tyranny and the people of Mississippi. He urged that the state "fight harder next time" and pledged to "resist the integration of any school anywhere in Mississippi."[52]

But the disaster at Ole Miss had finally liberated dissenters, and for virtually the first time in a decade, voices of moderation were heard in Mississippi, calling for open schools and peaceful compliance with court orders. In March 1963, Mississippi State participated in a racially mixed NCAA basketball tournament, and another "impregnable barrier" to desegregation fell. After running a defiant campaign, Governor Johnson's inaugural address sang a different tune. He declared that "hate, or prejudice, or ignorance will not lead Mississippi while I sit in the governor's chair," and he seemed to acknowledge the inevitability of desegregation, insisting that he would not fight a "rear-guard defense of yesterday" but rather would pursue Mississippi's "share of tomorrow." In the fall of 1964, Mississippi became the last state to desegregate its grade schools.[53]

One of Brown's principal effects was to radicalize southern politics. By encouraging extremism, Brown increased the likelihood that once direct-action protest developed, it would incite a violent response. In the early 1960s, civil rights demonstrators often sought racial reforms that were less controversial than school desegregation, including voting rights, desegregated lunch counters, and more jobs for blacks. If not for the retrogression that Brown produced in southern politics, such demands might have been received sympathetically or at least without unrestrained violence. Brown ensured that when street demonstrations came, politicians such as Bull Connor, Jim Clark, Ross Barnett, and George Wallace were there to meet them.

8

Why Massive Resistance?

Why did *Brown* so radicalize southern politics in the short term, leading candidates for public office to compete for the most extreme segregationist positions? There were white racial moderates in the South—people who favored compliance with court orders, opposed school closures, and would have tolerated gradual desegregation. *Brown II* had consciously appealed to such moderates and sought to empower them. Why did that strategy fail so abysmally? Why were so few moderate voices heard in the South after *Brown*?

One explanation focuses on southern politicians. Either because they miscalculated their constituents' preferences or because they demagogically capitalized on their constituents' fears, politicians became extremists and created an environment that chilled the expression of moderate sentiment. On this view, massive resistance was not inevitable, at least outside of the Deep South. Politicians could have espoused more moderate positions without losing office, and in so doing, they might have mobilized more vocal support from the large bloc of moderates, who instead fell silent.

It is true that some politicians had incentives for extremism, regardless of their constituents' preferences. In Virginia, the Byrd machine had reason to emphasize race issues, which could distract voters from debates over public services, which were gradually weakening its political position. But in most of the South, it was not politicians who were primarily responsible for massive resistance. The political dynamics of the segregation issue combined with certain features of southern politics to propel public debate toward extremism, independently of the machinations of politicians. Most officials, including those who were ordinarily inclined toward racial moderation, became more extremist to survive, and those few who resisted were generally destroyed.

Several factors helped to foster massive resistance. Diehard segregationists had stronger preferences than did most moderates. They also had the capacity and the inclination to use repressive tactics to create the appearance of white unity behind massive resistance. Diehard states similarly exerted pressure on more moderately inclined neighbors. Further, legislative malapportionment exaggerated the political power of extremists. Perhaps most important, the desire of nearly all southern whites to preserve segregation if possible virtually ensured an attempt at massive resistance. Differences among whites concerned the burdens that they were willing to bear to preserve segregation, not their preference for it. Finally, the use of federal troops, which proved to be necessary to suppress massive resistance, ironically bolstered it in the short term.

Although many white southerners were prepared to comply with *Brown,* and a few actually agreed with it, hard-core segregationists tended to be more intensely committed. Ardent segregationists tended to come from rural areas with large black populations or from working-class urban neighborhoods that were not rigidly segregated. By virtue of their strong preferences, these extreme segregationists usually controlled southern racial policy. Legislative commissions that were appointed to recommend responses to *Brown* were generally dominated by Black Belt segregationists. The legislator who chaired Virginia's commission, Garland Gray, came from Southside, and he had already recorded his "unalterable opposition" to the Court's "monstrous" decision. All five members of the Arkansas legislative committee that recommended policy on school segregation represented the delta region, which had the state's largest black population.[1]

Diehard segregationists were not only more intensely committed than were their adversaries, but they also had the inclination and the capacity to silence dissent. Massive resisters wanted to suppress opposition because they believed that only by presenting a united front could they induce the Court and the nation to retreat from *Brown*.

This issue arose mainly in the context of whether to allow local-option desegregation. If given a choice, portions of many southern states—northwestern Arkansas, West Texas, northern and western Virginia, eastern Tennessee, the city of Atlanta—were prepared to comply with *Brown*. But massive resisters in state government were determined to eliminate that choice for fear that any deviation from universal segregation would make integration appear to be inevitable, embolden the National Association for the Advancement of Colored People, and undermine the campaign to convince northern integrationists that the South would never tolerate *Brown*.

Thus, the Virginia legislature revoked Arlington County's right to elect school board members as punishment for the board's 1956 vote to desegregate, and it rejected the Gray Commission's initial proposal for local-option desegregation. In 1957, the Texas legislature required local communities to conduct referendums before desegregating or else lose their state education funds. More than 120 school districts in Texas had desegregated before this law was passed, but almost none did so for several years thereafter. Massive resisters in Georgia worried that Atlanta, with its "wrecking crew of extremists, ultra-liberals and renegade politicians," could prove to be the "Achilles' heel in the fight to keep segregation." When Mayor William B. Hartsfield asked the state legislature to adopt local option, Governor Marvin Griffin declared that the mayor "cannot throw in the towel for me or any other Georgian." The Southern Manifesto was a highly successful effort by diehard segregationists to coerce moderates into maintaining a united front.[2]

Their incentive to suppress dissent is clear, but why were massive resisters so effective at doing so? The answer, in short, is that the South was not an open society characterized by robust debate on racial issues. In 1960, a law school dean in Mississippi pointed out that "[f]riends won't argue among themselves" about segregation, and "you can't think out loud hardly." James Silver, a history professor at Ole Miss, charged that Mississippi had "erected a totalitarian society which has eliminated the ordinary processes through which change can come about." A South Carolina minister, noting that people were afraid even to protest the beating of a local band teacher for his allegedly integrationist statements, observed, "Fear covers South Carolina like the frost." In such an environment, white moderates were "immobilized by confusion and fear," and they mostly went into hiding.[3]

In the mid-1950s, massive resisters were a majority in much of the South, and thus they could use the levers of government to suppress dissent. Public school teachers and university professors lost their jobs or were harassed by legislative investigating committees for daring to support integration or even for urging obedience to the law or criticizing mob violence. Unwilling to tolerate such assaults on academic freedom, many of them resigned and moved elsewhere, which only exacerbated the problem of the closed society. Integrationist university students faced similar harassment and expulsion. Hundreds of them, both black and white, were suspended or expelled for participating in direct-action protests in the 1960s.

Some southern states targeted speech as well as speakers, removing offensive books from circulation. When the Georgia board of education banned textbook statements that charged whites with discrimination against blacks, the chair explained, "There is no place in Georgia schools at any time for anything that disagrees with our way of life." An Alabama legislator sparked a national controversy by demanding that public libraries ban a popular children's book about the marriage of two rabbits, one white and one black. Even the staunchly segregationist *Montgomery Advertiser* thought this was "idiocy," but the legislator defended himself on the ground that "the South has room for only one viewpoint."[4]

Dissent was suppressed through private as well as public action. Citizens' councils applied economic pressure to blacks who pursued integration and to whites who were deemed to be insufficiently committed to segregation. The U.S. Civil Rights Commission had difficulty enlisting Mississippi whites to serve on the state's advisory committee after a citizens' council leader warned, "[A]ny scalawag southerner who fronts for our mortal enemies will face the well-deserved contempt and ostracism that any proud people would feel for a traitor." White students who initially befriended the Little Rock Nine were condemned as "nigger lovers," and Ole Miss faculty and administrators who were civil to James Meredith were frequently harassed. When a few white families refused to boycott desegregated schools in New Orleans in 1960, they received death threats, homes were vandalized, and parents were fired from jobs; at least one family gave up and moved north.[5]

Violence was the last resort for compelling white conformity. When a white woman contributed an essay to the moderate publication *South Carolinians Speak*, in which she urged gradual desegregation, her home was bombed. A mob beat up a white minister in Clinton, Tennessee, for escorting black students to the desegregated school. A northern white minister attending the University of Alabama was kidnapped and beaten for inviting a black minister and his congregants to attend a meeting with white students.

Such pressure suppressed the traditional organs of moderate racial opinion. Newspapers that advocated desegregation or simple compliance with the law were boycotted and sometimes shut down. The editor of the only South Carolina newspaper that urged compliance with *Brown* was driven out of the state, as was the editor of one of the few Mississippi newspapers that criticized Governor Ross Barnett's antics at Ole Miss. A student editor at Auburn University had a cross burned on his lawn for supporting the Freedom Rides.

Southern ministers who advocated integration, or simply protested against extremist resistance, were usually evicted by their congregations. In 1963, twenty-eight Methodist ministers in Mississippi signed a statement supporting school desegregation, and all but seven of them were gone within a year. Many other ministers simply suppressed their private convictions that segregation was immoral.

Under pressure from public officials, some southern universities stopped inviting integrationist speakers. Citizens' councils harassed social clubs that expressed interest in hearing opposing viewpoints. Some television stations refused to air national programs that discussed integration, explaining that they were "not running a propaganda machine for the NAACP."[6]

If southern society was closed for whites, it was hermetically sealed for blacks. Because blacks were the most integrationist of southerners, suppressing their viewpoint was critical to maintaining the veneer of solid support for segregation. Blacks were subject to the same forms of segregationist pressure as whites, but the coercion was often more intense. Citizens' councils announced, "We intend to make it difficult, if not impossible, for any Negro who advocates desegregation to find and hold a job, get credit, or renew a mortgage." Police harassed integrationist blacks, broke up their meetings, and sometimes beat them. During the Montgomery bus boycott, public officials who were pursuing a "get tough" policy arrested scores of blacks on phony traffic charges and tried to disbar the black lawyer who filed the bus desegregation suit and to alter his draft classification. The most aggressive black integrationists were targets of extraordinary white violence. Daisy Bates, leader of Little Rock's desegregation forces, had her home fire-bombed seven times within two years.[7]

Southern society was closed; Mississippi verged on totalitarianism. The state sovereignty commission spied on civil rights workers and channeled public funds to citizens' councils. The legislature made it a crime to incite a breach of the peace by urging "nonconformance with the established traditions, customs, and usages of the State of Mississippi," and Governor James Coleman threatened to prosecute speakers who entered Mississippi to agitate the race issue. A white newspaper editor, who was sued for libel for criticizing law enforcement officers who mistreated blacks, observed, "[I]n much of Mississippi, we live in an atmosphere of fear." When the long-time Ole Miss history professor James Silver criticized the state as a "closed society" in 1963, public officials, failing to perceive the irony, announced that "it is time to get rid" of Silver and "to stifle his degrading activities."[8]

In many parts of Mississippi, blacks still faced "systematic racial terrorism." A visitor to Jefferson County reported, "It is all but unbelievable to see the fear that is shown by the Negro people." In many counties, not a single black person dared to register to vote. In the early 1960s, civil rights workers in Mississippi were routinely beaten, bombed, shot at, and occasionally killed. Local officials permitted the Klan to operate virtually without restraint.[9]

Racial moderates had neither the inclination nor the capacity to use such methods. They did not control state or local governments, and thus they could not fire segregationist teachers, expel segregationist students, or use the law enforcement apparatus to harass citizens' council members. Nor did moderates make harassing phone calls to segregationists, burn crosses on their lawns, or blow up their homes. When Robert Williams, the president of the NAACP branch in Union County, North Carolina, advocated that blacks meet "violence with violence" in the wake of Mack Parker's lynching in Mississippi in 1959, the national office immediately suspended him. Thus, hard-core segregationists were not only more intensely committed to their position than were moderate whites, but they were also more willing to use coercive measures to achieve victory. The suppression of moderate opinion had a cascading effect: As some people were intimidated into silence, the pressure on others to conform intensified.[10]

Just as within one state diehard segregationists could pressure moderates by denying the inevitability of desegregation, so could extremist states pressure their moderate neighbors. Politicians had difficulty explaining to constituents why they had to desegregate when neighboring states were not doing so.

This dynamic partially explains Governor Orval Faubus's dilemma over school desegregation in Little Rock in 1957. Alabama and Texas had flouted desegregation orders in the previous year, and the segregationist governor of Georgia, Marvin Griffin, had visited Little Rock two weeks before schools were scheduled to open and expressed shock that any governor with troops at his disposal would allow integration. Citizens approached Faubus on the street, demanding to know, "[I]f Georgia doesn't have integration, why does Arkansas?" On other occasions, citizens' councils asked why Faubus remained silent, while governors in South Carolina and Georgia were denouncing antisegregation court decisions. Alabama citizens' councils pressured their representatives in Congress "to join us in this fight, so we won't have to go to Mississippi, Georgia or South Carolina" to find real segregationists.[11]

Comprehending this dynamic and the importance of maintaining regional unity, diehard states in the Deep South pressured their more moderate neighbors to conform to massive resistance. The Columbia *State* criticized states that were abandoning segregation without a fight, because "surrender of some states makes it harder for the others to hold the line." Soon after he had fomented violent resistance to desegregation in Clinton, Tennessee, John Kasper, the South's leading peripatetic troublemaker, told Birmingham segregationists, "We want trouble and we want it everywhere we can get it." When sixteen Clintonians were arrested in connection with Kasper's disturbances, several attorneys general from southern states agreed to defend them—an expression of regional solidarity.[12]

[margin note: Extremists spread their influence throughout South]

Senator James Eastland of Mississippi also traveled through the South, speaking to mass segregationist rallies, warning against efforts "to pick [us] off one by one under the damnable doctrine of gradualism," and criticizing "border states [that] have weak-kneed politicians at the Capitol . . . [and] weak governors." The perceived importance of maintaining regional unity led Virginians to criticize North Carolina's token integrationism as "abject surrender" and Alabamans to regard Virginia's abandonment of massive resistance as a "crippling blow."[13]

Extremists also benefited from legislative malapportionment, which in every state favored rural districts that contained the most committed white supremacists. In Alabama and Georgia, Black Belt counties enjoyed nearly twice the representation that their populations warranted, meaning that whites in those counties, where blacks were generally disfranchised, exercised even more disproportionate political power. Moreover, such counties tended to reelect the same representatives for decades, which enhanced their legislative seniority and thus further augmented the political power of diehard segregationists.

[margin note: legislative districts]

[margin note: voting patterns]

Moderate racial opinion in cities was often nullified by malapportionment. For example, Atlanta had little clout in the rural-dominated Georgia legislature. Georgia's unique county-unit system, which extended malapportionment to elections for state executive offices, explains the extremism of governors such as Herman Talmadge and Marvin Griffin. Roy Harris conceded, "The county unit system is absolutely essential in order to maintain the pattern of segregation in Georgia."[14]

In other states, which elected executive officers on the principle of one person, one vote, governors often tried to force legislative reapportionment, but their efforts came to naught. When Governors James E. Folsom and LeRoy Collins called special legislative sessions in Alabama and Florida in the mid-1950s to consider reapportionment, legislators instead enacted massive resistance measures. Had *Brown* been decided after *Reynolds v. Sims* (1964) invalidated malapportionment in state legislatures, rather than before, massive resistance might have played out rather differently.

Yet the most important explanation for the temporary triumph of massive resistance may be this: Many southern whites—perhaps a majority outside of the Deep South—preferred token integration to school closures, but very few favored token integration over segregation. Thus, opinion polls on *Brown* revealed minimal support among southern whites, but referendums on school closures showed substantial white opposition. Consequently, until it became clear that preserving segregation entailed school closures, moderate whites had every reason to allow massive resistance to run its course, as they too preferred to avoid desegregation. The difference between white "moderates" and "extremists" was not in their preference for segregation, but in the sacrifices they were prepared to make to maintain it.

From this perspective, the crucial development of the mid-1950s was the growing conviction among white southerners that *Brown* could be successfully defied and segregation preserved. Massive resisters may have been emboldened by the fierce and successful opposition to desegregation put up by whites in Milford, Delaware, in the fall of 1954. If border state whites could frustrate desegregation, how could it possibly be imposed on the real South? *Brown II* furthered this conviction, as many southern whites sensed the beginnings of a judicial retreat. President Eisenhower's obvious lack of enthusiasm for *Brown*, his statements rejecting the use of federal troops to enforce desegregation orders, and his refusal to intervene against violent resistance to desegregation in Texas, Alabama, and Tennessee in 1956 encouraged southern whites to question the inevitability of integration.

Historical memories of the first Reconstruction, when southern whites had worn down the (never intense) commitment of northern whites to protecting the political and civil rights of southern blacks, inspired hope that determined resistance could nullify *Brown*. One segregationist editor, urging white southerners to "shape their destiny and control their way of life, just as they did in the far more dangerous period of Reconstruction," triumphantly concluded: "Our forefathers saved white men's civilization. We can do it again." Senator Eastland similarly noted, "Southern people have been tested in the past and have not been found wanting," and he predicted a new "golden hour of Southern history." Analogies to Prohibition also offered solace to southern whites: Many Americans, in the North and the South, had drawn the lesson from that historical episode that national efforts to coerce social reform against strong resistance were doomed to failure.[15]

One cannot know how many white southerners genuinely believed that *Brown* could be nullified and segregation preserved. But many southern politicians spoke this way, and their constituents may well have believed what they wanted to. Governor J. Lindsay Almond of Virginia had "faith that the decision ultimately will be reversed," and Senator Harry Byrd thought that "if people are firm enough and determined enough," the justices might change their minds. The segregation czar of Louisiana, Willie Rainach, promised that school closures would be unnecessary because the mere threat of them would be sufficient to block desegregation, and he predicted that the Court would reverse itself within a decade. Another Louisiana legislator observed, "When those birds in the Supreme Court realize we mean business, we'll find we won't have to change our entire school system." A South Carolina judge expressed confidence that "this decision will be eventually reversed, though it may take years." The principal purposes of the Southern Manifesto included convincing white southerners that desegregation was not inevitable and convincing northerners that the South would not capitulate. Efforts at undermining the perceived inevitability of desegregation also had a cascading effect: The fewer people who accepted desegregation as inevitable, the less so it became.[16]

Political rhetoric challenging the inevitability of desegregation clearly had an effect. A circular from a white supremacist organization declared:

> The fact that the Supreme Court has ruled as it has, in favor of the black man, is no sign that the whole thing is settled. Many times in the past the Supreme Court has reversed itself, and many other times it has merely overlooked enforcing its rulings.

A reporter from Norfolk, Virginia, noted that after the "general air of calm resignation" following *Brown I,* the notion had developed "that the fatal day would be delayed for many years," and "in some quarters there was actual belief that integration would never come." Political journalist Samuel Lubell, who was interviewing white southerners during this period, reported, "By the spring of 1957 the segregationists, emboldened by the lack of opposition to their efforts, had come to believe that nullification of the Supreme Court's decision was in sight." According to Gallup polls, the number of white southerners who believed that school desegregation was inevitable fell from 55 percent early in 1956 to 43 percent in August 1957.[17]

Once Eisenhower used federal troops at Little Rock, however, only school closures could prevent desegregation. As several schools closed in Virginia and in Little Rock in 1958, white southerners had to confront a previously avoided question: What costs were they prepared to incur in order to preserve segregation?

The speed with which massive resistance crumbled outside of the Deep South after schools were closed suggests one of two possibilities: Either many whites had endorsed school closures only as a bluff to induce a retreat by the Court and by integrationist northerners, or they had genuinely supported closures but without carefully calculating the costs. Once the bluff was called, and the costs of school closures were made concrete, the attitudes of white southerners toward school desegregation changed rapidly. Parents' groups that were dedicated to saving public education sprang up across the South, and some local chambers of commerce mobilized against school closures.

A post–Little Rock poll revealed that two out of three whites in Virginia would rather close schools than integrate them. Reflecting that opinion, in 1958, Governor Almond closed schools in Charlottesville, Norfolk, and Warren County, while continuing to give fiery speeches that endorsed massive resistance. But private school arrangements quickly proved to be unsatisfactory, especially in Norfolk, where a federal judge enjoined public employees from teaching in private schools and thousands of children went uneducated. Public opinion in Virginia changed rapidly as a result. By November, newspapers that had formerly supported massive resistance were calling for "speedy abandonment" of that "futile" strategy and the adoption of a "new approach." James J. Kilpatrick, editor of the *Richmond News Leader* and the principal force behind the interposition movement three years earlier, now called for "new weapons and new tactics" and endorsed token integration.[18]

Public officials soon reflected that opinion shift. Although Southside politicians continued to endorse "massive resistance all the way," Governor Almond changed his tune virtually overnight. After federal and state courts invalidated school closures in January 1959, Almond repudiated massive resistance in favor of local option and token integration. He criticized proposals to abandon public education as "going back to the dark ages" and warned that Virginia "cannot secede from the Union [or] overthrow the federal government." An opinion poll showed that two out of three Virginians now supported the governor's new policy.[19]

Attitudes toward school desegregation also changed quickly in Little Rock. Governor Faubus had promised an easy transition from public to private education, and in September 1958, Little Rock voters supported school closures in a referendum by a margin of greater than 5–2. But the white private school quickly proved to be unsatisfactory, especially after a federal court blocked its use of public money and public school buildings. In December, school board elections showed that voters were evenly divided between candidates of the citizens' council and those of more moderate businesspeople. In February 1959, the 2,000 members of the Little Rock Chamber of Commerce voted by a margin of better than 3–1 to reopen high schools with token integration. The business community could easily count the costs of school closures: Ten businesses had relocated to Little Rock in the two years before September 1957, but not a single one had done so since.

In May 1959, city voters narrowly recalled segregationist school board members in retaliation for their purges of moderate teachers and replaced them with token integrationists. By the time Little Rock public high schools reopened with a few blacks in attendance that fall, the private school corporation had gone bankrupt. In 1960, Samuel Lubell discovered that the same Little Rock whites who two years earlier had preferred to see Central High burned down rather than "infested with niggers" now favored token integration over school closures.[20]

Because their moment of truth arrived later, Georgians were able to learn vicariously from the tribulations of others. Little Rock officials and business leaders visited Atlanta to warn of the economic and social costs entailed by diehard segregationism. In his 1958 gubernatorial campaign and then repeatedly over the next two years, Governor Ernest Vandiver rejected local option and token integration in favor of school closures. Yet public opinion began to shift as school closures loomed once Judge Frank Hooper ordered Atlanta to desegregate in 1960, which he later postponed until 1961. Parents' organizations, business leaders, and most newspapers preferred token integration to school closures.

Reflecting this opinion shift, Vandiver encouraged the legislature to appoint the Sibley Commission, which searched for an honorable means of retreat. By early 1961, as the desegregation crisis hit the University of Georgia, Vandiver was declaring, "We cannot abandon public education," and urging the repeal of statutes that required integrated schools to close and their replacement with provisions for local option and public tuition grants for students to attend private schools. Henceforth, Vandiver insisted that federal court orders must be obeyed, and he bragged that his administration had kept the schools open.[21]

These dramatic turnabouts in Virginia, Arkansas, and Georgia help to explain the political dynamics of massive resistance. Until attempted, nobody knew whether it could succeed. School closures were a cheap threat, and the costs, if implemented, were hard to calculate in advance. After Little Rock, however, only school closures could preserve segregation. Once they were tried, public opinion turned rapidly against them because of the harm to education and to business development. Moderates, who had previously possessed little incentive to oppose massive resistance, now asserted themselves, and the debate rapidly swung in their favor. Token integration, though "still . . . objectionable," was "not intolerable," and it was preferable to school closures. Moreover, this dynamic, which favored moderation, was as self-reinforcing as the earlier one, which had supported extremism. As the first moderates asserted themselves and demanded open schools, others found it easier to follow.[22]

Yet the realism that was impelled by Little Rock, New Orleans, and Ole Miss had little immediate effect on Governors John Patterson, George Wallace, and Ross Barnett. In the late 1950s, diehard resisters may genuinely have believed that desegregation could be avoided and the Court induced to back down. Explaining their behavior in 1962–1963 is more difficult, as they surely understood by then that they could not preserve "segregation forever" and that to "fight harder next time" was no formula for success.[23]

The reason that politicians continued to make such pledges is probably that voters in Alabama and Mississippi continued to reward them for doing so. For example, Wallace plainly anticipated political gain from fomenting a desegregation fight with the federal government, even though his stand in the schoolhouse door in Tuscaloosa was a carefully orchestrated charade.

The real question is why voters rewarded such irresponsible pledges once desegregation had become inevitable. Perhaps they were so embittered at the prospect of externally coerced racial change that they preferred, in the best southern tradition, to fight futile battles rather than to capitulate. Many whites in Mississippi and Alabama, though conceding that "you can't fight the Federal government and win," still insisted, "[W]e'll never accept it voluntarily," and "they'll have to force it on us." As William Faulkner pointed out, Mississippi whites "will accept another civil war, knowing they're going to lose."[24]

Finally, massive resistance could end only after Eisenhower had proved his willingness to use federal troops to enforce desegregation orders. Yet, ironically, the deployment of these forces bolstered massive resistance in the short term. Historically, white southerners have been especially sensitive to outside interference with their "way of life." Thus, when Eisenhower sent federal troops into Little Rock, moderate white southerners united with extremists in assailing the president. Although Little Rock should have discouraged extremism by demonstrating the futility of massive resistance, its immediate effect was to further radicalize southern opinion and to empower politicians who promised defiance of "federal tyranny."

On statewide television, Faubus referred to Little Rock as an "occupied" city, implicitly appealing to the bitter historical memories that Arkansas whites had of the Civil War and of Reconstruction, when federal troops invaded the South. Southern political opinion overwhelmingly supported Faubus and condemned Eisenhower. A North Carolina representative asserted, "The issue of integrated schools is dwarfed by the precipitous and dictatorial stab at the rights of an individual state."[25]

Several southern politicians compared the use of federal troops at Little Rock to the Soviet Union's invasion of Hungary in 1956. Governor George Timmerman of South Carolina criticized the president for "trying to set himself up as a dictator." Senator Richard Russell condemned the use of "storm troopers." Circuit judge George Wallace compared Eisenhower to Hitler and accused the president of substituting "military dictatorship for the Constitution of the United States."[26]

President Kennedy's use of federal forces to desegregate Ole Miss in the fall of 1962 had a similar, albeit less dramatic, effect on southern politics. Political leaders in Arkansas rallied behind Mississippi governor Barnett, even though their state's public universities had desegregated nearly fifteen years earlier. After Ole Miss, the Republican candidate for the U.S. Senate in Alabama, James Martin, urged voters to "go to the polls with a Rebel yell," and he tried to associate his opponent, Senator Lister Hill, with the Kennedy administration. Martin came within one percentage point of becoming the state's first Republican senator since Reconstruction. In 1963, Paul Johnson won the governorship of Mississippi by denouncing the use of federal troops to desegregate Ole Miss.[27]

These are the reasons that *Brown* radicalized southern politics and induced candidates for public office to adopt extreme segregationist positions. Fire-breathing resistance to federal authority translated into political gain. Politicians calculated that white voters would reward stalwart resistance to racial change, even if it resulted in violence.

9

Brown, Violence, and Civil Rights Legislation

Before the Freedom Rides, Birmingham, Freedom Summer, and Selma (discussed below), some of the most violent racial episodes in the South involved school desegregation. Virtually every year after *Brown*, school desegregation generated violent resistance somewhere: Milford, Delaware, in 1954; Hoxie, Arkansas, in 1955; Tuscaloosa, Alabama; Clinton, Tennessee; Mansfield, Texas; and Clay and Sturgis counties, Kentucky, all in 1956; Little Rock, Arkansas, and Nashville, Tennessee, in 1957; Clinton (again) in 1958; New Orleans, Louisiana, in 1960; Athens, Georgia, in 1961; Oxford, Mississippi, in 1962; and Birmingham, Alabama, in 1963. Thus, in addition to radicalizing southern politics in ways that enhanced the likelihood of racial violence, *Brown* created concrete occasions for such outbreaks.

Violent episodes involving school desegregation tarnished the national and international image of white southerners. Resisting court orders to desegregate inevitably placed them on the wrong side of the law. Most Americans believed that judicial rulings should be obeyed, even by those who strongly disagreed with them; the alternative was anarchy.

President Dwight D. Eisenhower capitalized on this widespread conviction, insisting that the federal troops he sent to Little Rock were there "to support our federal court system—not to enforce desegregation." When President John F. Kennedy sent federal troops into Oxford, Mississippi, he likewise emphasized his duty "to implement the orders of the court," which was necessary to preserve "a government of laws, and not of men."[1] For individuals to violate court orders was bad enough, but mob resistance was even worse. Few things offended national opinion more than substituting the rule of the mob for that of the law.

In addition, violent confrontations over school desegregation tended to reveal blacks at their best and whites at their worst. The few blacks who had been handpicked as desegregation pioneers were almost always middle class, bright, well dressed, well mannered, and nonviolent. The mobs that sought to exclude them from white schools tended to be lower class, vicious, obscene, unruly, and violent. Photographic images of these confrontations, according to a *New York Post* editorial, showed "quiet, resolute Negro children defying jeers and violence and sadism." To the extent that Americans formed their views on school desegregation and Jim Crow from watching televised scenes of mob violence from Little Rock or New Orleans, southern whites were bound to lose the battle for public opinion.[2]

Some violent outbreaks over desegregation were brief, as it did not take long to bomb schools in Clinton and Nashville. Other episodes were protracted, such as Little Rock and New Orleans. Lengthy desegregation confrontations attracted media attention. Confrontation and violence play well on television, and extended conflict gives photographers and reporters time to assemble. Few Americans owned television sets in 1950. By the time of Little Rock, most of them did, and by the time of New Orleans and Oxford, the vast majority did. Live footage of white mobs assailing black students profoundly affected national opinion.

In February 1956, a mob numbering more than a thousand, throwing rocks and eggs and threatening a lynching, drove Autherine Lucy out of the University of Alabama. One northern newspaper condemned mob violence in opposition to court decisions and proclaimed, "Shame falls on Alabama." Adlai Stevenson, not known for his strong statements on civil rights, denounced the mob violence as "deplorable" and "intolerable." A South Carolina newspaper called the riot a "public disgrace," which "has given the South another black eye" and "played right into

Figure 9.1. A white man kicks black newspaper reporter Alex Wilson as a mob watches outside of Little Rock's Central High School, September 23, 1957. Wilson said, "I fought for my country, and I'm not running from you," as he was attacked. Arkansas History Commission.

the hands of professional South-baiters." Compared with the mob, blacks had been models of "discipline, patience, and understanding." The *Washington Post* predicted that the incident would "outrage opinion even in areas where extreme views against integration prevail." Roy Wilkins, head of the National Association for the Advancement of Colored People, cited the riot as evidence of the need for civil rights legislation to protect against mob violence and to withhold federal funds from defiant educational institutions in the South.[3]

Little Rock was a much larger event; it lasted for weeks and culminated in the use of federal troops to protect black students from an enormous mob surrounding Central High School. Outside of the South, public opinion overwhelmingly condemned the mob violence and supported the president. Governor Orval Faubus was widely ridiculed— "the sputtering sputnik from the Ozarks," according to Maryland governor Theodore McKeldin. Gloster Current of the NAACP "[t]hank[ed] God for Gov. Faubus. He has hastened integration five years by opening the eyes of the country to the kind of thinking that will call out the National Guard to keep nine Negro students out of Little Rock High School." Wilkins similarly labeled Faubus a "valuable enemy" who has "aroused and educated to our point of view millions of people in America." Ironically, though Faubus alienated northern opinion, southern whites hailed him as a hero, thus ensuring that other southern politicians would mimic his behavior and further repulse northern opinion.[4]

In November 1960, similarly ugly scenes were repeated in New Orleans. But this time, the targets of the mob were six-year-olds. Night after night, nationwide television audiences watched hundreds of vicious protestors, their faces contorted by hate, spitting, snarling, and yelling "kill them niggers" at first-graders walking to school in their Sunday best. The author John Steinbeck, who happened to be traveling through New Orleans at the time, called the mob's rantings "bestial and filthy and degenerate," and he compared them to the "vomitings of demoniac humans." The *New York Times*, which thought that the efforts of a "racist rabble . . . to subvert the Constitution and substitute anarchy for law" were "degrading and dangerous," warned that the "conscience of America" would not tolerate the "mobsters" or the "insurrectionary histrionics" of the state's elected officials. A Miami woman reported that the "appalling sight and sound . . . [made her] sick—almost physically ill," while a German-born doctor compared the scenes from New Orleans to those enacted in Nazi Germany in the 1930s.[5]

Much of the southern white-on-black violence of the 1950s occurred in the context of court-ordered school desegregation. To the extent that such violence helped to transform national opinion on race, *Brown* was directly responsible.

Brown helped to foment violence in other ways as well. The simple existence of *Brown* may have inspired white vigilantes to attack blacks. *Brown* led extremist politicians to use inflammatory rhetoric that may have indirectly incited violence. *Brown* even led some officeholders to calculate the political benefits of violently suppressing civil rights protest.

Polls taken after *Brown* revealed that 15–25 percent of southern whites favored violence, if necessary, to resist school desegregation. The post-*Brown* rebirth of the Ku Klux Klan in the South—Klan rallies in 1956 drew hundreds, even thousands, in parts of South Carolina, Georgia, Alabama, and Florida—suggests a greater willingness among whites to use violence. One Klan leader reported that *Brown* created "a situation loaded with dynamite" and "really gave us a push." Now that the justices had "abolished the Mason-Dixon line," Klansmen vowed to "establish the Smith and Wesson line." In 1957, six Birmingham Klansmen castrated a randomly selected black man after taunting him for "think[ing] nigger kids should go to school with [white] kids."[6]

In the late 1940s, Mississippi whites had threatened and beaten blacks for their suffrage activities, but in 1955, the Reverend George Lee in Belzoni and Lamar Smith in Brookhaven were killed for voting or encouraging other blacks to do so. The annual number of reported lynchings in Mississippi had dropped to zero in the years before *Brown*, but in 1955, in addition to the Lee and Smith murders, fourteen-year-old Emmett Till was killed for allegedly whistling at a white woman in Money, Mississippi. That year, the NAACP published a pamphlet entitled *M Is for Mississippi and Murder*.[7]

lynchings
murders

Connecting these killings to *Brown* is speculative, but the timing suggests a possible linkage, and some contemporaries inferred a causal connection. The *Herald* of Yazoo City, Mississippi, declared that the blood of Till was on the hands of the justices. The unwillingness of white jurors to indict or convict the clearly guilty white murderers of blacks is even more plausibly linked to *Brown*'s impact on southern white opinion. One Mississippi white declared, "There's open season on the Negroes now. They've got no protection, and any peckerwood who wants can go out and shoot himself one, and we'll free him."[8]

Till's funeral in Chicago attracted thousands of mourners, and a photograph of his mutilated body in *Jet* seared the conscience of northerners. Segregating black school children was one thing, lynching them quite another. Wilkins condemned Mississippi's "political murders" and the "system that permits the shooting down of little boys." Republican representative Hugh Scott of Pennsylvania called for legislation to "eliminate this kind of horror from American life."[9]

Mississippi was not the only southern state to become more racially violent after *Brown*. Birmingham, Alabama, where civic leaders in the early 1950s had tried to clean up the city's image by suppressing violence, once again became "Bombingham" after *Brown*. Between 1955 and 1963, Birmingham blacks were the targets of twenty-one bombings, none of which the police were able to solve. In Montgomery, the homes and churches of several black ministers and other civil rights leaders were bombed during and after the bus boycott.

bombings

One study counted more than a hundred violent incidents in the South connected to civil rights activity between January 1, 1955, and May 1, 1958. Most of these involved the bombing of homes, schools, and churches, and some Jewish synagogues were also targeted. The victims were usually black, but moderate whites were occasionally attacked as well. After listening to a judge denounce the Supreme Court's "asinine" decisions for an hour, a grand jury in Camden, South Carolina, declined to indict six men who were charged with beating the white director of a school band for allegedly making integrationist statements. Synagogue bombings attracted special attention and condemnation in the North. Both New York senators visited Atlanta after a temple was bombed in late 1958, and they demanded legislation that would authorize federal intervention in such cases.[10]

The lynching of Mack Parker in April 1959, which captured front-page headlines in major newspapers, stunned Americans. Whites had seized Parker, who was scheduled to stand trial for allegedly raping a white woman, from the jail in Poplarville, Mississippi, and killed him—the state's first old-style lynching since World War II. At least one Mississippi newspaper blamed the Supreme Court and drew the lesson that "force must not be used in pushing revolutionary changes in social custom. Every such action produces equal and opposite reaction." The judge who presided over the grand jury that was investigating the lynching urged its members to "have the backbone to stand against any tyranny . . . [even including] the Board of Sociology setting [sic] in Washington, garbed in Judicial Robes, and 'dishing out' the 'legal precedents' of Gunnar Myrdal."[11]

Many southern politicians condemned the lynching but expressed the hope that the South "won't be punished by civil rights legislation for what a handful have done." Citizens' council guru Judge Tom Brady predicted that the NAACP would "rejoice in this highly regrettable incident" and "will urge passage of vicious civil rights measures." He was at least partially right. Wilkins declared that Parker's lynching was the "natural consequence of an organized campaign of law defiance" by southern politicians and that it demonstrated the "necessity of further and stronger protection of civil rights . . . by the federal government."[12]

Constituents wrote to their representatives in Congress to express horror and to demand federal legislation to curb such atrocities. Prominent liberals, such as Senators Hubert Humphrey, Paul Douglas, and Jacob Javits, made forceful calls for federal civil rights legislation. Attorney General William Rogers announced that he was studying the need for such legislation in light of Parker's lynching and the unwillingness of a local grand jury to indict known participants, which he thought "as flagrant and calculated a miscarriage of justice as I know of."[13]

Diehard segregationists identified and promoted a linkage between *Brown* and white vigilante violence against blacks. In 1956, John Kasper traveled through Alabama, attacking the racial moderation of Governor James E. ("Big Jim") Folsom and calling for "marching bands" and "roving forces" to converge on any area threatened with desegregation. A Dallas minister told a large citizens' council rally that if public officials would not block integration, plenty of people were prepared to "shed blood if necessary to stop this work of Satan." A member of the Tuskegee citizens' council warned, "We will stop integration if it takes bloodshed!" A handbill that was circulated at a huge citizens' council rally in Montgomery denounced desegregation and declared, "When in the course of human events it becomes necessary to abolish the Negro race, proper methods should be used," including guns and knives.[14]

It was difficult to pin collective blame on white southerners for random acts of violence committed by white vigilantes against blacks. However, when public officials incited such violence, many northerners deemed national civil rights legislation to be a plausible response. Southern politicians fomented violence by explicitly encouraging it, by predicting it, and by using extremist rhetoric that inspired it.

Most southern politicians avoided explicit exhortations to violence, and many affirmatively discouraged it, either to immunize themselves from criticism when violence occurred or because they rightly understood that violence would "do irreparable harm to our cause and turn public opinion against us." One southern congressman warned that the gains made in convincing northerners that *Brown* was lawless "can be swept away by one shotgun blast, by one explosion of dynamite touched off in the heat of passion."[15] Still, a few politicians could not restrain themselves. An Alabama legislator declared that whites must leave the state, "stay here and be humiliated, or take up our shotguns." A Mississippi legislator stated that "a few killings" now could "save a lot of bloodshed later on." Others promoted violence more discreetly. A few days after a raging mob had driven Autherine Lucy out of Tuscaloosa, Senator James Eastland of Mississippi told an enormous citizens' council rally that he knew "you good people of Alabama don't intend to let the NAACP run your schools."[16]

Rather than explicitly promoting violence, many southern politicians simply predicted it, which Martin Luther King, Jr., pointed out was a "conscious or unconscious invitation to [it]." The attorney general of South Carolina warned, "[O]ur patience may become exhausted and when that happens, God knows what the results will be." Roy Harris predicted that integrationist efforts would produce "hatred and bloodshed," and Judge Tom Brady endorsed the view of the *Jackson Daily News* that "[h]uman blood may stain Southern soil in many places because of

[*Brown*]." Diehard segregationists, after hearing enough of such predictions, were likely to make good on them. The failure of public officials to condemn violence also had the effect of encouraging it. Rather than denouncing a mob in Mansfield, Texas, that blocked court-ordered desegregation and called for the blood of black students, Governor Allan Shivers commended the "orderly protest against a situation instigated and agitated by the [NAACP]."[17]

Other officials repudiated violence, while using extremist rhetoric that probably encouraged it. Governor Marvin Griffin of Georgia condemned violence but also insisted that "no true Southerner feels morally bound to recognize the legality of this act of tyranny [*Brown*]," and he proclaimed that the South "stands ready to battle side-by-side for its sacred rights . . . but not with guns." One of that state's U.S. senators, Herman Talmadge, likened *Brown* to a coup d'etat by a foreign dictator, and he called it "judicial tyranny" and the "greatest single blow ever . . . struck against constitutional government." After the temple bombing in Atlanta, Griffin and Talmadge called for severe punishment of the perpetrators—probably "Communists," they said—yet in the same breath they denied that *Brown* was the law of the land and vowed that the South would never "surrender."[18]

Senator Eastland cautioned, "Acts of violence and lawlessness have no place," and he insisted, "The fight that we wage must be a just and legal fight." But he also condemned *Brown* as "illegal, immoral," "dishonest," and a "disgrace," and he proclaimed, "[R]esistance to tyranny is obedience to God." Congressman James Davis of Georgia likewise insisted, "There is no place for violence or lawless acts," right after he had called *Brown* a "monumental fraud which is shocking, outrageous and reprehensible," warned against "meekly accept[ing] this wrongful usurpation of power," and denied any obligation of "the people to bow the neck to this new form of tyranny." These politicians either knew that such rhetoric was likely to incite violence, or they were criminally negligent for not knowing it.[19]

In terms of influencing national opinion, whether political demagoguery produced violence was less important than the perception that it did. The NAACP constantly asserted such a linkage, blaming southern politicians for fostering a climate that was conducive to the lynching of Mack Parker and insisting that the bombers of southern synagogues "were made bold by groups of so-called respectable people which have urged publicly that the courts be defied." James Meredith blamed the assassination of Medgar Evers in 1963 on "governors of the Southern states and their defiant and provocative actions."[20]

Figure 9.2. Medgar Evers, the NAACP's field secretary in Mississippi, was murdered in 1963 for his civil rights activities. Library of Congress, Prints and Photographs Division, *New York World-Telegram & Sun* Collection.

Others drew similar connections. A lawyer in Clinton, Tennessee, blamed school desegregation violence on the congressional representatives who signed the Southern Manifesto: "What the hell do you expect these people to do when they have 90 some odd congressmen from the South signing a piece of paper that says you're a southern hero if you defy the Supreme Court[?]" After Atlanta's temple bombing, Mayor William B. Hartsfield declared, "Whether they like it or not, every rabble-rousing politician is the godfather of the cross-burners and the dynamiters who are giving the South a bad name."[21]

The general connection between extremist politicians and violence is plausible, but the linkage between particular public officials and the brutality that inspired civil rights legislation is compelling. The principal players were Bull Connor, John Patterson, Ross Barnett, George Wallace, and Jim Clark. The violence that they cultivated, condoned, or unintentionally fomented proved to be critical to transforming national opinion on race.

Though the increased violence of southern whites against blacks in the late 1950s influenced national racial opinion, it was neither sufficiently sustained nor frequently enough captured on television to generate the widespread outrage needed for the enactment of transformative civil rights legislation. As of 1960, southern whites still tended to care more about preserving segregation than northern whites did about eliminating it. Civil rights leaders needed a new strategy for turning northern racial opinion in their favor.

In the 1950s, Martin Luther King, Jr., was still trying to convince southern whites that racial segregation was wrong—to "awaken a sense of moral shame in [them]." Within a few years, however, he had largely abandoned such efforts in favor of trying to win support from northern whites, most of whom already thought that segregation was wrong but were disinclined to do much about it. Lynchings, such as those of Till in 1955 or Parker in 1959, educated and energized northern whites by unveiling the violence at the core of white supremacy and belying the claims of southern whites that blacks endorsed the racial status quo. In 1961, a white New Yorker told the NAACP that he had sympathized with the association's cause for years but that it took the murders of Till and Parker to "crystallize my rage." Wilkins put the point more bluntly: Whenever "some outrage occurs, white people send the NAACP checks."[22] To transform northern opinion, then, southern civil rights leaders concluded that they had to provoke violence against themselves, especially in settings that were likely to attract national media attention. Direct-action protest would probably incite brutal repression, and if the conflict lasted long enough, the national media would pay attention and so would the nation.

The success of this strategy of "creative tension" depended on the presence of certain conditions. In 1960, most white Americans disapproved of direct-action protest. Many shared former president Harry S Truman's view that "[i]f anyone came into my store and tried to stop business, I'd throw him out." To win public support, then, protestors had to be unambiguously in the right and their adversaries in the wrong. Their behavior had to be impeccable and their objectives clearly legitimate. The contrast they sought to portray was between well-dressed, polite, studious blacks peacefully protesting and a "ragtail rabble, slackjawed, black-jacketed, grinning fit to kill" assaulting them.[23]

The demonstrators' success also required the "cooperation" of law enforcement officers. Peaceful arrests, even if illegal, dampened protest without generating violent confrontation; the media got bored, the demonstrators grew tired, and the Kennedy administration failed to intervene. Such was the lesson of Albany, Georgia, in 1961–1962, as Laurie Pritchett, the "nonviolent police chief," arrested hundreds of demonstrators and outlasted the movement. Violent assaults on protestors, by contrast, captured media attention, forced the administration to intervene, and outraged northerners. Thus, the Freedom Riders "count[ed] upon the racists of the South to create a crisis," and leaders of the Southern Christian Leadership Conference (SCLC) "calculated for the stupidity of a Bull Connor."[24]

T. Eugene "Bull" Connor was first elected to the Birmingham City Commission in 1937 on a pledge to crush the communist/integrationist threat posed by the unionization efforts of the Congress of Industrial Organizations. In 1938, he broke up the inaugural meeting of the Southern Conference for Human Welfare in Birmingham because it violated a local segregation ordinance. In the late 1940s, Connor's police department failed to take action in response to a wave of bombings that were directed at black families moving into contested neighborhoods.

By 1950, however, civic leaders had come to view Connor as an embarrassment. A committee to encourage business relocations was hampered by the city's racial violence and the extremism of politicians such as Connor. Some businesspeople orchestrated his public humiliation through an illicit sexual encounter, and Connor retired from politics in 1953. Birmingham then saw some racial progress, including the establishment of the first hospital for blacks, the desegregation of elevators in downtown office buildings, and serious efforts toward desegregating the police force.

After *Brown*, however, Birmingham's racial progress ground to a halt. In 1955, the city council rejected proposals to hire black police officers, which it said might lead to "serious racial trouble" in light of *Brown*. An interracial committee disbanded in 1956; consultation between the races largely ceased; and Connor resurrected his political career. In 1957, he regained his seat on the city commission by promising that he would not permit "professional agitators and radicals to come into Birmingham and stir up racial strife" and by attacking his opponent, who insisted that "[i]t doesn't take AGITATION to maintain SEGREGATION," as weak on the race issue. In the late 1950s, a powerful Klan element wreaked havoc in Birmingham with a wave of unsolved bombings and brutality. The police, under Connor's control, declined to interfere and may well have covered up evidence about the perpetrators of the crimes.[25]

Standing for reelection in 1961, Connor cultivated extremists by offering the Klan fifteen minutes of "open season" on the Freedom Riders as they rolled into town. Promising the Klansmen through an intermediary that he would keep officers away from the scene, Connor reportedly beseeched them: "By God, if you are going to do this thing, do it right!" After horrific beatings were administered to media representatives as well as demonstrators, the *Birmingham News* wondered, "[W]here were the police?" Voters may have been less curious, having handed a landslide victory just two weeks earlier to Connor, who had invited the violence.[26]

police absent

When the Freedom Riders traveled on to Montgomery, the police again mysteriously disappeared, and the demonstrators were savagely beaten once more. Governor Patterson had promised safe passage, and thus he bore considerable responsibility for the violence.

Patterson was one of the most extreme southern politicians of the post-*Brown* era. Running for governor in 1958, he predicted that integration would cause "violence, disorder, and bloodshed," and as governor he warned that "enemies" of the South were launching an "all-out war to completely destroy our customs, traditions and way of life." After New Orleans erupted in violence over school desegregation in 1960, Patterson promised that the violence there would be nothing as compared with the consequences of forced integration in Alabama, where there would be "hell to pay." Patterson vowed that when the federal showdown came, "I'll be one of the first ones stirring up trouble, anyway I can." He blamed the Freedom Riders themselves—"professional agitators," he called them—for the violence they suffered. But Klansmen may have taken their lead from the governor, who could probably have prevented the violence had he been so inclined.[27]

Whether Patterson, Connor, and other public officials had incited violence against the Freedom Riders or merely failed to prevent it, public opinion generally deemed them to be responsible. Federal judge Frank Johnson, Attorney General Robert Kennedy, former governor Folsom, and many others blamed state and local officials for the brutality. *Time* wrote that Alabama officials, from "Governor John Patterson on down, abdicated their duties of maintaining law and order." The *Birmingham News* also singled out Patterson for blame, noting that he had "talk[ed] for months in a manner that could easily say to the violent, the intemperate . . . that they were free to do as they pleased when it came to the hated integrationists."[28]

Alabama politicians had handed the civil rights movement an important victory on a silver platter. Reflecting a visceral opposition to direct action, only about 24 percent of Americans had supported the Freedom Rides, while 64 percent disapproved. Critics viewed the demonstrators as "provocateurs, or inciters to disorder." David Brinkley of NBC television thought that the Freedom Riders, though within

Freedom Riders blamed by some

their legal rights, should cease their "exhibition," which was "doing positive harm" by "inflam[ing] . . . Southern opinion" and making "advances even more difficult than they already were."[29]

But the Freedom Riders were behaving nonviolently, exercising rights recently declared by the Supreme Court, and enduring vicious beatings. This was southern white supremacy at its ugliest—"the violent brutality of mobsters," as the NAACP described it. Senator Jacob Javits of New York stated, "[T]he whole country must be deeply shocked, appalled and . . . ashamed by the . . . violence," while Senate majority leader Mike Mansfield declared that the Alabama disorders "should cause us—as a Nation—to hang our heads in shame." Even in Montgomery and Birmingham, Alabama, leading newspapers criticized the "savage scene," the "howling mobs," and the "raging attack." Influenced by constituents who expressed horror at Alabama's treatment of the Freedom Riders, northern members of Congress took up once again the need for civil rights legislation.[30]

Congress acted [handwritten marginal note]

The fall of 1962, when James Meredith integrated Ole Miss, was the first time that people were killed in a desegregation riot. Governor Barnett did not openly advocate violence, and he probably hoped to avoid it. But his defiant rhetoric likely contributed to the bloodshed in Oxford, Mississippi, and it certainly fostered the perception that he was responsible.

Barnett had been elected governor in 1959 on a platform that implicitly endorsed violence: "We can stop this integration fight if we have the blood and guts of our forefathers." In a speech to the citizens' council after his nomination, Barnett declared:

Physical courage is a trait sadly lacking in altogether too many of the South's so-called leaders. We must separate the men from the boys. We must identify the traitors in our midst. We must eliminate the cowards from our front lines.

In his inaugural address, Barnett promised, "[O]ur schools at all levels must be kept segregated at all costs."[31]

As court-ordered desegregation became imminent at Ole Miss in the summer of 1962, Barnett was trapped. His defiant vows made retreat politically unpalatable. Rather than preparing Mississippians for the inevitable, he continued to breathe defiance, threatened to arrest federal officers who interfered with state officials in the performance of their duties, and called for the resignation of all state officials who were unwilling to go to jail for defying federal authority in this "righteous cause." After twice physically blocking Meredith's entrance to the university,

Barnett privately negotiated an agreement with the Justice Department that would enable him to avoid contempt sanctions by retreating in the face of a public display of federal force.[32]

Yet his defiant ravings had created a frenzied atmosphere in which Barnett could not prevent violence. A race riot involving as many as 3,000 people broke out in Oxford on September 30, 1962, killing two and injuring several hundred. Barnett blamed federal marshals for the fiasco, but most commentators and national politicians pinned the responsibility on him. Whether or not Barnett had sought the violence, he reaped political benefits from it and became the "dominant political figure in Mississippi as long as he live[d]." Barnett was ineligible to succeed himself in office, but in 1963 voters rewarded the futile defiance that had caused deadly violence by electing Paul Johnson, who campaigned on the role that he had played as lieutenant governor in blocking Meredith's admission.[33]

Meanwhile, after the failed demonstrations in Albany, Georgia, in 1961–1962, the leadership of the SCLC was searching for a city with a police chief who was unlikely to duplicate Laurie Pritchett's restraint. They selected Birmingham, perhaps the South's most violent city, where Bull Connor, as commissioner of public safety, had already achieved notoriety by allowing the Klan to beat Freedom Riders. King was much criticized for refusing to delay the Birmingham demonstrations until after he had attempted to negotiate with the new mayor, Albert Boutwell, who had recently defeated Connor for the post. But local black minister Fred Shuttlesworth was urging King to act quickly, before Connor had vacated the office of police commissioner. King's lieutenant Wyatt Walker later explained: "We knew that when we came to Birmingham that if Bull Connor was still in control, he would do something to benefit our movement. We didn't want to march after Bull was gone."[34]

The strategy worked brilliantly. After some initially uncharacteristic restraint, Connor unleashed police dogs and fire hoses against the demonstrators, many of whom were children. Television and newspaper coverage featured images of police dogs attacking unresisting demonstrators, including one that President Kennedy reported made him "sick." Members of Congress condemned the "shocking episodes of police brutality." Newspaper editorials called the violence "a national disgrace." Citizens voiced their "sense of unutterable outrage and shame" and demanded that politicians take "action to immediately put an end to the barbarism and savagery in Birmingham." Within ten weeks, spin-off demonstrations spread to more than a hundred cities, as Birmingham sparked a "revolution . . . in the mind, heart and soul of Negroes all over America."[35]

Figure 9.3.
One of Bull
Connor's
police dogs
attacks a black
bystander
during street
demonstra-
tions. President
John Kennedy
said this
photograph
made him
"sick."
*Birmingham
News.*

Televised brutality against peaceful civil rights demonstrators in Birmingham dramatically altered northern opinion on race and enabled the passage of the 1964 Civil Rights Act. Comparing the Kennedy administration's civil rights policy before and after Birmingham demonstrates the transformative effect of that episode.

When Kennedy was elected president in 1960, he was not a civil rights enthusiast, and his victory depended on the support of southern whites. At the outset of the Kennedy administration, the NAACP was not expecting legislation to accelerate the pace of school desegregation. The administration warned against congressional efforts to condition the receipt of federal education funds on progress being made toward school desegregation, and polls showed that Americans were opposed to such measures by a 3–1 margin. Critics called the administration "timid and reluctant" and accused it of "dragging its feet" on civil rights, but polls showed that two-thirds of Americans thought the pace of desegregation was "[t]oo fast" or "[a]bout right," and only 11 percent thought it "[n]ot fast enough."[36]

When Kennedy finally proposed civil rights legislation in February 1963—two months before the Birmingham demonstrations began—his bill focused on voting rights. With regard to school desegregation, the administration proposed only technical and financial assistance to desegregating districts—a proposal that even Eisenhower had supported in the late 1950s. Kennedy did not endorse the proposals of liberals to grant the attorney general authority to institute desegregation suits or to empower the president to terminate federal education funds for school districts that remained segregated. Administration critic William F. Buckley rightly observed that the landmark civil rights bill proposed by Kennedy in the summer of 1963 "was not even conceived of as recently as a year ago."[37]

Outside of the school desegregation context, the administration had also been cautious on civil rights before Birmingham. After promising during the 1960 campaign that civil rights legislation would be his first priority, during his first two years in office, Kennedy repeatedly declared that he would not seek such legislation because Congress would not pass it. For those two years, Kennedy also delayed fulfilling a campaign pledge to eliminate race discrimination in federally assisted housing with the "stroke of a presidential pen." Kennedy placated southern Democrats with atrocious judicial appointments, including William Harold Cox, Senator Eastland's college roommate, who later referred to blacks from the bench as "niggers" and "chimpanzees."[38]

The Kennedy Justice Department negotiated the resolution of racial conflicts with white southerners behind the scenes, rather than confronting them openly, prosecuting wrongdoers, and compelling the enforcement of civil rights. Rather than supporting the Freedom Riders' exercising of their federal rights to nonsegregated transportation, the administration privately authorized Mississippi officials to illegally jail them in exchange for promises to avoid violence. After convincing civil rights workers in Mississippi to redirect their energies toward voter registration, which was assumed to be less provocative than Freedom Rides or street demonstrations, the administration broke its apparent promise to protect them from violence. By 1962, congressional liberals and black leaders were regularly criticizing the administration for failing to take a vigorous stand on civil rights. Birmingham changed everything.

Opinion polls revealed that the percentage of Americans who deemed civil rights to be the nation's most urgent issue rose from 4 percent before Birmingham to 52 percent afterward. Bishops now announced that the nation's 45 million Catholics had a "strict moral duty" to support civil rights. A majority of Americans now favored expansive civil rights legislation. President Kennedy overhauled his earlier civil rights proposals to include broader voting rights protections, the desegregation of public accommodations, authority for the attorney general to bring school desegregation suits, and the termination of federal funding for programs that engaged in race discrimination. Only after the police dogs and fire hoses of Birmingham did Kennedy announce on national television that civil rights was a moral issue "as old as the scriptures and . . . as clear as the American Constitution."[39]

That fall, after a quarter of a million Americans had marched on Washington, D.C., in support of civil rights and after four black youngsters had been blown up in Birmingham's Sixteenth Street Baptist Church, congressional representatives toughened the administration's bill, adding prohibitions on employment discrimination and broadening the attorney general's authority over desegregation suits. Just five days after Kennedy's assassination on November 22, 1963, President Lyndon Johnson told a joint session of Congress that "no memorial oration or eulogy could more eloquently honor President Kennedy's memory than the earliest possible passage of the civil rights bill for which he fought so long." With Johnson's strong backing, the bill became law in the summer of 1964, after withstanding the longest filibuster in Senate history.[40]

Congress

LBJ

Alabama's governor, George Wallace, had played a minor role in suppressing the Birmingham demonstrations and would play a more substantial role in the violence that lay ahead. Perhaps more than any other individual, Wallace personified the post-*Brown* racial fanaticism of southern politics. Early in his political career, in the late 1940s and early 1950s, Wallace had been criticized as "soft" on segregation. Unlike Connor, he was in the half of the Alabama delegation that did not walk out of the 1948 Democratic National Convention over the civil rights plank, and in 1954 he had been Folsom's campaign manager for southern Alabama.[41]

By the mid-1950s, however, Wallace felt the changing political winds, broke with Folsom, and cultivated conflict with federal authorities over race issues in his position as Barbour County circuit judge. After his defeat in the 1958 gubernatorial election, Wallace vowed never to be "out-nigger[ed]" again, and in 1962 he made good on that promise. Though some Alabama officials repudiated massive resistance after the riot at Ole Miss, Wallace continued to denounce federal "tyranny" and to promise "segregation forever." Like most southern politicians, he publicly condemned violence. Yet Wallace's actions from 1963 to 1965 directly and indirectly encouraged the brutality that helped to transform national opinion on race.[42]

During the Birmingham demonstrations in the spring of 1963, Wallace dispatched several hundred state troopers to the city, and they supplemented Bull Connor's brutality with some of their own. He also publicly praised Connor for forcefully suppressing the demonstrations. That summer in Tuscaloosa, Wallace fulfilled his pledge to stand in the schoolhouse door, physically blocking the university's entrance before, in a carefully planned charade, stepping aside in the face of superior federal force—more than 15,000 members of the federalized National Guard. Learning from Ole Miss, Wallace had warned that he "would not tolerate mob action," and massive security measures kept Tuscaloosa "peaceful and serene."[43]

Yet Wallace, like Barnett, had grown overconfident in his ability to spout defiant rhetoric without provoking violence. After Tuscaloosa, Wallace continued to promise a "forceful stand" against grade school desegregation, which federal courts had ordered in Alabama for the fall. In September, Wallace used state troopers to block school desegregation in Birmingham, Mobile, Huntsville, and Tuskegee—action that was contrary to the wishes of most local officials, who called Wallace a "dictator" for preventing them from complying with court orders to desegregate.[44]

In Birmingham, white mobs demonstrated outside the schools that were scheduled to desegregate; the home of a black lawyer who was heavily involved in school desegregation litigation was bombed; and a minor race riot erupted in which police killed one black man and roughly twenty others were injured. Wallace had encouraged extremist groups to wage a "boisterous campaign" against school desegregation, and now he defended the rioters, who he insisted are "not thugs—they are good working people who get mad when they see something like this happen."[45]

Threatened with contempt citations by all five Alabama district judges and overmatched by President Kennedy's federalization of the state National Guard, Wallace relented. The schools desegregated, but Wallace had, according to the *New York Times*, "stirred up a devil's brew of racial hatred that [could] erupt any minute into further violence." Within a week, tragedy had struck. Birmingham Klansmen, possibly inspired by the governor's protestations that "I can't fight federal bayonets with my bare hands," dynamited the Sixteenth Street Baptist Church, killing four black schoolgirls. Within hours of the bombing, two other black teenagers were killed, one by white hoodlums and the other by the police.[46]

It was the largest death toll of the civil rights era, and Wallace received much of the blame. Wilkins charged the governor with encouraging a "deliberate mass murder," while King blamed Wallace for "creat[ing] the climate that made it possible for someone to plant that bomb." Alabama attorney general Richmond Flowers linked the carnage to Wallace's defiance: "The individuals who bombed the Sixteenth Avenue [*sic*] Church in their way were standing in the schoolhouse door." President Kennedy noted a "deep sense of outrage and grief" and thought it "regrettable that public disparagement of law and order has encouraged violence which has fallen on the innocent." Wallace may not have sought the violence, but his provocative rhetoric probably contributed to it, and he certainly took no measures to prevent it.[17]

Most of the nation was appalled by the murder of innocent school children. One week after the bombing, tens of thousands of people across the United States participated in memorial services and marches. Northern whites wrote to the NAACP to join, to condemn, and to apologize. A white lawyer from Los Angeles wrote, "Today I am joining the NAACP; partly, I think, as a kind of apology for being caucasian, and for not being in Birmingham to lend my physical support." Another white woman in the North condemned those Birmingham whites who were involved in the bombing or who condoned it as the "worst barbarians," and she said that she was "ashamed to think that

Figure 9.4. The Sixteenth Street Baptist Church in Birmingham after it was bombed on September 15, 1963. Birmingham Public Library, Department of Archives and Manuscripts, no. 85.1.22.

I bear their color skin." She also declared that the bombing had "certainly changed my attitude," which previously had been "somewhat lukewarm" on civil rights. A white youngster from New Rochelle wrote: "How shall I start? Perhaps to say that I am white, sorry, ashamed, and guilty. . . . Those who have said that all whites who, through hatred, intolerance, or just inaction are guilty are right."[48]

A black veteran of World War I from South Carolina, who had "seen many things that have been irksome" in his seventy years, including the lynchings of Till and Parker, told the NAACP that "nothing in my life has had the effect upon me that the bombing of the Church and the Murder of the six Negroes in Birmingham [had]." He prayed that God would not "let these children die in vain," and he enclosed money to be divided among the families of the murdered youngsters. The NAACP urged its members to "flood Congress with letters in support of necessary civil rights legislation to curb such outrages," and Wilkins demanded that the federal government "cut off every nickel" going to Alabama. Northern members of Congress reflected the outrage of their constituents by introducing amendments to strengthen the administration's pending civil rights bill.[49]

Wallace's critics in Alabama attacked his schoolhouse door routine at Tuscaloosa as "the greatest production since Cleopatra," and they accused him of making a "monkey of himself" and a "mockery" of Alabama. But most voters apparently disagreed. Wallace remained enormously popular, and in January 1964 he won an important victory when the state Democratic executive committee instructed the Alabama delegation to the 1964 national convention to support Wallace as a favorite-son candidate for president. Meanwhile, Wallace continued to rail against the "shocking" pronouncements of federal "judicial tyrant[s]" and to urge local authorities to resist desegregation, though he refrained from any more schoolhouse door stands. But the linkage between Wallace and civil rights violence had not ended, as Selma was still in the future.[50]

Before Selma, though, the civil rights stage shifted back to Mississippi, where movement leaders during the summer of 1964 successfully repeated the Birmingham strategy. Civil rights activists in Mississippi, after struggling for years against horrific violence to organize the state, decided to import hundreds of mostly white northern college students for a Freedom Summer of civil rights activity. They understood that bringing "outside agitators" to Mississippi would probably elicit a deadly response, and they calculated that the national media and the Johnson administration would lavish attention on relatively affluent white students from the nation's most prestigious universities.

Freedom Summer

BROWN V. BOARD OF EDUCATION AND THE CIVIL RIGHTS MOVEMENT

The strategy worked even more effectively and more tragically than they had anticipated. Within days, three civil rights workers had disappeared. For much of the summer, FBI agents and national media representatives blanketed the state searching for them. Their murders, combined with dozens of church bombings, shootings, beatings, and other atrocities, taught an attentive nation unforgettable lessons about Jim Crow, Mississippi-style. The groundwork was laid for further civil rights legislation. Selma brought it to fruition.

Situated in the heart of Alabama's Black Belt, Selma was home to the state's first citizens' council, which had quickly enrolled nearly a quarter of Dallas County's white males. Early in 1965, SCLC leaders brought their voter registration campaign to Selma, which they chose partly because of the presence there of a law enforcement officer with Bull Connor–like proclivities. Sheriff Jim Clark had a temper which "could be counted on to provide vivid proof of the violent sentiments that formed white supremacy's core."[51]

The result was another resounding success for the civil rights movement. After initially displaying restraint, which disappointed SCLC workers, Clark eventually returned to form and brutalized nonresisting demonstrators. The violence culminated in Bloody Sunday, March 7, 1965, when county and state law enforcement officers viciously assaulted marchers as they crossed the Edmund Pettus Bridge on the way to Montgomery.

Governor Wallace had promised that the march would be broken up by "whatever measures are necessary," and Colonel Al Lingo, Wallace's chief law enforcement lieutenant, insisted that the governor himself had given the order to attack. That evening, ABC television interrupted its broadcast of *Judgment at Nuremberg* for a lengthy film report of peaceful demonstrators being assailed by stampeding horses, flailing clubs, and tear gas. Two white volunteers from the North were killed in the events surrounding Selma: a Unitarian minister from Boston and a mother of five from Detroit.[52]

Most of the nation was repulsed by the ghastly scenes from Selma that they watched on television. *Time* reported, "Rarely in history has public opinion reacted so spontaneously and with such fury." Over the following week, huge sympathy demonstrations took place across the country. Hundreds of clergy from around the nation flocked to Selma to show their solidarity with King and his comrades. Citizens demanded remedial action from their representatives, scores of whom condemned the "deplorable" violence and the "shameful display" of Selma and then endorsed voting rights legislation.[53]

Prior to Selma, administration officials had been divided over whether to pursue voting rights legislation in the near term. One week after Bloody Sunday, however, President Johnson proposed such legislation before a joint session of Congress. Seventy million Americans watched on television as the president beseeched them to "overcome the crippling legacy of bigotry and injustice" and declared his faith that "we shall overcome."[54]

Although most Americans were appalled by the violence at Birmingham and Selma, the politicians who were partly responsible for it calculated—usually correctly—that Alabama voters would reward them for their roles in fostering it. Contemporaries speculated that Connor's violent suppression of civil rights demonstrations in Birmingham was calculated to earn him support among segregationist voters should he run for state office. Indeed, the following year, Connor was elected state public service commissioner, as he capitalized on the name recognition he had achieved during the Birmingham demonstrations.

George Wallace remained enormously popular among whites in Alabama, in spite of—or perhaps because of—his partial responsibility for the violence at Birmingham and Selma. When he provoked a showdown with the Kennedy administration over the desegregation of grade schools in several Alabama cities in the fall of 1963 (the episode that culminated in the bombing of Birmingham's Sixteenth Street Baptist Church), Wallace was apparently hoping to generate support for a change in the state constitution that would enable him to serve a second consecutive term as governor.

Sheriff Clark calculated that his brutality against demonstrators in Selma would translate into a viable gubernatorial candidacy in 1966. He withdrew from that race only after Wallace, who was barred from succeeding himself, announced the candidacy of his wife, Lurleen, who then won the election. Clark rightly appreciated that nobody could outflank Wallace as a symbol of resistance to racial change.

The violent suppression of peaceful black demonstrations may have enhanced the political prospects of segregationist officials in the South, but it repulsed national opinion and led directly to the passage of landmark civil rights legislation. *Brown* was less directly responsible than is commonly supposed for putting those demonstrators on the streets, but it was more directly responsible for the violent reception they encountered.

The post-*Brown* racial fanaticism of southern politics produced a situation that was ripe for violence, while *Brown* itself created concrete occasions on which violent opposition to school desegregation was likely. Some of the ensuing violence was mainly attributable to white vigilantes, but much of it was encouraged, directly or indirectly, by extremist politicians, whom voters rewarded for the irresponsible rhetoric that fomented atrocities. Even before the violent outbreaks of the 1960s, most white northerners had agreed with *Brown* in the abstract, but they were disinclined to push hard for its enforcement; many of them agreed with Eisenhower that the NAACP should rein in its demands for immediate desegregation. It was the televised scenes of officially sanctioned brutality against peaceful black demonstrators that transformed northern opinion on race.

By helping to lay bare the violence at the core of white supremacy, *Brown* accelerated its demise. President Eisenhower, Justice Hugo L. Black, and many southern moderates had foreseen that *Brown* would retard southern racial progress and destroy southern political liberalism. Justice Robert H. Jackson, too, had warned, "When the Court has gone too far, it has provoked reactions which have set back the cause it is designed to advance." Though these individuals rightly anticipated *Brown*'s backlash, they failed to foresee the ensuing counterbacklash that would develop as northerners were repulsed by the violence of southern whites against blacks and endorsed landmark civil rights legislation in response. The harder that southern whites fought to maintain Jim Crow, the more they seemed to accelerate its demise.[55]

[handwritten margin note: anticipated violence reaction, so.]

Would the same violence have confronted civil rights demonstrators without *Brown*? One cannot know for certain. But without *Brown*, school desegregation would probably not have been a pressing issue in the 1950s. Southern blacks generally had other priorities, including ending police brutality, securing voting rights, gaining access to decent jobs, and equalizing public funding of black schools. Moreover, before *Brown*, southern whites had proved willing to make small concessions on racial issues that were less important to them than school segregation. Without *Brown*, negotiation might have continued to produce gradual change without inciting white violence.

How southern whites in this counterfactual universe would have responded if and when black street demonstrations erupted is impossible to tell. In the absence of post-*Brown* political fanaticism, however, one can imagine Freedom Riders arriving in Birmingham and Montgomery without police commissioners inviting Klansmen to beat them, and one can imagine blacks demonstrating for voting rights in Selma without law enforcement officers brutalizing them. By the early 1960s, most southern whites could probably have tolerated desegregated transportation and black suffrage had *Brown* not converted all racial challenges, in their minds, into fundamental assaults on Jim Crow.

Whether and how southern schools would have desegregated in this counterfactual scenario is anybody's guess, but it almost certainly would not have happened as quickly as it did under the 1964 Civil Rights Act. Only the violence that resulted from *Brown*'s radicalization of southern politics enabled transformative racial change to occur as rapidly as it did.

CONCLUSION

Brown v. Board of Education was possible in 1954 because dramatic changes in racial attitudes and practices had already occurred. The justices who decided the case understood this, commenting on the "spectacular" advances, the "great changes," and the "constant progress" being made in race relations. In the absence of such changes, *Brown* would not have been decided as it was.

These changes were caused both by factors that were internal to the South and by those that were external to it. Because southern whites were generally resistant to changes in racial practices, pressure was required to effect them. Southern blacks supplied some of that pressure, aided by improvements in education, the growth of a black middle class, greater militancy resulting from World War II, and the more tolerant racial norms that existed in the urban, as opposed to the rural, parts of the South.

But Jim Crow was so ruthless and pervasive that internally generated change was difficult to accomplish. Because southern whites did not permit blacks to become very well educated, there were few black lawyers available to challenge the system in court. Because southern blacks were generally not permitted to vote, internal change through politics was nearly impossible. Because whites controlled the livelihoods of most blacks, protest generally resulted in severe economic reprisals. The system was ultimately secured by the threat and the reality of physical violence against those blacks (and whites) who dared to challenge it.

It is nearly impossible to change such a system without external pressure. That pressure was supplied by the National Association for the Advancement of Colored People and, eventually, by national public opinion and the intervention of the federal government. Threatened and actual lawsuits induced southern states to begin equalizing spending on black education and permitting blacks to register to vote. Pressure by the national government helped to create an environment in which southern blacks could engage in racial protest with some measure of physical security. Ultimately, landmark civil rights legislation in the 1960s supplied coercive mechanisms that accelerated the downfall of formal Jim Crow. External pressure was produced by a combination of factors: the Great Migration, the rising prosperity and political clout of northern blacks, the ideology of World War II, and the Cold War imperative for racial change.

The Second World War was a watershed in the history of U.S. race relations. Returning black veterans became the vanguard of the modern civil rights movement. The ideological ramifications of the war against fascism, combined with the ensuing Cold War imperative for racial change, profoundly influenced the racial views of millions of white Americans. As huge numbers of blacks migrated to the North to take advantage of novel economic opportunities, northern blacks began to exert considerable influence over national racial policy.

Long-term forces such as urbanization, industrialization, and better education also fostered progressive racial change. Urbanization enabled blacks to become better educated, thus ensuring eventual challenges to Jim Crow. Urban blacks commanded greater economic resources, which provided more funds for social protest, dramatized the disparities between the economic and the social status of blacks, and created a weapon—economic boycotts—with which to extract changes in racial practices.

Urban blacks also created institutions, such as churches and colleges, which helped to overcome collective-action barriers to social protest, which better urban transportation and communication also facilitated. More relaxed racial mores in cities opened space for black protest by reducing the threat of physical violence and enabling blacks to vote and thus enjoy a modicum of political influence. No civil rights movement was possible at a time when most blacks picked cotton on southern plantations.

Better-educated whites in the South were less intensely committed to preserving traditional racial practices. Moreover, as the South became less insular, racial change became harder to resist. World War II exposed millions of southerners, white and black, to novel racial attitudes and practices. The growth of the mass media exposed millions more to outside influences, which tended to erode traditional racial mores. Media penetration also prevented white southerners from limiting outside scrutiny of their treatment of blacks. Northerners did not see southern lynchings on television, but Bull Connor's brutalization of peaceful black demonstrators came directly into their living rooms.

Long-term international trends also advanced the cause of progressive racial change in the United States. The decolonization of Africa inspired American blacks to demand their political and civil rights. Postwar competition with the Soviet Union for the allegiance of non-white Third World nations forced Americans to improve their domestic racial practices in order to demonstrate that democratic capitalism was not synonymous with white supremacy. This Cold War imperative influenced the racial policies of presidential administrations from the 1940s to the 1960s and may have influenced the justices who were most preoccupied with national security concerns

Finally, a decrease in white-on-black violence in the South was critical to progressive racial change. The heightened black militancy that grew out of World War I was crushed by a crescendo of white violence, including scores of lynchings and several racial massacres. A southern civil rights movement was almost inconceivable in such an environment. By contrast, in the 1960s, civil rights demonstrators and litigants often faced economic reprisals and threats, but usually not actual violence. Ironically, the relative decline in white-on-black violence, which made civil rights protest possible, ensured that any residual violence would stand out, especially with the assistance of the national media. White southerners lynched a hundred blacks a year around 1900, yet most northerners showed little concern. But isolated lynchings in the 1950s— Emmett Till's in 1955, Mack Parker's in 1959—appalled most northerners (and many southerners too) and rallied support for civil rights legislation.

Street demonstrations were possible in Birmingham in 1963 partly because greater constraints on white violence had created a more secure physical environment. As Martin Luther King, Jr., put it, "The striking thing about the nonviolent crusade of 1963 was that so few felt the sting of bullets or the clubbing of billies and nightsticks." Yet law enforcement's brutalization of peaceful protestors, piped directly into American homes by television, profoundly influenced national opinion and led directly to the enactment of transformative civil rights legislation.[1]

What does the Court's racial jurisprudence tell us about the nature of judicial decision making? How much is it a product of legal factors, such as text, original intent, and precedent, and how much of political factors, such as the values of judges, social and political context, and external political pressure?

We have seen that all judicial decisions are products of both law and politics. When the legal sources are relatively determinate, the justices tend to adhere to them, unless their political preferences to the contrary are very strong. The justices invalidated the grandfather clause in *Guinn* (1915) and the phony false-pretenses law that supported peonage in *Bailey* (1911) because these were transparent evasions of constitutional constraints. Had the Fourteenth Amendment explicitly barred segregation, *Plessy* might well have come out the other way.

Yet legal sources alone can never determine a constitutional interpretation, because judges always have to choose whether to adhere to them. When the justices' personal preferences are strong, they may reject even relatively determinate law. *Brown* illustrates this point. To the justices who were most committed to the traditional legal sources, *Brown* should have been an easy case—for *sustaining* school segregation. Jackson candidly conceded that barring segregation could be defended only in political, not legal, terms. Yet, in 1954, most of the justices considered racial segregation—the doctrine that Hitler had preached—to be evil, and they were determined to forbid it, regardless of whether conventional legal sources sanctioned that result.

Guinn and *Bailey* are unusual in that constitutional violations are rarely that transparent. The text of the Constitution fails to supply determinative answers to most questions. "Equal protection" does not plainly forbid separate but equal. Precedent could supply greater clarity, yet the justices feel free to overrule past decisions, and they lack any clear legal standard that prescribes when to do so. The justices seem to overrule decisions that strike them as *really* wrong, which is obviously more of a political criterion than a legal one. *Grovey* (1935), which sustained the constitutionality of white primaries, proved unpalatable to the justices in 1944, not because its legal reasoning was faulty but because during World War II, they found black disfranchisement to be offensive.

Another reason that constitutional law is generally indeterminate is the absence of consensus regarding which sources of interpretation are legitimate. For example, Justice Hugo L. Black claimed to be a textualist and an originalist, but Stanley F. Reed expressly defended the notion of a living Constitution, and Frank Murphy seems to have thought that the justices must take account of morality. That justices who disagreed about the permissible sources of interpretation would reach different interpretive results seems inevitable. Moreover, even if consensus did exist regarding the permissible sources of interpretation, in the absence of an accepted hierarchy for resolving conflicts between them, interpretive disagreement would be unavoidable.

The upshot is that justices engaged in constitutional interpretation have substantial room to maneuver; they cannot help but be influenced by their personal values and the social and political contexts of their times. Thus, we should not be surprised that the justices in the early twenty-first century divided 5–4, along consistent political lines, over most of the interesting and important constitutional issues, including federalism, abortion, affirmative action, minority voting districts, school prayer, religious-school vouchers, campaign finance reform, picking presidents, and others. These divisions are indicative not of bad faith, but of constitutional law's indeterminacy. On such issues, where personal preferences tend to be strong, only very determinate law could be constraining, and constitutional law is rarely that.

Because of constitutional law's indeterminacy, social and political context matters greatly to constitutional interpretation, as the Court's decisions in the race area demonstrate. Between *Plessy* (1896) and *Brown* (1954), the conventional constitutional sources that were pertinent to the segregation issue did not change. Nor was *Plessy* an obviously wrong legal interpretation. The Equal Protection Clause does not plainly bar segregation, and the original understanding of the Fourteenth Amendment probably permitted it. Abundant legal precedents and deeply entrenched social customs supported segregation. On the conventional legal materials, *Plessy* was at least plausible, and it was arguably right. As the justices in 1896 almost certainly thought that segregation was good policy, the case was easy.

Fifty-eight years later, the Court came out the other way—unanimously—despite the doubts of several justices as to whether invalidating segregation could be legally justified. The social and political context of race had changed so dramatically, as had the personal racial attitudes of the justices, that even a relatively weak legal case could not deter them from invalidating segregation.

Because social and political context plays such a substantial role in the justices' constitutional decision making, the romantic image of the Court as savior of the weak and oppressed is probably unrealistic. The justices reflect dominant public opinion too much for them to protect truly subordinated groups. Not only did the Court fail to intervene against slavery before the Civil War, but it extended positive constitutional protection to the institution. The justices validated the internment of Japanese Americans during World War II and the persecution of political leftists during the McCarthy era. And, during the heyday of Jim Crow, the justices approved segregation and disfranchisement.

Constitutional law generally has sufficient flexibility to accommodate dominant public opinion, which the justices have little inclination, and limited power, to resist. As a result, courts are likely to protect only those minorities that are favorably regarded by majority opinion. Ironically, when a minority group suffering oppression is most in need of judicial protection, it is least likely to receive it. The justices would not have dreamed of protecting women or gays under the Equal Protection Clause before the women's movement and the gay rights movement. Similarly, segregation and disfranchisement began to seem objectionable to the justices only as blacks became a vital New Deal constituency, achieved middle-class status and professional success, and earned federal judgeships, a military generalship, and a Nobel Peace Prize.

None of this is to suggest that the justices perfectly reflect national opinion. Many famous cases confirm that they do not. When the Court invalidated school prayer or criminal prohibitions on flag burning, and when the justices protected certain procedural rights of criminal defendants, they were plainly frustrating dominant opinion. When this happens, it is usually a product of the culturally elite values of the justices. On certain issues, differences of opinion correlate with socioeconomic status. All of the justices are very well educated, and most of them are reasonably affluent. This may explain why, on issues such as school prayer and flag burning, their views seem systematically more liberal than those of average Americans. In the middle of the twentieth century, race was an issue on which popular and elite opinions significantly diverged.

Because of their culturally elite biases, the justices may have found *Brown* (politically) easier than most Americans did. Still, by 1954, background forces for racial change had already altered public opinion enough so that half the nation endorsed *Brown* from the day it was decided. Because the justices found *Brown* so difficult to justify legally, perhaps they would not have decided it as they did had it not been so easy politically. By 1954, segregation seemed like such an egregious evil to the nation's cultural elite that the justices simply could not make themselves sustain it.

Though the justices generally reflect elite opinion, there are some obvious exceptions. Correlations exist between high socioeconomic status and liberal political positions on certain cultural issues, but they are not perfect. On the Court in the early twenty-first century, Justices Antonin Scalia and Clarence Thomas, although members of the cultural elite, certainly do not share its liberal political propensities.

Thus, constitutional rulings always reflect some element of fortuity in the composition of the Court. Had there been five Justice Reeds, *Brown* almost certainly would not have been decided as it was. Nor is it inconceivable that there could have been five justices in 1954 whose views were like Reed's. The South remained a vital part of the New Deal political coalition and Presidents Franklin D. Roosevelt and, to a slightly lesser extent, Harry S Truman had been virtually oblivious to the racial attitudes of their appointees to the Court.

This suggests another element of fortuity in Court decision making. Important constitutional issues often change across generations, and sometimes unpredictably so. Few could have forecast in the late 1930s, when Roosevelt began reconstituting the Court, that school segregation would become the biggest constitutional issue of the twentieth century. Yet it did, and within just fifteen years.

Although more justices of Reed's persuasion could easily have been serving in 1954, it is noteworthy that even Reed was not impervious to broad forces for racial change. Had he been so, he would probably have stood his ground and dissented in *Brown*. Yet Reed authored opinions invalidating the white primary and segregation in interstate travel, which suggests that he shared some culturally elite values, though of the southern variety.

Congressional representatives are presumably members of the cultural elite as well, yet they lagged far behind the justices in achieving progressive racial results. Why?

First, members of Congress have to respond to their constituents in order to be reelected, while the justices enjoy lifetime tenure. Of course, justices are not completely removed from public influence, but their relative insulation affords them some leeway to respond to their own culturally elite values, whereas representatives have to attend more closely to popular opinion or risk early retirement. Second, the U.S. Congress—especially the Senate—is far from majoritarian. Though national opinion plainly supported antilynching legislation in the 1930s and anti–poll-tax legislation in the 1940s, Senate filibusters regularly defeated such measures and all other civil rights proposals until 1957.

 *Congress elected officials*

The antimajoritarianism of the Senate raises the interesting possibility that the Court's race decisions from the 1920s onward may have reflected national opinion better than did Congress's (in)action. In the 1920s and 1930s, the justices intervened several times against southern lynch law, while southern Democrats in the Senate thrice killed antilynching bills that had passed the House. The Court invalidated the white primary in the 1940s. In that same decade, the House passed an anti–poll-tax bill every two years, and the Senate killed them all. Opinion polls revealed that half the nation supported *Brown* at a time when Congress would not have dreamed of legislating against school segregation.

Southern politics was even more absurdly antimajoritarian. It is ironic that during their deliberations in *Brown*, the justices expressed anxiety about usurping the functions of representative government, given how unrepresentative southern legislatures were in the 1950s. Eighty percent of southern blacks were still disfranchised in 1952, and legislatures were badly malapportioned in favor of rural whites, who were the most committed to maintaining white supremacy.

Thus, *Brown* was not only consistent with what half of all Americans thought about segregation, but it was not drastically inconsistent with what a properly functioning southern political system might have produced. This raises the interesting question of whether *Brown* might have been unnecessary had southern blacks been fully enfranchised and had one-person, one-vote principles been in operation. One cannot know for sure, but most southern whites were so committed to preserving school segregation that they would probably have outvoted blacks favoring integration. The equalization of black schools would have been a likelier scenario than legislative desegregation. But the question is hypothetical because southern whites would not permit most blacks to vote until Congress forced them to do so. And Congress would not act until national opinion demanded it, which happened only after *Brown* had elicited and exposed the most brutal aspects of Jim Crow, to the horror of national television audiences.

Though the culturally elite values of the justices open space for them to deviate from popular opinion in their constitutional interpretations, that space is limited. The fact that the justices live in the same historical moment and share the same culture as the general population is probably more important to their constitutional interpretations than the fact that they occupy a distinct socioeconomic subculture.

Even if *Brown* in 1954 was politically easier for the justices than it was for average Americans because they held culturally elite values, as few as ten years earlier the justices would probably have lacked the inclination to invalidate school segregation. At a time when the vast majority of white Americans believed in white supremacy, so did most justices. *Plessy* had been an easy case for them. In 1896, the justices were just as culturally elite as they would be in 1954, but at the turn of the twentieth century even well-educated, relatively affluent whites generally supported segregation and disfranchisement.

Personal values and the broader social and political context are important components of judicial decision making, but one must not neglect the occasional influence of more direct external political constraints. *Brown II* was plainly shaped by the justices' awareness that their power is limited. They did not wish to issue an unenforceable ruling, and they were dubious, with good reason, as to whether Congress and the president would enforce orders for immediate desegregation. The justices were also consciously appealing to southern moderates for support. Such strategic considerations also influenced the justices' decision to vacate the school desegregation field for nearly a decade thereafter.

What lessons shall we draw from this study about the consequences of Court rulings? To begin, we should be humble in our convictions: We have no way of precisely measuring the impact, direct or indirect, of Court decisions. However, although this is not science, something useful can still be said on the subject.

Both polar positions in the scholarly debate should be rejected. *Brown* did not "change . . . the whole course of race relations in the United States," nor did it create the civil rights movement. But neither was *Brown* irrelevant. The Court's ruling plainly raised the salience of school segregation, encouraged blacks to litigate against it, changed the order in which racial practices would otherwise have been contested, mobilized extraordinary resistance to racial change among southern whites, and created concrete occasions for street confrontations and violence.[2]

As to direct effects, some Court decisions plainly matter more than do others. *Smith v. Allwright*, the white primary decision, launched a revolution in politics in the urban South, and *Sweatt v. Painter* integrated public universities outside of the Deep South. *Brown*, however, was almost completely nullified for a decade south of the border states. The efficacy of Court decisions depends on certain social and political conditions.

One reason that *Smith* was more effectively implemented than was *Brown* is that blacks were more united behind and more intensely committed to voting rights than they were to integrated schools. Voting protects other rights, and many civil rights leaders insisted that if the suffrage rights

Direct Consequences =

of southern blacks were adequately assured, they could secure other rights for themselves through politics. The right to vote was also more directly implicated by the democratic ideology of World War II than was the right to nonsegregated education: How could one possibly justify denying suffrage rights to soldiers who had just risked their lives fighting to defend democracy?

Moreover, blacks were historically far more divided over whether to pursue integrated education than whether to pursue the right to vote. Segregated schools, if they could be made genuinely equal, offered several advantages to blacks: job opportunities for black teachers in an era when few white-collar occupations were open to blacks; an educational environment that was relatively free from the stereotyping, insults, and humiliation that characterized the experiences of black children in integrated schools; and sympathetic portrayals of black history and culture.

Blacks were more divided over some rights than others, but they were more militant about enforcing all of their rights after World War II than before. This greater militancy was partly a product of greater physical security. Constitutional rights are not worth much when asserting them is likely to get one beaten or killed. Had *Plessy* come out the other way, southern railroads would likely have remained segregated. Blacks who tested such a right to nonsegregated travel would have jeopardized their lives in an era of rampant lynching.

By contrast, in 1950, lynchings were nearly obsolete, and postwar black litigants were far more likely to face economical reprisal than physical violence. The national government now monitored and occasionally intervened against violence directed toward blacks exercising their constitutional rights, and most southern whites no longer countenanced lynchings or extreme violence. Even in the 1950s, it took great courage to litigate against Jim Crow in the Deep South, but the reduced risk of reprisal in the form of physical violence enabled blacks to assert their rights more aggressively than would have been conceivable in earlier decades.

The intensity of opponents' resistance is another important factor in whether Court decisions prove to be efficacious. Southern whites were much less resistant to black suffrage than they were to integrated grade school education. Black disfranchisement has always occupied a lower rung on the hierarchy of preferences of white supremacists than has school segregation, which is one reason that many southern blacks were not disfranchised until the 1890s, whereas southern public schools were almost universally segregated even during Reconstruction. By the 1940s, many moderate white southerners had a hard time justifying black disfranchisement to themselves in light of improved black education and the democratic ideology of World War II. By contrast, most white southerners ferociously resisted grade school desegregation, which involved the race mixing of young children, male and female, and thus for most whites had inevitable connotations of miscegenation.

Some constitutional rights are easier to circumvent than others partly because alleged denials turn on facts that are relatively difficult to establish. Early on, white southerners discovered that the most effective means of evading federal constitutional constraints was to delegate unfettered discretion to local administrators, who could maintain white supremacy without openly violating the Constitution. This was the means by which southern blacks were excluded from jury service, disfranchised, and cheated out of their fair share of public education funds.

Over time, however, some of these administrative schemes for perpetuating white supremacy became more difficult to sustain than others. As blacks became better educated, registrars had a harder time seriously maintaining that black voter applicants had flunked literacy tests that less well educated whites were generally passing. By contrast, a black defendant who crossed swords at trial with a white sheriff over whether his confession was voluntarily given or induced by a beating had a much harder time convincing white fact finders that his account was true. Thus, the disparate evidentiary burdens inherent in establishing violations of particular rights may help to explain why Court decisions protecting black suffrage were more efficacious than those forbidding coerced confessions. Then too, judges and jurors are likely to find some rights bearers more sympathetic than others. Black criminal defendants—indigent, often illiterate, frequently guilty of some crime even if not the one charged—were less attractive rights bearers than were the middle-class, well-educated blacks endeavoring to vote or seeking admission to public universities from which blacks were excluded.

The relative availability of sanctions against violators also influences the efficacy of Court decisions that protect particular rights. In the 1940s, law enforcement officers and jury commissioners had little direct incentive to abide by the constitutional rights of black defendants, because civil and criminal sanctions were generally unavailable. After *Screws v. United States* (1945), it was far from certain that the justices would approve the imposition of federal criminal liability on sheriffs who beat defendants into confessing. Nor was it clear in the 1940s that courts would authorize the imposition of monetary liability under federal civil rights statutes against public officers who contravened state law while violating the federal Constitution; and every state barred the use of physical force to obtain confessions.

By contrast, voter registrars and party officials who interfered with the voting rights of blacks were more vulnerable to federal legal sanctions. After *Smith v. Allwright*, officials who refused to allow blacks to participate in party primaries were committing clear constitutional violations, which would probably qualify for federal criminal prosecution even under the restrictive standard of *Screws*. The NAACP constantly threatened registrars and party officials with criminal liability if they defied *Smith*.

Civil suits for damages were also more realistic in voting rights cases. The Court's first two white primary decisions sustained damages actions under federal statute against public officials who refused to allow blacks to participate in Democratic primaries. One reason that southern school boards were able to resist *Brown* for so long is that the first school desegregation lawsuits never sought money damages. One reason that they did not was the well-founded supposition that white jurors in the South would never impose liability on public officials for resisting school desegregation. (Suits asking for injunctive relief, as opposed to money damages, are heard by judges, not juries.) Indeed, the constitutional guarantee of a jury trial before the imposition of criminal or civil liability was a huge impediment to the enforcement of any civil right, so long as blacks were excluded from southern juries and most whites opposed blacks' civil rights.

On a related matter, the public enforcement of civil rights is likely to be more efficacious than is private enforcement. The Justice Department commanded far greater resources than did the NAACP or individual black litigants; it monopolized criminal enforcement; and it did not bear the same risks of economic reprisal and physical retaliation for challenging traditional racial practices. One reason that *Smith* proved so effective is that the Justice Department made credible threats to enforce it. Similarly, the pace of school desegregation accelerated dramatically after the 1964 Civil Rights Act authorized federal enforcement. Public action also offers enforcement mechanisms that are unavailable to private litigants, such as threats to terminate public funds for rights violators and the appointment of federal administrators to replace recalcitrant state officials.

Yet, public enforcement generally depends on public support for the underlying right. The political branches of the national government do not tend to support Court decisions simply because the justices have spoken. Rather, they respond to public opinion, which may or may not endorse the Court's handiwork. Congress and the president ultimately

Public opinion

got behind *Brown*, not because of *Brown*, but because the civil rights movement had altered public opinion on school segregation.

The availability and the quality of lawyers also play a role in the enforcement of rights. One underappreciated reason that civil rights victories had such disappointing results before World War II is that there were few black lawyers practicing in the South and those who were frequently were badly educated and poorly trained. Most white lawyers would not take civil rights cases because of the odium that attached to them. The NAACP had limited resources; it was absent from much of the South until the 1940s; and it could not intervene without the assistance of local counsel. Constitutional rights are worth little without effective lawyers to raise them.

The nature of the court in which rights violations are litigated also affects enforceability. State appellate and federal judges were more likely than state trial judges to vindicate the constitutional rights of southern blacks, because they were better educated, more professionalized, and more independent of local opinion, which often proved to be hostile to the rights. Cases of black criminal defendants usually did not proceed beyond trial courts, mainly because state provision of counsel did not generally extend to appeals, but also because procedural defaults frequently insulated trial errors from appellate review. Many black criminal defendants suffered egregious violations of their rights that were never reviewed by any court that was likely to be sympathetic toward enforcement. By contrast, blacks litigating voting rights violations were free to choose their forum—usually federal court. They also frequently commanded the resources that were necessary to pursue appeals to courts that were more likely to sympathize with their claims.

Moreover, judges themselves were influenced by the traditional hierarchy of white supremacist values. Southern judges were far more likely to sympathize with, and thus to liberally construe, *Smith v. Allwright* or *Sweatt v. Painter* than *Brown v. Board of Education*. The willingness of lower court judges to apply *Smith* in a "broad and discerning" manner, rather than in a "narrow and literal" one, proved to be critical to its implementation, given the multiple evasions attempted by southern officials.[3]

The clarity of legal instructions also influences lower court implementation. Even though most federal judges in the South thought that *Brown* was wrongheaded, their sense of professional obligation generally deterred them from defying it. Almost all of them acknowledged that formal school segregation had to end, whether or not they agreed with *Brown*. Yet *Brown II* was so vague as to be meaningless. It provided southern judges with no political cover, which made it difficult for them to adopt broad constructions even if they were inclined to do so, which few of them were, given their personal opposition to school desegregation. Instead, most judges countenanced delay and evasion.

Constitutional litigation can only redress those problems that are grounded in law. Because white supremacy depended less on law than on entrenched social mores, economic power, ideology, and physical violence, the amount of racial change that litigation could produce was inevitably limited. Invalidating white primaries could enroll only so many voters at a time when in many Deep South counties blacks still risked economic and physical reprisals for attempting to vote. Invalidating residential segregation ordinances and barring the judicial enforcement of racially restrictive covenants had little effect on segregated housing patterns, which had numerous extralegal causes. Even school desegregation litigation ultimately had limited integrative effect because of segregated housing patterns and white flight to suburbs and to private segregated academies.

Brown was difficult to enforce for another reason: Resistance was geographically concentrated. *Roe v. Wade*, which invalidated most criminal prohibitions on abortion, divided national opinion in approximately the same way that *Brown* did. But opposition to *Roe* was spread throughout the nation, not concentrated in one region, as it was with *Brown*. Virtually all white southerners disagreed with *Brown*, and in the 1950s, whites still held most of the political, economic, social, and physical power in the South. This meant that virtually all officials who were responsible for enforcing *Brown*—school board members, judges, jurors, politicians, and law enforcement officers—disagreed with it. Those southerners who endorsed *Brown*—mainly blacks—held little power. Under such circumstances, the enforcement of rights is bound to be precarious.

Brown was more difficult to enforce than *Roe* for another reason as well. Regardless of how much opposition existed to abortion, capitalism ensured the development of a market to supply what those exercising the *Roe* right demanded: abortion services. By contrast, *Brown* created no favorable market opportunities to facilitate enforcement, because essentially no southern whites wanted grade school desegregation. Anyone who established private integrated schools after *Brown*, performing a market function analogous to that of abortion clinics after *Roe*, would have done a very poor business indeed.

Political, social, and legal conditions ensured that *Brown* would be difficult to enforce. Most power holders in an entire region thought the decision was wrong and were intensely mobilized against it; this included the actors who were initially responsible for its enforcement.

Black beneficiaries of the ruling were neither united behind the right nor as intensely committed to its enforcement as they were with regard to some other rights. Congress and the president were unenthusiastic about implementing the decision. A multitude of techniques for evading the right were available, and sanctions against violators were mostly unobtainable.

Given these constraints on enforcement, it is ironic that southern whites, who had eschewed open confrontation with the Court over black jury service and black suffrage while completely sabotaging those rights through administrative discrimination, chose to openly defy *Brown*. Rather than follow North Carolina's lead and use similarly fraudulent mechanisms to circumvent school desegregation, the white South declared war on the Court, nullified *Brown*, and deployed state troops and encouraged vigilante mobs to block the enforcement of desegregation orders. Such open defiance forced President Eisenhower's hand, alienated national opinion, radicalized southern politics, fostered violence, and irritated the justices.

[margin handwriting: open defiance]

One cannot know how long token school desegregation might have persisted had white southerners played their hand differently, but in retrospect, massive resistance almost certainly proved to be a mistake from their perspective. The nature of southern politics may have impelled that mistake. Southern politicians reaped rewards for adopting extremist positions. Governor Orval Faubus won four more terms in office because he called out the militia to block the desegregation of Little Rock schools, and state legislators across the South saw political profit in passing interposition resolutions. The electoral incentives of southern politicians led them to respond to *Brown* in ways that ultimately facilitated its enforcement.

What can be said about the indirect consequences of litigation, which may be even harder to measure than are direct effects, though they may be just as real? It seems indisputable that *Brown* raised the salience of school segregation. Politicians, political parties, and social organizations were forced to take a position on the issue, which they had previously been able to avoid doing. For northern liberals and for many religious groups, taking a position on school segregation in 1954 inevitably meant opposing it. *Brown* also forced southern politicians to take a position on the issue, which many of them would have preferred to avoid doing. Given dominant public opinion in the South, however, the only conceivable position that they could take was to support segregation and to condemn *Brown*. By shifting the racial debate from other issues to school segregation, *Brown* clearly had an effect.

[margin handwriting: indirect consequences]

Brown also plainly inspired blacks. To have the Court declare segregation to be unconstitutional was symbolically important, and it furthered the hope and the conviction that fundamental racial change was possible. *Brown* directly inspired southern blacks to file petitions and lawsuits seeking school desegregation—something that almost certainly would not have happened in the mid-1950s, at least not in places such as Mississippi or South Carolina, had it not been for *Brown*. Thus, *Brown* shaped the agenda of southern blacks and shifted the focus to school desegregation and away from other issues that had preoccupied them before the Court's ruling: voting rights, school equalization, police brutality, and employment discrimination. This agenda-setting effect mattered, because southern whites were much more resistant to school desegregation than to many of these other reforms.

Brown's educational effect, as distinguished from its motivational consequences, is probably overstated. There is little evidence to suggest that many Americans changed their position on school segregation because of the justices' moral influence. White southerners bitterly denounced *Brown*. Most white northerners supported it, but more because they already agreed with its principles than because they were educated by the decision. Moreover, in the mid-1950s, their endorsement was fairly tepid. Few white northerners were prepared to support aggressive enforcement of *Brown* until the early 1960s. Northern opinion on race was educated far more by the civil rights movement than by *Brown*.

The limited educational influence of *Brown* is consistent with that of other landmark Court rulings. *Roe v. Wade* (1973) apparently did not educate many Americans to support abortion rights, as the country remained divided roughly down the middle three decades later. *Furman v. Georgia* (1972), which invalidated the arbitrary enforcement of the death penalty, plainly has not educated many Americans to oppose capital punishment, given opinion polls showing public support at 70 percent or higher. *Engel v. Vitale* (1962), which invalidated voluntary, nondenominational prayer in public schools, has consistently been opposed by 60–70 percent of the American public. Apparently, relatively few Americans take moral instruction on pressing policy questions from the justices.

Indeed, to the contrary, many landmark Court rulings seem to have generated backlashes rather than support. *Dred Scott v. Sandford* (1857), which essentially declared the Republican party to be unconstitutional by forbidding the federal regulation of slavery in national territories, seemed to help the party politically rather than annihilate it. *Furman* apparently mobilized support for the death penalty, as thirty-five states responded to the Court's ruling within four years by amending their death penalty statutes in the hope of satisfying the constitutional qualms of the justices. *Roe* mobilized antiabortion activists, who had not previously played a significant role in American politics. In 1993, the Hawaii Supreme Court ruled that marriage could not be limited to heterosexuals; within a few years, thirty states and Congress had passed "defense of marriage" acts in opposition. A similar ruling by the Massachusetts Supreme Court in 2003 generated a dramatic backlash in the 2004 elections.

Brown produced precisely this sort of effect. As southern blacks, inspired by the Court's ruling, filed school desegregation petitions and lawsuits, southern whites mobilized extraordinary resistance in response. Politics moved dramatically to the right, moderates collapsed, and extremists prospered. In the mid-1950s, racial retrogression characterized the South, as progress that had been made in black voting, university desegregation, and the integration of athletic competitions was halted and then reversed. Politicians used extremist rhetoric that encouraged violence, and some of them, such as Bull Connor and Jim Clark, correctly calculated that the violent suppression of civil rights protest would win votes. Court-ordered desegregation also created concrete occasions for violence, usually in settings that ensured that white supremacists would come off badly.

Yet backlashes themselves sometimes have unpredictable ramifications. The violence ignited by *Brown*, especially when directed at peaceful protestors and broadcast on television, produced a counterbacklash. In 1954, most northerners agreed with *Brown* in the abstract, but their preferences were not strong enough to make them willing to face down the resistance of southern whites. It was southern violence against civil rights demonstrators that transformed national opinion on race. By the early 1960s, northerners were no longer prepared to tolerate the brutal beatings of peaceful black demonstrators, and they responded to such scenes by demanding civil rights legislation that attacked Jim Crow at its core.

To judge the success or failure of a litigation campaign based solely on the concrete consequences of Court decisions is mistaken, given the capacity of litigation itself to mobilize social protest. The NAACP's lawyers educated blacks about their constitutional rights and instilled hope that racial conditions were malleable. Many branches formed around litigation, which also proved to be an excellent fundraising tool. Black lawyers served as role models to black audiences in courtrooms, as they jousted with whites in the only southern forum that permitted racial interactions on a footing of near-equality, and they demonstrated forensic skills that belied conventional white stereotypes of black inferiority. For NAACP lawyers such as Charles Hamilton Houston and Thurgood Marshall, these indirect effects of litigation were nearly as important as Court victories themselves.

Before World War II, alternative forms of protest—political mobilization, economic boycotts, street demonstrations, and physical resistance—were largely unavailable to southern blacks, who lived under a ruthlessly repressive regime of Jim Crow. At that time, litigation did not compete with alternative protest strategies for scarce resources, and it offered the advantages of not requiring large-scale participation to succeed and of taking place in the relative safety of courthouses rather than on the streets.

Yet there was a risk of exaggerating the contributions that litigation could make to social reform. In the 1930s, civil rights leaders appreciated that Court decisions required social support to be efficacious. Charles Houston warned, "We cannot depend upon the judges to fight . . . our battles," and he urged, "The social and public factors must be developed at least along with and, if possible, before the actual litigation commences."[4]

By the 1950s, though, litigation had secured such impressive Court victories and the NAACP was riding so high on its success that direct-action protest may have been discouraged, even though it had now become a viable option given the greater physical security enjoyed by southern blacks. Litigation and direct action now competed for scarce resources, and litigation seemed to have the edge in the 1950s, until the effective nullification of *Brown* by white southerners demonstrated the limited capacity of lawsuits alone to produce social change.

Though litigation had performed valuable service in mobilizing racial protest and securing Court victories, it could not fulfill all of the functions of direct action. Sit-ins, Freedom Rides, and street demonstrations fostered black agency much better than did litigation, which encouraged blacks to place their faith in elite black lawyers and white judges rather than in themselves. In addition, direct-action protest more reliably created conflict and incited opponents' violence, which ultimately proved to be critical to transforming national opinion on race.

Brown played a role both in generating direct action and in shaping the responses it received from white southerners. Any social protest movement must overcome a formidable hurdle in convincing potential participants that change is feasible, and *Brown* made Jim Crow seem to be more vulnerable. *Brown* raised the hopes and expectations of black Americans, which were then largely dashed by massive resistance; this demonstrated that litigation alone could not produce meaningful social change. *Brown* inspired southern whites to try to destroy the NAACP, with some temporary success in the Deep South, and this unintentionally forced blacks to support alternative protest organizations, which embraced philosophies more sympathetic to direct action. Finally, the southern white backlash that was ignited by *Brown* increased the chances that once civil rights demonstrators appeared on the streets, they would be greeted with violence rather than with gradualist concessions.

Court decisions do matter, though often in unpredictable ways. But they cannot fundamentally transform a nation. The justices are too much products of their time and place to launch social revolutions. And, even if they had the inclination to do so, their capacity to coerce change is too heavily constrained.

The justices were not tempted to invalidate school segregation until a time when half the nation supported such a ruling. They declined to aggressively enforce the *Brown* decision until a civil rights movement had made northern whites as keen to eliminate Jim Crow as southern whites were to preserve it. And while *Brown* did play a role in shaping both the civil rights movement and the violent response it received from southern whites, deep background forces ensured that the United States would experience a racial reform movement regardless of what the Supreme Court did or did not do.

NOTE ON SOURCES

In this abridged version of *From Jim Crow to Civil Rights: The Supreme Court and the Struggle for Racial Equality* (Oxford University Press, 2004), the endnotes provide sources only for quotations. Anyone interested in further documentation should consult the larger volume, which takes a much more comprehensive approach to citations.

NOTES

CHAPTER 1

1. Stephen Kantrowitz, *Ben Tillman and the Reconstruction of White Supremacy* (Chapel Hill, N.C., 2000), 168–69.

2. Holden v. Hardy, 169 U.S. 366, 398 (1898).

3. Alfred Holt Stone, *Studies in the American Race Problem* (New York, 1908), 64 ("enlightened public policy"); Leslie H. Fishel, Jr., "The North and the Negro, 1865–1900" (Ph.D. diss., Harvard University, 1953), 396–97 ("more unthinkable today").

4. Amasa M. Eaton, "The Suffrage Clause in the New Constitution of Louisiana," *Harvard Law Review* 13 (Dec. 1899): 288 ("greatest crime"); Paul H. Buck, *The Road to Reunion, 1865–1900* (Boston, 1937), 287 ("very extremity of permissible action").

5. McCulloch v. Maryland, 4 Wheat. 316, 423 (1819).

6. Williams v. Mississippi, 170 U.S. 213, 225 (1898).

7. Clarence H. Poe, "Suffrage Restrictions in the South: Its Causes and Consequences," *North American Review* 175 (July 1902): 541.

8. Stone, *American Race Problem*, 351 ("greatest self-confessed failure"); "Disfranchising a Race," *Nation* 66 (26 May 1898): 398–99 ("varied assortment of inferior races").

9. John M. Mathews, *Legislative and Judicial History of the Fifteenth Amendment* (Baltimore, Md., 1909), 126.

10. Mississippi Code Ann. § 2358 (1892), reproduced in Williams v. Mississippi, 170 U.S. 213, 218–19 (1898).

11. Margaret Law Callcott, *The Negro in Maryland Politics, 1870–1912* (Baltimore, Md., 1969), 135.

12. Horace Calvin Wingo, "Race Relations in Georgia, 1872–1908" (Ph.D. diss., Emory University, 1962), 202 ("on the wrong track"); *Crisis* 1 (Jan. 1911): 7 ("greatest mistake").

13. Louis R. Harlan, *Separate and Unequal: Public School Campaigns and Racism in the Southern Seaboard States, 1901–1915* (Chapel Hill, N.C., 1958), 131.

14. James D. Anderson, *The Education of Blacks in the South, 1860–1935* (Chapel Hill, N.C., 1988), 225–26 ("negro jobs"); Sheldon Hackney, *Populism to Progressivism in Alabama* (Princeton, N.J., 1969), 163 (McKinley); *Crisis* 2 (June 1911): 49 (Taft).

15. William Alexander Mabry, "Louisiana Politics and the 'Grandfather Clause,'" *North Carolina Historical Review* 13 (Oct. 1936): 304 ("weak and transparent subterfuge"), 306 ("grossly unconstitutional").

16. *Washington Post*, 23 June 1915, p. 6 ("so obvious an evasion"); *New York Times* (*NYT*), 23 June 1915, p. 10 ("nullify the Constitution"); Julien C. Monnet, "The Latest Phase of Negro Disfranchisement," *Harvard Law Review* 26 (Nov. 1912): 57 ("so thin a gauze").

17. Benno C. Schmidt, Jr., "Principle and Prejudice: The Supreme Court and Race in the Progressive Era. Part 3: Black Disfranchisement from the KKK to the Grandfather Clause," *Columbia Law Review* 82 (1982): 879.

18. Ibid. ("slightest political importance"); *Crisis* 10 (Aug. 1915): 172 ("not exactly the same thing"); *NYT*, 23 June 1915, p. 10 ("white man will rule his land").

19. State v. Armstead, 60 So. 778, 780 (Miss. 1913).

20. John Dittmer, *Black Georgia in the Progressive Era, 1900–1920* (Urbana, Ill., 1977), 81 ("shocking extent"); "Slavery," *Crisis* 22 (May 1921): 6 ("soul destroying slavery").

21. Chicago Commission on Race Relations, *The Negro in Chicago: A Study of Race Relations and a Race Riot* (Chicago, 1922), 99.

22. *Crisis* 18 (May 1919): 14 (Du Bois); Raymond Gavins, "Urbanization and Segregation: Black Leadership Patterns in Richmond, Virginia, 1900–1920," *South Atlantic Quarterly* 79 (Summer 1980): 270–71 ("lawless Ku Klux Klan").

CHAPTER 2

1. Neil A. Wynn, *The Afro-American and the Second World War* (New York, 1976), 45 (Roosevelt); Michael Barone, *Our Country: The Shaping of America from Roosevelt to Reagan* (New York, 1990), 160 (Knox); Hirabayashi v. United States, 320 U.S. 81, 110 (1943) (Murphy, J., concurring).

2. Richard M. Dalfiume, *Desegregation of the U.S. Armed Forces: Fighting on Two Fronts, 1939–53* (Columbia, Mo., 1969), 110 ("Hitlers in America"); John Morton Blum, *V Was for Victory: Politics and American Culture During World War II* (New York, 1976), 217–18 ("Hitler's Way"); Jessie Myles to NAACP, 30 July 1945, NAACP Papers (Frederick, Md., University Publications of America 1982), part 4, reel 9, frame 12 ("good enough to vote"); Jules Tygiel, *Baseball's Great Experiment: Jackie Robinson and His Legacy* (New York, 1983), 69, 74 ("organized base-ball").

3. James Hinton to Thurgood Marshall, 21 July 1942, NAACP, part 4, reel 10, frame 735 ("aroused as never before"); Numan V. Bartley, *The New South, 1945–80: The Story of the South's Modernization* (Baton Rouge, La., 1995), 14 ("except in the rarest instances").

4. Eric Foner, *The Story of American Freedom* (New York, 1998), 242.

5. Robert J. Norrell, *Reaping the Whirlwind: The Civil Rights Movement in Tuskegee* (New York, 1985), 61.

6. Howard W. Odum, "Social Change in the South," in Taylor Cole and John H. Hallowell, eds., *The Southern Political Scene 1938–1948* (Gainesville, Fla., 1948), 247 ("universal message"); G. M. Johnson to Nora Windon, 18 Aug. 1948, NAACP, part 4, reel 8, frame 592 ("social order").

7. *To Secure These Rights: The Report of the President's Committee on Civil Rights* (New York, 1947), 148 ("democratic ideal"); Dalfiume, *Desegregation of the U.S. Armed Forces*, 138–39 ("under observation" and "top dog").

8. Robert L. Harris, Jr., "Racial Equality and the United Nations Charter," in Armstead L. Robinson and Patricia Sullivan, eds., *New*

Directions in Civil Rights Studies (Charlottesville, Va., 1991), 126 ("part and parcel"), 137 ("tide of change").

9. Alexander Heard, *A Two Party South?* (Chapel Hill, N.C., 1952), 148.

10. Jennifer E. Brooks, "Winning the Peace: Georgia Veterans and the Struggle to Define the Legacy of World War II," *Journal of Southern History* 66 (Aug. 2000): 574.

11. Walter White to Frank Murphy, 4 Dec. 1925, NAACP, part 5, reel 3, frame 230.

12. Kevin M. Kruse, "Personal Rights, Public Wrongs: The Gaines Case and the Beginning of the End of Segregation," *Journal of Supreme Court History* (1997): 120.

13. United States v. Carolene Products Co., 304 U.S. 144, 152–53 n. 4 (1938).

14. Smith v. Allwright, 321 U.S. 649, 664 (1944).

15. *New York Times* (NYT), 5 Apr. 1944, p. 18.

16. John M. Lofton, Jr., to Thurgood Marshall, 19 Nov. 1947, NAACP, part 4, reel 9, frame 957 ("Bill of Rights"); Dorothy Q. Rainey to J. Lon Duckworth, 20 June 1944, ibid., reel 7, frames 592–93 ("cruel and shameful").

17. Elmore v. Rice, 72 F. Supp. 516, 527 (E.D.S.C. 1947).

18. Justice Harold Burton conference notes, *Terry v. Adams*, 17 Jan. 1953, Box 244, Burton Papers, Library of Congress.

19. Ibid.

20. Ibid. ("can't see where"); Justice Jackson, draft dissent, Terry v. Adams, 3 Apr. 1953, p. 1 ("hateful little local scheme"), p. 9 ("sound principle[s]"), Box 179, Jackson Papers, Library of Congress.

21. R. Scott Baker, "Ambiguous Legacies: The NAACP's Legal Campaign against Segregation in Charleston, South Carolina, 1935–1975" (Ph.D. diss., Columbia University, 1993), 124.

22. Sweatt v. Painter, 339 U.S. 629, 634–35 (1950).

23. NYT, 6 June 1950, p. 28.

24. Justice Clark conference notes, *McLaurin* and *Sweatt*, Box A2, Clark Papers, Tarlton Law Library, University of Texas.

25. Justice Burton conference notes, *McLaurin* and *Sweatt*, Box 204, Burton Papers, Library of Congress ("no basis" and "amending the Constitution"); Justice Robert Jackson to Professor Charles Fairman, 5 Apr. 1950, Jackson Papers ("fill gaps" and "deliberately and intentionally excluded").

26. Jackson to Fairman, 5 Apr. 1950 ("segregation system"); Justice Clark, Memorandum to Conference (draft), Apr. 1950, p. 3, Box A2, Clark Papers ("forces of progress"); Mark V. Tushnet, *Making Civil Rights Law: Thurgood Marshall and the Supreme Court, 1936–1961* (New York, 1994), 140 ("much point").

27. John P. Frank, "The United States Supreme Court, 1949–50," *University of Chicago Law Review* 18 (Autumn 1950): 34; Mary Frances Berry, *Security, Stability, and Continuity: Mr. Justice Burton and Decision-Making in the Supreme Court, 1945–1958* (Westport, Conn., 1978), 150.

28. Justice Clark, Memorandum to Conference ("groundless"); Justice Burton conference notes, *McLaurin* and *Sweatt*, Box 204, Burton Papers ("no great harm"); *Crisis* 46 (Feb. 1939): 51 ("treated like a dog").

29. Justice Clark, Memorandum to Conference.

30. Harry S. Ashmore, "Racial Integration with Special Reference to Education in the South," *Journal of Negro Education* 21 (Summer 1952): 252.

31. Burton conference notes, *McLaurin* and *Sweatt*, Box 204, Burton Papers ("wholly unreasonable" and "reasonable segregation"); Clark, Memorandum to Conference, p. 3 ("at this time"), p. 6 ("[s]hould they arise"); Clark conference notes, *McLaurin* and *Sweatt*, Box A2, Clark Papers ("[W]e can meet").

32. Clement V. Vose, *Caucasians Only: The Supreme Court, the NAACP, and the Restrictive Covenant Cases* (Berkeley, Calif., 1959), 171 (emphases in original).

33. Lawrence B. DeGraaf, "Significant Steps on an Arduous Path: The Impact of World War II on Discrimination against African Americans in the West," *Journal of the West* 35 (Jan. 1996): 30.

34. Henderson v. United States, 339 U.S. 816, 825 (1950).

35. Burton conference notes, *Henderson v. United States*, Box 204, Burton Papers ("impossible to say"); Douglas conference notes, *Henderson v. United States*, 8 Apr. 1950, Box 195, Douglas Papers ("we must amend"); Frankfurter to Conference, memorandum, 31 May, 1950, p. 1, ibid. ("inconceivable").

36. Brief for Appellant, p. 28, Morgan v. Virginia, 328 U.S. 373 (1946) (No. 704).

37. Armistead L. Boothe, "Civil Rights in Virginia," *Virginia Law Review* 35 (Nov. 1949): 969 ("keynote to tragedy"); Benjamin Muse, "Segregation Losing Popularity," *Washington Post*, 19 Feb. 1950, sec. B, p. 8 ("idiotic and evil").

CHAPTER 3

1. Unidentified and undated press clipping (probably 1958), NAACP, part 20, reel 11, frame 27.

2. I have consulted and am quoting from the conference notes of Justices Burton, Clark, Douglas, and Jackson. The notes are broadly similar, and I will intersperse quotes from them without giving specific citations. The conference notes are not transcriptions. I am quoting from the notes, but one should not assume that they perfectly captured what was said at conference. On the whole, however, they appear to be quite accurate. Burton conference notes, Segregation Cases, 13 Dec. 1952, Box 244, Burton Papers, Library of Congress; Clark conference notes, *Brown v. Board of Education*, Box A27, Clark Papers, Tarlton Law Library, University of Texas; Douglas conference notes, *Brown v. Board of Education* and *Bolling v. Sharpe*, 13 Dec. 1952, case file: Segregation Cases, Box 1150, Douglas Papers, Library of Congress; Jackson conference notes, 12 Dec. 1952, Box 184, Jackson Papers, Library of Congress. See also Del Dickson, ed., *The Supreme Court in Conference, 1945–1985: The Private Discussions behind Nearly 300 Supreme Court Decisions* (New York, 2001), 646–54; Richard Kluger, *Simple Justice: The History of* Brown v. Board of Education *and Black America's Struggle for Equality* (New York, 1976), chap. 23; Mark Tushnet, "What Really Happened in *Brown v. Board of Education*," *Columbia Law Review* 91 (Dec. 1991): 1867–1930; Dennis J. Hutchinson, "Unanimity and Desegregation: Decision Making in the Supreme Court, 1948–1958," *Georgetown Law Journal* 68 (Oct. 1979): 34–44.

3. Jackson draft concurrence, 6 Jan. 1954, Box 184, Jackson Papers, Library of Congress.

4. Brief for the United States as Amici Curiae, *Brown v. Board of Education*, p. 6, in Philip B. Kurland and Gerhard Casper, eds., *Landmark Briefs and Arguments of the Supreme Court of the United States* (Washington, D.C., 1975–), 49:121 ("Communist propaganda mills"); *Chicago Defender*, 22 May 1954, p. 5 ("firmer basis" and "eyes of the world").

5. John D. Fassett, *New Deal Justice: The Life of Stanley Reed of Kentucky* (New York, 1994), 561.

6. Douglas, memorandum for the file, Segregation Cases, 17 May 1954, Box 1149, Douglas Papers.

7. Frankfurter to Reed, 20 May 1954, Reed Papers ("no doubt" and "several opinions"); Douglas conference notes, *Brown II*, 16 Apr. 1955, Box 1150, Douglas Papers ("decided the other way").

8. Frankfurter to Reed, 20 May 1954.

9. Kluger, *Simple Justice*, 656.

10. Douglas conference notes, *Briggs v. Elliott*, 12 Dec. 1953, case file: Segregation Cases, Box 1149, Douglas Papers.

11. Frankfurter, memorandum on *Smith v. Allwright*, n.d., 3, Frankfurter Papers, part 1, reel 10, frame 167 ("soldier"); Frankfurter to Reed, 20 May 1954 ("hard struggle" and "great good").

12. Jackson draft dissent, *Terry v. Adams*, 3 Apr. 1953, pp. 1, 9, Box 179, Jackson Papers.

13. Douglas conference notes, *McLaurin v. Oklahoma*, 8 Apr. 1950, Box 192, Douglas Papers.

14. Melvin I. Urofsky, *Division and Discord: The Supreme Court under Stone and Vinson, 1941–1953* (Columbia, S.C., 1997), 109 n. 112 ("debatable opinions"), 130 ("legal principles"), 217 ("merely personal judgment"), 223 ("disciplined thinking").

15. Frankfurter, memorandum (first draft), n.d., p. 1, Frankfurter Papers, part 2, reel 4, frame 378.

16. Alexander M. Bickel to Frankfurter, 22 Aug. 1953, Frankfurter Papers, part 2, reel 4, frames 212–14.

17. Mary Frances Berry, *Stability, Security, and Continuity: Mr. Justice Burton and Decision-Making in the Supreme Court 1945–1958* (Westport, Conn., 1978), 142 ("most influential factor"); Douglas conference notes, *Briggs v. Elliott* ("*Plessy* is right").

18. Jackson to Charles Fairman, 13 Mar. 1950, Fairman file, Box 12, Jackson Papers.

19. For this and the following paragraphs, see Jackson draft concurrence, School Segregation Cases, 15 Mar. 1954, pp. 1–2, case file: Segregation Cases, Box 184, Jackson Papers.

20. EBP [E. Barrett Prettyman] to Jackson, n.d., pp. 1, 3, Box 184, Jackson Papers.

21. Ibid. ("ashamed"); Burton conference notes, School Segregation Cases, 12 Dec. 1953, Box 244, Burton Papers ("congenial political conclusion," "judicial act," and "political decision").

22. Robert H. Jackson, *The Supreme Court in the American System of Government* (Cambridge, Mass., 1955), 80.

23. For this and the next paragraph, see Jackson, draft concurrence, School Segregation Cases, 7 Dec. 1953, pp. 8–11, case file: Segregation Cases, Box 184, Jackson Papers.

24. Clark cited in Douglas conference notes, *Briggs v. Elliott*, 12 Dec. 1953.

25. Jackson to Fairman, 13 Mar. 1950.

26. WHR [William H. Rehnquist], "A Random Thought on the Segregation Cases," Box 184, Jackson Papers.

27. Burton conference notes, School Segregation Cases, 12 Dec. 1953, Box 244, Burton Papers ("would be better"); Clark conference notes, *Brown v. Board of Education*, Box A27, Clark Papers ("up to Congress").

28. Jackson to Fairman, 13 Mar. 1950 ("almost any Congressional Act"); Jackson, draft concurrence, 7 Dec. 1953, pp. 7–8 ("However desirable"); Douglas conference notes, *Briggs v. Elliott* ("representative government has failed").

29. Jackson, draft concurrence, 15 Mar. 1954, pp. 1, 19–21.

30. Frankfurter, memorandum ("great changes" and "pace of progress"); Burton conference notes ("different world").

31. Burton conference notes ("much progress"); Douglas conference notes, *Brown v. Board of Education*, 13 Dec. 1952, case file: Segregation Cases, Box 1150, Douglas Papers ("constant progress").

32. Burton conference notes.

33. Douglas memorandum, 25 Jan. 1960, cited in Melvin I. Urofsky, ed., *The Douglas Letters: Selections from the Private Papers of Justice William O. Douglas* (Bethesda, Md., 1987), 169.

34. Douglas conference notes, *Brown v. Board of Education* ("gradually disappearing"); Jackson draft concurrence, 15 Mar. 1954, p. 1 ("early extinction").

35. Jackson draft concurrence, 15 Mar. 1954, p. 1.

36. Jackson conference notes, Segregation Cases, 12 Dec. 1952, Box 184, Jackson Papers.

37. Derrick Bell, "*Brown v. Board of Education*: Forty-Five Years after the Fact," *Ohio Northern University Law Review* 26, no. 2 (2000): 172.

38. Frankfurter, memorandum to justices, 15 Jan. 1954, p. 1, Reed Papers ("transform" and "not a wand"); Jackson, draft concurrence, 15 Mar. 1954, p. 13 ("weak reed" and "contempt"); Clark conference notes ("can't close our eyes").

39. Clark conference notes (Vinson); Jackson conference notes (Reed).

CHAPTER 4

1. Brown v. Board of Education (*Brown II*), 349 U.S. 294, 298–301 (1955).

2. *Southern School News*, Jan. 1955, p. 5 ("generous in the extreme"); "Law Clerks' Recommendations for Segregation Decree"

("Clerks' Recommendations"), 10 Apr. 1955, p. 6, Box 337, Burton Papers, Library of Congress ("greatly weaken" and "half a generation"). My account of the internal deliberations in *Brown II* relies on the conference notes of Burton, Douglas, Frankfurter, and Warren. See Warren conference notes, *Brown II*, case file: Segregation Cases, Box 574, Warren Papers, Library of Congress; Burton conference notes, Segregation Cases, 16 Apr. 1955, Box 244, Burton Papers, Library of Congress; Douglas conference notes, *Brown II*, 16 Apr. 1955, case file: Segregation Cases, Box 1149, Douglas Papers, Library of Congress; Frankfurter conference notes, *Brown II*, 16 Apr. 1955, File 4044, Box 219, Frankfurter Papers, Library of Congress.

3. Frankfurter to Warren, 8 July 1954, Box 184, Jackson Papers, Library of Congress ("warm friend" and "chaotic").

4. Jackson, draft concurrence, School Segregation Cases, 15 Mar. 1954, p. 2 ("universal understanding"), p. 5 ("justified in understanding"), p. 22 ("framing the decree"), case file: Segregation Cases, Box 184, Jackson Papers; Douglas conference notes, *Brown v. Board of Education* and *Bolling v. Sharpe*, 13 Dec. 1952, case file: Segregation Cases, Box 1150, Douglas Papers ("long line of decisions").

5. Frankfurter to Brethren, 14 Apr. 1955, Box 337, Burton Papers ("how we do," "educational," and "self-righteous"); Jackson, draft concurrence, 15 Mar. 1954, p. 4 ("retard acceptance"); Brief for the United States on the Further Argument of the Questions for Relief, *Brown v. Board of Education*, p. 8 ("understanding and good will").

6. "Clerks' Recommendations," pp. 5, 9 ("would indicate to the South"); EBP [Prettyman] to Jackson, Note re Segregation Cases, p. 4, Box 184, Jackson Papers ("jam a new social order"); Prettyman to Warren, bench memorandum, Segregation Cases, p. 17, case file: Segregation Cases, Box 574, Warren Papers ("meat-ax decree" and "castor oil").

7. Douglas conference notes, *Brown II* ("not fond" and "how many students"); Frankfurter conference notes, *Brown II* ("5 or 10" and "disappear"); *Brown II*, 349 U.S. 301 ("parties to these cases"); Warren conference notes, *Brown II* ("nothing should be said").

8. Jackson, draft concurrence, 15 Mar. 1954, p. 2 ("coerced out," "coerced into," and "sincerity and passion"), p. 4 ("needlessly"); Del Dickson, ed., *The Supreme Court in Conference*, 1940–1985: *The Private Discussions behind Nearly 300 Supreme Court Decisions* (New York, 2001), 639 ("Hitler's creed"); Douglas conference notes, *Brown v. Board of Education* and *Bolling v. Sharpe* (Reed).

9. Douglas conference notes, *Brown v. Board of Education* and *Bolling v. Sharpe* ("no definite time"); Warren conference notes, *Brown II* ("not suggest a date"); Frankfurter, Memorandum on the Segregation

Decree, 14 Apr. 1955, p. 2, file: Segregation Cases, Box 574, Warren Papers ("arbitrary" and "tend to alienate").

10. Frankfurter, Memorandum on the Segregation Decree, p. 2 ("local difficulties" and "mere imposition"), p. 3 ("super–school board"); JDF to Reed, n.d. (probably in the summer of 1954), Reed Papers ("carpetbaggers"); WBM to Burton, memorandum, *Brown II*, p. 28, Box 248, Burton Papers ("judicial branch").

11. Douglas conference notes, *Brown v. Board of Education* and *Bolling v. Sharpe* (Black); Frankfurter conference notes, *Brown II* ("let them flounder" and "rather cruel"); Frankfurter, Memorandum on the Segregation Decree, p. 1 ("unload responsibility" and "drawn-out"); Frankfurter, "Segregation Considerations," n.d., p. 2, Frankfurter Papers ("local pressures"); "Clerks' Recommendations," p. 2 ("superior authority").

12. Warren conference notes, *Brown II* ("less we say" and "deliberate"); Frankfurter, Memorandum on the Segregation Decree, p. 2 ("invite evasion"), p. 3 ("leave room"); Burton conference notes, *Brown II* ("latitude").

13. WBM to Burton, p. 36 ("carry the ball").

14. Ibid., p. 35 ("a premium"); Warren conference notes, *Brown II* ("should not be mentioned"); Douglas conference notes, *Brown II* ("a fact").

15. Jackson, draft concurrence, 15 Mar. 1954, p. 17.

16. *Southern School News* (SSN), June 1955, p. 3 ("feasible"), p. 4 ("mildest decree"), p. 5 ("as soon as feasible").

17. Ibid., p. 3 ("most recalcitrant"); Report of Secretary to NAACP Board of Directors, May 1955, p. 2, NAACP, part 1, 1951–1955 supp., reel 1, frame 766 (NAACP quotes).

18. Report of Secretary to NAACP Board of Directors, May 1955, p. 2, NAACP, part 1, reel 2, frame 766 ("doesn't believe"); James L. Hicks, "Voters Vineyard," *Afro-American* (Baltimore, Md.), 11 June 1955, p. 4; John H. McCray, "Need for Changing," ibid.

19. SSN, June 1955, p. 2 ("intended to appeal"), p. 3 ("obnoxious decision"), p. 4 ("mistake"), p. 5 ("moderate and reasonable"), p. 8 ("to be thankful for"), p. 10 ("turmoil and violence").

20. Ibid., p. 3 ("made a mistake"), p. 7 ("hot potato").

21. SSN, Feb. 1956, p. 1 ("no effect"); Apr. 1956, p. 2 ("clear abuse" and "lawful means"); Lucas A. Powe, Jr., *The Warren Court and American Politics* (Cambridge, Mass., 2000), 60 ("illegal encroachment").

22. WBM to Burton, p. 34.

23. SSN, Jan. 1955, p. 2 ("bedroom doors"); Nov. 1955, p. 9 ("mongrelize").

24. WAN [William A. Norris] to Douglas, certiorari memorandum, *Naim v. Naim*, 24 Oct. 1955, office memos, nos. 350–399, Box 1164, Douglas Papers ("obvious"); WAN to Douglas, supplemental memorandum, *Naim v. Naim*, n.d., ibid. ("blur any distinction"); Gregory Michael Dorr, "Principled Expediency: Eugenics, Naim v. Naim, and the Supreme Court," *American Journal of Legal History* 42 (Apr. 1998): 149 ("insubstantial"); Dennis J. Hutchinson, "Unanimity and Desegregation: Decision Making in the Supreme Court, 1948–1958," *Georgetown Law Journal* 68 (Oct. 1979): 63 ("chance to burn down").

25. Frankfurter memorandum, *Naim v. Naim*, Frankfurter Papers, part 2, reel 17, frames 588–90.

26. WAN to Douglas, certiorari memorandum, *Naim v. Naim*, 1 Mar. 1956, case file: office memos, numbers 350–399, Box 1164, Douglas Papers.

27. Naim v. Naim, 350 U.S. 985 (1956).

28. TON to Justice Burton, certiorari memo, Box 270, Burton Papers.

29. Burton conference notes, *Williams v. Georgia*, Box 270, Burton Papers.

30. Harlan, Memorandum for the Conference, 23 Apr. 1955, folder 412, Box 2, Harlan Papers, Princeton University Library ("aggravating facts" and "straining to vindicate"); Burton conference notes, *Williams v. Georgia* ("to stand pat").

31. Williams v. State, 88 S.E. 2d 376, 377 (Ga. 1955) ("supinely surrender"); Barrett Prettyman, Jr., *Death and the Supreme Court* (New York, 1961), 290 ("go to hell").

32. SSN, Oct. 1956, p. 6.

33. Statement by Roy Wilkins to *New York Post*, 1 Feb. 1957, NAACP, part 21, reel 13, frame 7 ("violence and terror"); SSN, Oct. 1956, p. 6 ("extremists on both sides"); *New York Times* (NYT), 6 Sept. 1956, p. 1 ("whole matter settled today"); Robert Fredrick Burk, *The Eisenhower Administration and Black Civil Rights* (Knoxville, Tenn., 1984), 192 ("set back progress"); SSN, Aug. 1959, p. 1 ("morally wrong").

34. SSN, Mar. 1956, p. 13 ("very shy" and "very severe case"); July 1956, p. 4 ("No responsible person"); Walter A. Jackson, "White Liberal Intellectuals, Civil Rights, and Gradualism, 1954–60," in Brian Ward and Tony Badger, eds., *The Making of Martin Luther King and the Civil Rights Movement* (New York, 1996), 104 (Stevenson).

35. Quoted in C. Vann Woodward, "Great Civil Rights Debate," *Commentary* 24 (Oct. 1957): 291.

36. "Go Slow, Now," *Life,* 12 Mar. 1956, p. 37; Jackson, "White Liberal Intellectuals," 105 (Roosevelt); "The Autherine Lucy Case," *St. Louis Globe-Democrat,* 4 Mar. 1956, NAACP, part 20, reel 6, frame 237.

37. Benjamin Muse, "Moderates and Militants," *New Republic,* 2 Apr. 1956, p. 8 ("cooling-off period"), p. 9 ("violence and bloodshed").

38. SSN, Oct. 1957, p. 15.

39. *NYT,* 18 July 1957, p. 12.

40. Aaron v. Cooper, 163 F. Supp. 13, 21, 29 (E.D. Ark. 1958).

41. SSN, July 1958, p. 11 ("immediate and jubilant"), p. 12 ("wonderful"), p. 16 ("really works").

42. C. Vann Woodward, "The South and the Law of the Land," *Commentary* 26 (Nov. 1958): 370.

43. Clark, draft dissent, Box A73, Clark Papers ("push button action"); Brennan to Clark, 23 May 1963, Box 97, Brennan Papers, Library of Congress ("shade less offensive").

44. Minutes of the NAACP Board of Directors' meeting, Oct. 1959, p. 6, NAACP, part 1, Supp. 1956–60, reel 2, frame 200.

45. Douglas memorandum, *Shuttlesworth v. Birmingham Board of Education,* 17 Nov. 1958, p. 8, Box 1211, Douglas Papers ("maintain segregation"); Shuttlesworth v. Birmingham, 162 F. Supp. 372, 381 (N.D. Ala. 1958) ("lightly reach").

46. SSN, Dec. 1957, p. 11.

47. Douglas, handwritten memo to the file regarding *Shuttlesworth,* Box 1211, Douglas Papers.

48. SSN, Dec. 1958, p. 3 ("handle our own affairs"); Jan. 1959, p. 10 (Long and Rainach).

49. SSN, Jan. 1960, p. 1 ("Court Backs Stairstep"), p. 3 ("immeasurably pleased"); Mar. 1960, p. 6 ("clear hope" and "save face"); Martin Luther King, Jr., *Why We Can't Wait* (New York, 1964), 19 ("tokenism").

50. SSN, May 1957, p. 4.

51. SSN, Apr. 1957, p. 3 ("integrationist"); Mar. 1957, p. 16 ("surrendering" and "weakling"); Nov. 1958, p. 15 ("abject surrender" and "eyedropper integration").

52. Hutchinson, "Unanimity and Desegregation," 76–77, 84 ("exemplars of understanding" and "important implications"); Frankfurter to conference, memorandum, 20 Feb. 1959, Box 1200, Douglas Papers ("defiance," "creditable judicial document," and "respectful").

53. Black to Douglas, handwritten note, *In re Harrison*, n.d., Box 1208, Douglas Papers.

54. *NYT*, 28 Aug. 1958, p. 10 ("something about 'slower'"); SSN, Sept. 1958, p. 5 ("backward"); Jeffrey R. Young, "Eisenhower's Federal Judges and Civil Rights Policy: A Republican 'Southern Strategy' for the 1950s," *Georgia Historical Quarterly* 78 (Fall 1994): 564 ("looking for opportunities" and "necessarily be permanent").

55. SSN, Mar. 1959, p. 16 ("heartening," "very proud," and "extreme"); Apr. 1959, p. 6 ("tremendous development," "more harm than good," "Virginia's experience," and "keep our eyes open"); Mar. 1960, p. 16 ("surprisingly good").

56. SSN, Aug. 1956, p. 13.

57. SSN, Dec. 1962, p. 16 ("wide gulf"); Mar. 1963, p. 1 ("legally and morally right" and "often painfully so").

58. Watson v. Memphis, 373 U.S. 526, 530 (1963).

59. Goss v. Board of Education, 373 U.S. 683, 689 (1963); Griffin v. County School Board, 377 U.S. 218, 229, 234 (1964).

60. Burton conference notes, *Brown II*.

61. SSN, June 1964, p. 10.

62. Burton memorandum as to Segregation Cases for Conference, 16 Apr. 1955, Box 337, Burton Papers.

CHAPTER 5

1. *Southern School News* (SSN), Oct. 1954, p. 15.

2. Ibid., p. 16.

3. Douglas conference notes, *Brown v. Board of Education* and *Bolling v. Sharpe*, 13 Dec. 1952, case file: Segregation Cases, Box 1150, Douglas Papers, Library of Congress; Jackson, draft concurrence, 7 Dec. 1953, Box 184, Jackson Papers, Library of Congress.

4. SSN, Aug. 1958, p. 11 ("excuse"); Oct. 1954, p. 3 ("luxury"); Dec. 1954, p. 7 (McKeldin).

5. SSN, Aug. 1955, p. 19.

6. SSN, Mar. 1958, p. 12.

7. Robert M. Palumbos, "Student Involvement in the Baltimore Civil Rights Movement, 1953–63," *Maryland Historical Magazine* 94 (Winter 1999): 472.

8. SSN, Oct. 1955, p. 5.

9. SSN, June 1957, p. 8.

10. Douglas conference notes, *Brown II*, 16 Apr. 1955, Box 1149, Douglas Papers.

11. SSN, Jan. 1958, p. 3 ("represent the people"); Dec. 1958, p. 13 ("whipping boys").

12. SSN, June 1956, p. 7.

13. SSN, Aug. 1958, p. 4 ("slow to accept it"); Oct. 1961, p. 12 ("alarmed at the instances").

14. Louis E. Lomax, *The Negro Revolt* (New York, 1962), 30.

15. WBM to Burton, memorandum, *Brown II*, p. 29, Box 248, Burton Papers; SSN, Oct. 1959, p. 7 ("chaos and disorder").

16. Douglas conference notes, *Brown II*.

17. SSN, Jan. 1958, p. 6 (first Atwell quote); Jan. 1957, p. 10 (second Atwell quote); Aug. 1960, p. 8 (Davidson); Sept. 1959, p. 10 (first Timmerman quote); Feb. 1958, p. 7 (second Timmerman quote); Mar. 1963, p. 14 (West).

18. SSN, Mar. 1963, p. 14 ("distasteful"); Oct. 1956, p. 8 ("no right to reverse"); June 1963, p. 6 ("free agent[s]"); May 1959, p. 7 ("most unfortunate").

19. SSN, June 1957, p. 4 ("arrogance"); Apr. 1962, p. 3 ("scallawagging").

20. SSN, Nov. 1962, p. 11.

21. Christopher W. Schmidt, "J. Waties Waring and the Making of Liberal Jurisprudence in Postwar America," in Peter F. Lau, ed., *From the Grassroots to the Supreme Court*: Brown v. Board of Education *and American Democracy* (Durham, N.C., 2004), 175.

22. SSN, May 1959, p. 12 ("total and immediate"); Jan. 1960, p. 16 ("so speedily"); Sept. 1960, p. 2 ("terrorism").

23. SSN, Feb. 1957, p. 6 ("racial tension"), p. 11 ("sympathetic understanding"); Mar. 1956, p. 5 ("overnight").

24. Briggs v. Elliott, 132 F. Supp. 776, 777 (E.D.S.C. 1955).

25. Burton memorandum as to Segregation Cases for conference, 16 Apr. 1955, p. 1, Box 337, Burton Papers ("mere admission"); SSN, Aug. 1957, p. 16 ("such extensive changes").

26. Robert A. Leflar and Wylie H. Davis, "Segregation in the Public Schools: 1953," *Harvard Law Review* 67 (Jan. 1954): 416.

27. SSN, Feb. 1961, p. 8.

28. SSN, Oct. 1958, p. 9.

29. Walter A. Jackson, "White Liberal Intellectuals, Civil Rights and Gradualism, 1954–60," in Brian Ward and Tony Badger, eds., *The Making of Martin Luther King and the Civil Rights Movement* (New York, 1996), 109 ("Model for the South"); SSN, Apr. 1960, p. 5 ("very encouraging").

30. SSN, Aug. 1959, p. 10 ("token compliance"); Nov. 1960, p. 12 ("unbelievably slow"); Apr. 1960, p. 2 ("bored and disgusted"); Aug. 1961, p. 14 ("stairstep integration").

31. Report of Secretary to the NAACP Board of Directors, Apr. 1960, part 1, supp. 1956–60, reel 2, frame 357.

32. SSN, Mar. 1961, p. 3.

33. SSN, Apr. 1961, p. 10.

34. SSN, July 1963, p. 17.

35. SSN, Jan. 1964, p. 2.

CHAPTER 6

1. J. Harvie Wilkinson, *From Brown to Bakke: The Supreme Court and School Integration: 1954–1978* (New York, 1979), 6 ("most important"); Howard A. Glickstein, "The Impact of *Brown v. Board of Education* and Its Progeny," *Howard Law Journal* 23, no. 1 (1980): 55 ("foundation"); Aryeh Neier, *Only Judgment: The Limits of Litigation in Social Change* (Middletown, Conn., 1982), 241–42 ("public debate"); David Goldfield, *Black, White, and Southern: Race Relations and Southern Culture 1940 to the Present* (Baton Rouge, La., 1990), 91–92 ("black awareness"); Harvard Sitkoff, *The Struggle for Black Equality, 1954–1992* (1981; rev. ed., New York, 1993), 35 ("black hope"); Glenn T. Eskew, "The Alabama Christian Movement for Human Rights and the Birmingham Struggle for Civil Rights, 1956–1963," in David J. Garrow, ed., *Birmingham, Alabama, 1956–1963: The Black Struggle for Civil Rights* (Brooklyn, N.Y., 1989), 11 ("new activism").

2. Geraldine Gardner to Justice Douglas, 21 May 1954, Box 1150, Douglas Papers.

3. *New York Times* (NYT), 4 July 1957, p. 1 ("[f]ederal bayonet[s]"), p. 20 ("didn't completely understand"); NYT, 18 July 1957, p. 13 ("rug is [being] pulled").

4. *Southern School News* (SSN), June 1955, p. 9 ("politicians and professors"); Helen L. Jacobstein, *The Segregation Factor in the Florida Democratic Gubernatorial Election of 1956* (Gainesville, Fla., 1972), 8 ("tortured the Constitution").

5. *Washington Post*, 18 May 1954, p. 2.

6. Report of Secretary to NAACP Board of Directors, Sept. 1955, p. 5, NAACP, part 1, supp. 1951–55, reel 2, frame 786.

7. SSN, Sept. 1954, p. 7.

8. SSN, June 1964, p. 2.

9. Benjamin Muse, *Ten Years of Prelude: The Story of Integration since the Supreme Court's 1954 Decision* (New York, 1964), 19 ("greatest victory"); *Chicago Defender*, 22 May 1954, p. 5 ("majestic break"); Aldon D. Morris, *The Origins of the Civil Rights Movement: Black Communities Organizing for Change* (New York, 1984), 81 ("danced in the streets"); Louis E. Lomax, *The Negro Revolt* (New York, 1962), 73 ("impossible for a white person").

10. Stewart Burns, ed., *Daybreak of Freedom: The Montgomery Bus Boycott* (Chapel Hill, N.C., 1997), 256 ("servility and passivity"), 315 ("sustained collective action").

11. Burns, *Daybreak of Freedom*, 96 ("determination and courage"), 117 ("organize and discipline"), 246 ("one unfortunate girl").

12. Muriel Symington, letter to the editor, *New York Post*, 9 Apr. 1956, p. 29.

13. Burns, *Daybreak of Freedom*, 63.

14. Ibid., 110.

15. Ibid., 19.

16. Ibid., 99 ("boasting of a victory"), 181 ("social fabric"), 188 ("piddling stuff").

17. SSN, June 1960, p. 10.

18. SSN, Apr. 1960, p. 2 ("panty-raid style"); Report of Secretary to NAACP Board of Directors, Feb. 1960, p. 4, part 1, supp. 1956–60, reel 2, frame 309 ("caught the imagination").

19. Burns, *Daybreak of Freedom*, 256.

20. Lomax, *Negro Revolt*, 77.

21. Answer to interrogatory, *NAACP v. Almond*, 13 Aug. 1957, pp. 1–2, NAACP, part 20, reel 12, frames 958–59.

22. Burns, *Daybreak of Freedom*, 340.

23. John A. Morsell, memorandum on program for 1960 convention, 2 May 1960, p. 2, NAACP, part 22, reel 9, frame 216 ("*really* got desegregated"); Mark V. Tushnet, *Making Civil Rights Law: Thurgood Marshall and the Supreme Court, 1936–1961* (New York, 1994), 305 ("rabble-rouser"); John Dittmer, "The Politics of the Mississippi Movement," in Charles W. Eagles, ed., *The Civil Rights Movement in America* (Jackson, Miss., 1986), 72 ("naturally discouraged").

24. Patricia Simon to Gloster Current, 24 Apr. 1958, p. 2, NAACP, part 22, reel 9, frame 624 ("eminently successful"); Morris, *Civil Rights Movement*, 37 ("don't march in the streets").

25. Carter to Wilkins, memo, 2 Mar. 1960, p. 2, NAACP, part 22, reel 9, frame 179 ("identify the organization"); Morsell, memorandum on program for 1960 convention, 2 May 1960, pp. 1–2, ibid., frames 215–16 ("outlived our usefulness" and "action organization"); Wilkins to Hon. Theodore Spaulding, 28 Mar. 1961, part 21, reel 22, frame 19 ("since the very beginning").

26. Morsell, memorandum on program for 1960 convention, 2 May 1960, p. 2, NAACP, part 22, reel 9, frame 216 ("chief sustainer and guide"); SSN, Mar. 1960, p. 3 ("dozing conscience"); undated and unidentified memorandum (probably from the fall of 1961), NAACP, part 22, reel 3, frame 375 ("one or two").

27. SSN, May 1960, p. 6 ("absolutely clear"); NAACP press release, 17 Mar. 1960, part 21, reel 22, frame 229 ("Nazi-like tactics").

28. James Farmer, *Lay Bare the Heart: An Autobiography of the Civil Rights Movement* (New York, 1985), 14 ("big mistake"); Medgar Evers to Gordon Carey, 4 May 1961, pp. 2–3, NAACP, part 21, reel 12, frames 230–31 ("possibly hamper"); Wilkins to presidents and advisors of NAACP college chapters, memo, 26 May 1961, ibid., frame 242 ("viciousness, crudity").

29. Dittmer, "Politics of the Mississippi Movement," 81.

30. Morris, *Civil Rights Movement*, 123.

31. Burns, *Daybreak of Freedom*, 335–36 ("daily rededication[s]" and "community spirit"); Morsell to McLucas, 28 Sept. 1960, NAACP, part 20, reel 11, frame 706 ("established agencies").

32. Taylor Branch, *Parting the Waters: America in the King Years 1954–63* (New York, 1988), 598.

33. "A Clear-Cut Victory," *Afro-American* (Baltimore, Md.), 11 June 1955, p. 4 ("long and laborious"); James L. Hicks, "Voters Vineyard," ibid. ("try our very souls").

34. SSN, Sept. 1955, p. 1 ("not later than").

35. Martin Luther King, Jr., *Why We Can't Wait* (New York, 1964), 18 ("slow pace"); Wilkins to Presidents of NAACP branches et al., memo, 2 Feb. 1961, NAACP, part 21, reel 22, frame 6 ("snail-like pace"); Wilkins, press conference transcript, pp. 7–8, ibid., reel 13, frames 65–66 ("this foolishness," "in a hurry," "so particular," and "mass demonstration"); Farmer, *Lay Bare the Heart,* 13 ("status remains quo").

36. SSN, Nov. 1962, p. 17 ("being a Negro"); July 1962, p. 1 (Mize and Wisdom).

37. Walter Jones, "I Speak for the White Race," *Montgomery Advertiser*, 4 Mar. 1957, NAACP, part 20, reel 4, frame 436; NAACP press release, 11 Aug. 1961, p. 2, ibid., reel 5, frame 48 ("shall never recover"); SSN, Apr. 1959, p. 3 ("would close every school").

38. Wilkins to W. Lester Banks, 20 Aug. 1957, NAACP, part 20, reel 12, frame 982 ("bunch of Republicans"); Muse, *Ten Years of Prelude*, 39 ("consuming hatred"); open letter from four black ministers, n.d., p. 2, part 20, reel 11, frame 185 ("as necessary as breathing"); SSN, July 1958, p. 16 ("southern expression of communism"); Dec. 1956, p. 9 ("subversive or Communist backgrounds").

39. Wilkins to Carter Wesley, 31 May 1957, NAACP, part 20, reel 12, frames 365–66.

40. Wilkins to Board of Directors, memo, 7 May 1957, NAACP, part 20, reel 12, frame 296 ("future operation"); Evers to Current, 2 Oct. 1956, ibid., reel 14, frames 96–97 ("economic pressures" and "pure in heart").

41. Current to Wilkins, memorandum, 18 June 1957, ibid., reel 12, frames 410 ("atmosphere of gloom"), 413 ("arresting our activities"); Francis L. Williams to Current, 20 June 1958, part 22, reel 9, frame 650 ("regain the confidence").

CHAPTER 7

1. Marshall Frady, *Wallace* (New York, 1968), 102 ("just alike"); George E. Sims, *The Little Man's Big Friend: James E. Folsom in Alabama Politics, 1946–1958* (University, Ala., 1985), 166 ("brotherly love"); *Southern School News* (SSN), Sept. 1955, p. 3 ("good colored people").

2. Alexander Heard, *A Two Party South?* (Chapel Hill, N.C., 1952), 148.

3. Kari Fredrickson, *The Dixiecrat Revolt and the End of the Solid South, 1932–1968* (Chapel Hill, N.C., 2001), 203.

4. Julian M. Pleasants and Augustus M. Burns III, *Frank Porter Graham and the 1950 Senate Race in North Carolina* (Chapel Hill, N.C., 1990), 99.

5. SSN, Sept. 1954, p. 2 (Cherry), p. 13 (Stanley), p. 14 (Clement).

6. C. Vann Woodward, "The 'New Reconstruction' in the South: Desegregation in Historical Perspective," *Commentary* 21 (June 1956): 503 ("live with change"); R. Ray McCain, "Reactions to the United States Supreme Court Segregation Decision of 1954," *Georgia Historical Quarterly* 52 (Dec. 1968): 372 ("on the way out").

7. *SSN*, Sept. 1954, p. 13 ("usurpation of power"); McCain, "Reactions," 381 (Talmadge); *New York Times (NYT)*, 18 May 1954, p. 1 (Eastland).

8. *Chicago Defender*, 25 Sept. 1954, p. 3 (Talmadge); *SSN*, Oct. 1954, p. 6 (Griffin).

9. Elizabeth Geyer, "The 'New' Ku Klux Klan," *Crisis* 63 (Mar. 1956): 139 ("uptown"); *SSN*, Feb. 1956, p. 6 ("force their demands").

10. *SSN*, Apr. 1956, p. 2.

11. Weldon James, "The South's Own Civil War: Battle for the Schools," in Don Shoemaker, ed., *With All Deliberate Speed: Segregation-Desegregation in Southern Schools* (New York, 1957), 23 ("mix the races"); *SSN*, Nov. 1954, p. 15 ("double crossers"); July 1956, p. 3 ("sugar-coated"); Oct. 1959, p. 3 ("cowards" and "traitors"); July 1957, p. 3 ("suicide"); Stan Opotowsky, "Dixie Dynamite: The Inside Story of White Citizens Councils," Jan. 1957, NAACP, part 20, reel 13, frame 685 ("takes guts").

12. Hamilton Basso, letter to the editor, *NYT*, 10 Apr. 1955, p. 10E ("foremost preoccupation"); *SSN*, Apr. 1955, p. 3 ("slumber"); Nov. 1959, p. 16 ("debt of gratitude").

13. Stewart Burns, ed., *Daybreak of Freedom: The Montgomery Bus Boycott* (Chapel Hill, N.C., 1997), 208.

14. *SSN*, Jan. 1956, p. 15.

15. Jim Johnson, "Let's Build a Private School at Hoxie," *Arkansas Faith*, Dec. 1955, p. 12, NAACP, part 20, reel 13, frame 307.

16. Dick Mansfield, "Local Report from Norfolk," 22 May 1958, p. 3, NAACP, part 22, reel 1, frame 518.

17. *SSN*, Mar. 1956, p. 13 ("orgy of race conflict" and "no useful purpose"); letter to the editor, *Tampa Morning Tribune*, n.d., NAACP, part 20, reel 7, frame 217 ("only issue"); Saunders to Wilkins, 7 May 1956, ibid., frame 198 ("segregation train"); *SSN*, June 1956, p. 9 ("moderation" and "understanding"), p. 12 ("every lawful means"); undated press clipping, *Florida Sentinel*, part 20, reel 13, frame 429 ("level-headed and far-sighted").

18. *SSN*, May 1956, p. 4 ("great deterioration"); Apr. 1956, p. 9 ("too outspoken" and "Negro cases"); *Tampa Morning Tribune*, 10 May 1956, part 20, reel 7, frame 200 ("crashing rebuke").

19. *SSN*, Feb. 1956, p. 6 ("bunch of hogwash"); July 1958, p. 11 ("scotch and soda").

20. *SSN*, June 1956, p. 10.

21. SSN, Apr. 1956, p. 11.

22. SSN, May 1956, p. 11 ("sudden and unexpected"); June 1955, p. 15 ("increasingly difficult").

23. "Able and Willing," *Montgomery Advertiser*, 8 July 1956, NAACP, part 20, reel 13, frame 376.

24. SSN, Oct. 1957, p. 8.

25. SSN, Dec. 1957, p. 10.

26. Dan T. Carter, *The Politics of Rage: George Wallace, the Origins of the New Conservatism, and the Transformation of American Politics* (New York, 1995), 96.

27. SSN, June 1958, p. 3 ("federal treasury"); Aug. 1958, p. 16 ("weak"); Oct. 1958, p. 17 ("two Confederate grandfathers" and "tool of the NAACP").

28. SSN, Mar. 1959, p. 3.

29. SSN, Sept. 1958, p. 10 ("old-fashioned segregationist"); Mar. 1959, p. 12 ("threw in the towel").

30. SSN, Nov. 1958, p. 10 ("surrender"); Dec. 1958, p. 5 (newspaper publishers), p. 15 ("determined and united").

31. SSN, Sept. 1958, p. 4 ("rot in a federal prison" and "will of the people"); Mar. 1959, p. 13 (Gartin).

32. SSN, Jan. 1956, p. 6 ("foolish" and "legal poppycock"); May 1956, p. 15 ("daily uproar"); Erle Johnston, *I Rolled with Ross: A Political Portrait* (Baton Rouge, La., 1980), 78 ("mongrelization"); SSN, Sept. 1959, p. 5 ("foot in the door," "good Lord," and "sane and sensible"); Feb. 1960, p. 7 ("all costs").

33. SSN, June 1956, p. 3 ("hotheads"); Aug. 1958, p. 3 ("1,000 percent" and "Nigger").

34. SSN, Dec. 1959, p. 15.

35. Matthew David Lassiter, "The Rise of the Suburban South: The 'Silent Majority' and the Politics of Education, 1945–75" (Ph.D. diss., University of Virginia, 1999), 217–18 ("just begun" and "division and discord"); SSN, Mar. 1959, p. 7 ("blow to our cause"); Feb. 1960, pp. 1–2 ("again and again").

36. SSN, June 1959, p. 9.

37. SSN, Feb. 1959, p. 16 ("a little integration" and "every ounce"); Mar. 1960, p. 6 ("sign of weakness").

38. SSN, Apr. 1960, p. 3.

39. SSN, Dec. 1962, p. 10.

40. Lassiter, "Rise of the Suburban South," 297 ("not a damned fool"); SSN, Mar. 1962, p. 12 ("compromise" and "inevitable").

41. SSN, Mar. 1963, p. 4 ("close every school"); Apr. 1963, p. 15 ("new look").

42. SSN, Feb. 1962, p. 12 ("nigger"); Mar. 1962, p. 12 ("weak-kneed").

43. SSN, Apr. 1962, p. 3 ("school house door"); May 1962, p. 6 ("throw him in jail").

44. SSN, Dec. 1963, p. 10 ("good fight"); William Doyle, *An American Insurrection: The Battle of Oxford, Mississippi, 1962* (New York, 2001), 65–66 ("your governor").

45. SSN, Jan. 1962, p. 15.

46. SSN, May 1963, p. 14 ("change of mood," "vicarious suffering," and "must not happen here"); Jan. 1963, p. 15 ("how reasonably").

47. SSN, Jan. 1963, p. 1.

48. SSN, Oct. 1962, pp. 13–14.

49. SSN, Oct. 1962, p. 14 ("bravado"); Nov. 1962, p. 11 ("another Oxford"); Dec. 1962, p. 3 ("one single utterance" and "wasting paper"); Feb. 1963, p. 11 ("toss the gauntlet").

50. SSN, Feb. 1963, pp. 10–11 ("fighting chance" and "bring disgrace"); Apr. 1963, p. 9 ("indecent and irresponsible" and "rebellion and riots").

51. SSN, Feb. 1964, p. 2.

52. Johnston, *I Rolled with Ross*, 102 ("Stand Tall with Paul"), SSN, Aug. 1963, p. 20 ("fight harder next time"); Nov. 1963, p. 1 ("any school anywhere").

53. SSN, Mar. 1963, p. 6 ("impregnable barrier"); NYT, 22 Jan. 1964, pp. 1, 28 (Johnson).

CHAPTER 8

1. *Southern School News* (SSN), Oct. 1954, p. 14 ("unalterable opposition"); Nov. 1954, p. 15 ("monstrous").

2. SSN, June 1958, p. 3 ("wrecking crew"); June 1956, p. 16 ("Achilles' heel"); Dec. 1958, p. 15 ("throw in the towel").

3. SSN, Mar. 1960, p. 7 ("[f]riends won't argue" and "think out loud"); Dec. 1963, p. 10 ("totalitarian society"); Stan Opotowsky, "Dixie Dynamite: The Inside Story of White Citizens Councils," *New York Post*, 12 Jan. 1957, NAACP, part 20, reel 13, frame 679 ("like the frost"); Stewart Burns, ed., *Daybreak of Freedom: The Montgomery Bus Boycott* (Chapel Hill, N.C., 1997), 168 ("immobilized").

4. SSN, June 1955, p. 18 ("no place in Georgia"); June 1959, p. 12 ("idiocy" and "only one viewpoint").

5. SSN, Mar. 1960, p. 7 ("scalawag southerner"); Jan. 1958, p. 8 ("nigger lovers").

6. *Birmingham Post-Herald*, 22 Dec. 1960, p. 12, NAACP, part 21, reel 22, frame 399.

7. NAACP press release, 25 July 1956, pp. 1–2, part 20, reel 4, frames 639 40.

8. Numan V. Bartley, *The Rise of Massive Resistance: Race and Politics in the South during the 1950s* (Baton Rouge, La., 1969), 211 ("nonconformance"); SSN, Jan. 1959, p. 13 ("atmosphere of fear"); Dec. 1963, p. 10 ("closed society"); Apr. 1964, p. 14 ("get rid" and "degrading activities").

9. Charles M. Payne, *I've Got the Light of Freedom: The Organizing Tradition and the Mississippi Freedom Struggle* (Berkeley, Calif., 1995), 7 ("systematic racial terrorism"); Robert L. T. Smith, "Visit to Jefferson County [Mississippi]," n.d., NAACP, part 20, reel 2, frame 166 ("all but unbelievable").

10. SSN, June 1959, p. 11.

11. SSN, Sept. 1957, p. 6 ("why does Arkansas?"); June 1956, p. 11 ("join us").

12. SSN, Oct. 1955, p. 3 ("hold the line"); Neil R. McMillen, "Organized Resistance to School Desegregation in Tennessee," *Tennessee History Quarterly* 30 (Fall 1971): 319 ("We want trouble").

13. SSN, May 1956, p. 15 ("damnable doctrine" and "weak-kneed politicians"); Nov. 1958, p. 15 ("abject surrender"); Mar. 1959, p. 15 ("crippling blow").

14. SSN, Apr. 1962, p. 11.

15. SSN, Dec. 1959, p. 14 ("shape their destiny"); Sen. James Eastland, "The South Will Fight!" *Arkansas Faith*, Dec. 1955, pp. 8, 27, NAACP, part 20, reel 13, frames 303 ("golden hour"), 322 ("not been found wanting").

16. James W. Ely, Jr., *The Crisis of Conservative Virginia: The Byrd Organization and the Politics of Massive Resistance* (Knoxville, Tenn., 1976), 61 (Almond and Byrd); SSN, July 1958, p. 16 ("When those birds"); July 1957, p. 4 ("eventually reversed").

17. Daniel L. McBroom of White Peoples [sic] Association to "All White People," n.d., NAACP, part 20, reel 13, frame 483 ("has reversed itself"); Dick Mansfield, "Local Report from Norfolk," 22 May 1958, p. 3, NAACP, part 22, reel 1, frame 518 ("calm resignation" and "fatal day

would be delayed"); Samuel Lubell, *White and Black: Test of a Nation* (New York, 1964), 96 ("believe that nullification").

18. SSN, Dec. 1958, p. 6.

19. Ibid. ("all the way"); Nov. 1959, p. 9 ("dark ages"); July 1959, p. 6 ("cannot secede").

20. Lubell, *White and Black*, 100 ("infested").

21. SSN, Feb. 1961, p. 8 ("abandon public education").

22. SSN, Mar. 1960, p. 6.

23. SSN, Feb. 1963, p. 10 ("segregation forever"); Aug. 1963, p. 20 ("fight harder next time").

24. Lubell, *White and Black*, 106–7 ("can't fight the Federal government," "never accept it," and "have to force it"); "But What of the Law?" *New Republic*, 2 Apr. 1956, p. 9 ("will accept another civil war").

25. SSN, Oct. 1957, p. 8.

26. SSN, Oct. 1957, p. 4 ("military dictatorship"), p. 13 ("dictator"), p. 15 ("storm troopers").

27. SSN, Dec. 1962, pp. 2–3.

CHAPTER 9

1. *Southern School News* (SSN), Nov. 1957, p. 5 ("our federal court system"); Oct. 1962, p. 12 ("government of laws").

2. *New York Post*, 24 Sept. 1956, NAACP, part 20, reel 12, frame 151.

3. "Shame Falls on Alabama," *Worcester* (Mass.) *Telegram*, 8 Feb. 1956, NAACP, part 20, reel 6, frame 121; *New York Times* (NYT), 12 Feb. 1956, p. 57 ("deplorable"), "A Riot: A Public Disgrace," *Cheraw* (S.C.) *Chronicle*, 9 Feb. 1956, part 20, reel 6, frame 122; "Failure in Alabama," *Washington Post*, 8 Feb. 1956, p. A12 ("outrage opinion").

4. SSN, Nov. 1957, p. 4 ("sputtering sputnik"), p. 15 ("Gov. Faubus"); Dec. 1958, p. 12 ("valuable enemy" and "aroused and educated").

5. Morton Inger, *Politics and Reality in an American City: The New Orleans School Crisis of 1960* (New York, 1969), 57–58 (Steinbeck); "Economic Lynching," *NYT*, 19 Nov. 1960, p. 20 ("racist rabble"); Adam Fairclough, *Race and Democracy: The Civil Rights Struggle in Louisiana, 1915–1972* (Athens, Ga., 1995), 252 ("appalling sight and sound").

6. N. K. Perlow, "KKK Leader Warns: 'We Mean Business,'" *Police Gazette* (Aug. 1956): 33, NAACP, part 20, reel 13, frame 444 ("loaded with

dynamite"); Stan Opotowsky, "Dixie Dynamite: The Inside Story of White Citizens Councils," Jan. 1957, NAACP, part 20, reel 13, frame 682 ("Smith and Wesson line"); Andrew Michael Manis, *A Fire You Can't Put Out: The Civil Rights Life of Birmingham's Reverend Fred Shuttlesworth* (Tuscaloosa, Ala., 1999), 147 ("nigger kids").

7. NAACP, *M Is for Mississippi and Murder*, NAACP, part 20, reel 2, frame 655.

8. John Dittmer, *Local People: The Struggle for Civil Rights in Mississippi* (Chicago and Urbana, Ill., 1994), 58.

9. Wilkins, Keynote Address to National Delegate Assembly for Civil Rights, 4 Mar. 1956, p. 6, NAACP, part 21, reel 12, frame 193; Rep. Hugh Scott, speech before the National Delegate Assembly for Civil Rights, 5 Mar. 1956, p. 3, ibid., frame 206.

10. Margaret Price, "Joint Interagency Fact Finding Project on Violence and Intimidation" (draft), NAACP, part 20, reel 11, frame 403.

11. SSN, May 1959, p. 8 ("equal and opposite"); Howard Smead, *Blood Justice: The Lynching of Mack Charles Parker* (New York, 1986), 175 ("Board of Sociology").

12. SSN, May 1959, p. 8.

13. Smead, *Blood Justice*, 181.

14. SSN, Oct. 1956, p. 9 ("marching bands"); Aug. 1957, p. 7 ("work of Satan"); Anonymous to Charles Gomillion, 26 Feb. 1959, NAACP, part 20, reel 6, frame 11 ("bloodshed"); handbill circulated at Montgomery citizens' council meeting, 10 Feb. 1956, ibid., reel 5, frame 126 ("abolish the Negro race").

15. 102 Congressional Record 6825 (23 Apr. 1956) (Rep. Davis) ("irreparable harm"); SSN, Mar. 1957, p. 16 ("shotgun blast").

16. NAACP press release, 1 Mar. 1956, part 20, reel 5, frame 168 ("shotguns"); James C. Cobb, *The Most Southern Place on Earth: The Mississippi Delta and the Roots of Regional Identity* (New York, 1992), 214 ("few killings"); SSN, Mar. 1956, p. 7 ("good people of Alabama").

17. Martin Luther King, Jr., *Stride toward Freedom: The Montgomery Story* (New York, 1958), 174; SSN, Jan. 1956, p. 5 ("patience may become exhausted"); Mar. 1956, p. 10 ("hatred and bloodshed"); Tom Brady, *Black Monday* (Winona, Miss., 1954), 41; statement by Gov. Allan Shivers, 31 Aug. 1956, in 1 R.R.L.R. 885 (1956).

18. SSN, Nov. 1954, p. 10 ("morally bound"); June 1956, p. 3 ("ready to battle"); Aug. 1956, p. 5 ("judicial tyranny"); July 1955, p. 1 ("greatest single blow"); Nov. 1958, p. 10 ("Communists" and "surrender").

19. Eastland, "The South Will Fight!!" pp. 7–9, 27, NAACP, part 20, reel 13, frames 302–4, 322; 102 Congressional Record 6822, 6825 (23 Apr. 1956) (Rep. Davis).

20. NAACP press release, 21 Mar. 1958, NAACP, part 20, reel 12, frame 6 ("so-called respectable people"); SSN, Aug. 1963, p. 20 ("defiant and provocative").

21. J. W. Peltason, *Fifty-Eight Lonely Men: Southern Federal Judges and School Desegregation* (New York, 1961), 138 ("southern hero"); Robert E. Bundy to executives of voluntary affiliate organizations, circular re recent bombing incidents, 20 Oct. 1958, NAACP, part 20, reel 6, frame 723 ("rabble-rousing politician").

22. King, *Stride toward Freedom*, 102; John P. Kavanagh to NAACP, 14 May 1961, part 20, reel 3, frame 120 ("my rage"); Wilkins to H. D. Monteith, 15 Nov. 1956, p. 2, ibid., reel 11, frame 177 ("white people").

23. SSN, Apr. 1960, p. 14 ("throw him out"); Miles Wolff, *Lunch at the Five and Ten: The Greensboro Sit-Ins: A Contemporary History* (New York, 1970), 152 ("ragtail rabble").

24. Morris, *Civil Rights Movement*, 242 (Pritchett); Henry Hampton and Steve Fayer, *Voices of Freedom: An Oral History of the Civil Rights Movement from the 1950s through the 1980s* (New York, 1980), 75 ("racists of the South"); David J. Garrow, *Bearing the Cross: Martin Luther King, Jr., and the Southern Christian Leadership Conference* (New York, 1988), 251 ("stupidity of a Bull Connor").

25. Manis, *A Fire You Can't Put Out*, 84 ("serious racial trouble"); William A. Nunnelley, *Bull Connor* (Tuscaloosa, Ala., 1991), 55 ("professional agitators"), 58 ("AGITATION").

26. Manis, *A Fire You Can't Put Out*, 265 ("By God"); Glenn T. Eskew, *But for Birmingham: The Local and National Movements in the Civil Rights Struggle* (Chapel Hill, N.C., 1997), 160 ("[W]here were the police?").

27. SSN, Mar. 1958, p. 13 ("violence"); Dec. 1959, p. 1 ("all-out war"); Jan. 1961, p. 5 ("hell to pay" and "stirring up trouble"); July 1961, p. 9 ("professional agitators").

28. *Time*, 26 May 1961, p. 16; 107 Congressional Record 9216 (29 May 1961) (Rep. Giaimo quoting from *Birmingham News*).

29. Roy Wilkins to branch officers, memo, 25 May 1961, NAACP Papers, part 21, reel 12, frame 241 ("provocateurs"); David Brinkley, statement, 25 May 1961, ibid., frame 240.

30. Wilkins to Branch Officers, memo, 25 May 1961, NAACP, part 21, reel 12, frame 241 ("brutality of mobsters"); 107 Congressional Record 8027 (16 May 1961) (Sen. Javits); ibid., 8498 (22 May 1961) (Sen. Mansfield), Jason Paul Clabaugh, "Reporting the Rage: An Analysis of

Newspaper Coverage of the Freedom Rides of May, 1961," *Southern Historian* 14 (Spring 1993): 50–51 ("savage scene," etc.).

31. SSN, Sept. 1957, p. 16 ("blood and guts"); Oct. 1959, p. 3 ("men from the boys"); Feb. 1960, p. 7 ("segregated at all costs").

32. SSN, Oct. 1962, p. 1.

33. Robert Sherrill, *Gothic Politics in the Deep South: Stars of the New Confederacy* (New York, 1968), 186.

34. Garrow, *Bearing the Cross*, 227–28.

35. David J. Garrow, *Protest at Selma: Martin Luther King, Jr. and the Voting Rights Act of 1965* (New Haven, Conn., 1978), 141 ("sick" and "national disgrace"); 109 Congressional Record 8125 (9 May 1963) (Rep. Lindsay) ("shocking episodes"); Rose V. Russell to Pres. Kennedy, 8 May 1963, NAACP, part 20, reel 4, frame 307 ("outrage and shame"); Nubar Esaian to Pres. Kennedy, 8 May 1963, ibid., frames 313–15 ("barbarism and savagery"); Martin Luther King, Jr., *Why We Can't Wait* (New York, 1964), 67 ("revolution").

36. SSN, June 1961, p. 11 ("timid and reluctant"); Mar. 1963, p. 1 ("dragging its feet"); George H. Gallup, *The Gallup Poll: Public Opinion 1935–1971* (New York, 1972), 3:1769 ("[t]oo fast," etc.).

37. Excerpts from various articles by William Buckley in *National Review*, p. 4, NAACP, part 21, reel 1, frame 154.

38. Carl M. Brauer, *John F. Kennedy and the Second Reconstruction* (New York, 1977), 437 ("presidential pen"); Dittmer, *Local People*, 223 ("niggers" and "chimpanzees").

39. SSN, Sept. 1963, p. 5 ("strict moral duty"); Brauer, *John F. Kennedy and the Second Reconstruction*, 260 ("old as the scriptures").

40. SSN, Dec. 1963, p. 1.

41. Donald S. Strong, "Alabama: Transition and Alienation," in William C. Havard, ed., *The Changing Politics of the South* (Baton Rouge, La., 1972), 451.

42. Carter, *Politics of Rage*, 96 ("out-nigger[ed]"); SSN, Feb. 1963, p. 10 ("tyranny" and "segregation forever").

43. SSN, June 1963, p. 5.

44. SSN, July 1963, p. 5 ("forceful stand"); Sept. 1963, p. 2 ("dictator").

45. Carter, *Politics of Rage*, 166 ("boisterous campaign"), 172 ("not thugs").

46. "Wallace's Defeat in 'Victory,'" NYT, 11 Sept. 1963, p. 42 ("devil's brew"); Carter, *Politics of Rage*, 173 ("federal bayonets").

47. *NYT*, 16 Sept. 1963, p. 26 ("deliberate mass murder"); *SSN*, Oct. 1963, p. 8 (Kennedy), p. 10 ("plant that bomb"); Nov. 1963, p. 2 ("standing in the schoolhouse door").

48. Donald B. Brown to Wilkins, 18 Sept. 1963, NAACP, part 20, reel 3, frame 941 ("apology for being caucasian"); Elouise May to NAACP, 16 Sept. 1963, ibid., frame 947 ("worst barbarians"); Robert E. Feir to Wilkins, 23 Sept. 1963, ibid., frame 959 ("sorry, ashamed, and guilty").

49. Manzie Ridgill to Wilkins, 17 Sept. 1963, NAACP, part 20, reel 3, frames 919–20 ("nothing in my life"); NAACP press release, 21 Sept. 1963, ibid., frame 986 ("flood Congress"); *SSN*, Oct. 1963, p. 11 ("cut off every nickel").

50. *SSN*, Nov. 1963, p. 2 ("since Cleopatra" and "mockery"); *NYT*, 9 Sept. 1963, p. 16 ("monkey"); *SSN*, Jan. 1964, p. 1 ("shocking" and "judicial tyrant[s]").

51. J. Mills Thornton, "Municipal Politics and the Course of the Movement," in Armstead L. Robinson and Patricia Sullivan, eds., *New Directions in Civil Rights Studies* (Charlottesville, Va., 1991), 60.

52. Stephen L. Longenecker, *Selma's Peacemaker: Ralph Smeltzer and Civil Rights Mediation* (Philadelphia, 1987), 176.

53. *Time*, 19 Mar. 1965, p. 24; 111 Congressional Record, 4984 (15 Mar. 1965) (Sen. Douglas) ("deplorable"); ibid., 4989 (15 Mar. 1965) (Sen. Scott) ("shameful display").

54. Lyndon Johnson, "Special Message to the Congress: The American Promise" (15 Mar. 1965), in *Public Papers of the Presidents of the United States: Lyndon B. Johnson, 1965* (Washington, D.C., 1966), 1:284.

55. Robert H. Jackson, *The Supreme Court in the American System of Government* (Cambridge, Mass., 1955), 80.

CONCLUSION

1. Martin Luther King, Jr., *Why We Can't Wait* (New York, 1964), 39.

2. Philip Elman, "The Solicitor General's Office, Justice Frankfurter, and Civil Rights Litigation, 1946–1960: An Oral History," *Harvard Law Review* 100 (Feb. 1987): 837.

3. "The Right to Vote," *New South* 4 (Feb. 1949): 1, NAACP, part 4, reel 7, frame 554.

4. Genna Rae McNeil, *Groundwork: Charles Hamilton Houston and the Struggle for Civil Rights* (Philadelphia, 1983), 135.

SELECT BIBLIOGRAPHY

All of the themes and topics in this book are further developed in Michael J. Klarman, *From Jim Crow to Civil Rights: The Supreme Court and the Struggle for Racial Equality* (New York, 2004), which contains a more comprehensive bibliography. For some criticisms of that book, see Paul Finkelman, "Civil Rights in Historical Context: In Defense of *Brown*," *Harvard Law Review* 118 (Jan. 2005): 973–1029; David E. Bernstein and Ilya Somin, "Judicial Power and Civil Rights Reconsidered," *Yale Law Journal* 114 (Dec. 2004): 591–657; and David J. Garrow, "'Happy' Birthday, *Brown v. Board of Education*? *Brown*'s Fiftieth Anniversary and the New Critics of Supreme Court Muscularity," *Virginia Law Review* 90 (Apr. 2004): 693–729.

Still indispensable on the history of civil rights litigation in the Supreme Court is Richard Kluger, *Simple Justice: The History of* Brown v. Board of Education *and Black America's Struggle for Equality* (New York, 1976). Also very important are Mark V. Tushnet, *Making Civil Rights Law: Thurgood Marshall and the Supreme Court, 1936–1961* (New York, 1994); and Jack Greenberg, *Crusaders in the Courts: How a*

Dedicated Band of Lawyers Fought for the Civil Rights Revolution (New York, 1994).

For a skeptical view of the capacity of courts to produce social change, see the important book by Gerald N. Rosenberg, *The Hollow Hope: Can Courts Bring about Social Change?* (Chicago, 1991). Rosenberg's controversial book has generated numerous responses and criticisms. See, e.g., David A. Schultz, ed., *Leveraging the Law: Using the Courts to Achieve Social Change* (New York, 1998).

On the general topic of the impact of Supreme Court decisions, see Stephen L. Wasby, *The Impact of the United States Supreme Court: Some Perspectives* (Homewood, Ill., 1970); Joel F. Handler, *Social Movements and the Legal System: A Theory of Law Reform and Social Change* (New York, 1978); and Jeffrey A. Segal and Harold J. Spaeth, *The Supreme Court and the Attitudinal Model* (New York, 1993), 333–55.

On the conditions necessary for social reform litigation to be successful, see Charles R. Epp, *The Rights Revolution: Lawyers, Activists, and Supreme Courts in Comparative Perspective* (Chicago, 1998). See also Marc Galanter, "Why the 'Haves' Come Out Ahead: Speculations on the Limits of Legal Change," *Law and Society Review* 9 (Winter 1975): 95–160.

For a sampling of the literature emphasizing the dependence of Court decisions on social and political contexts, see Robert G. McCloskey, *The American Supreme Court*, 2d ed., revised by Sanford Levinson (Chicago, 1994); and Robert A. Dahl, "Decision-Making in a Democracy: The Supreme Court as a National Policy-Maker," *Journal of Public Law* 6 (Fall 1957): 279–95. See also Barry Friedman, "Dialogue and Judicial Review," *Michigan Law Review* 91 (Feb. 1993): 577–682. My own views on that topic are developed in Michael J. Klarman, "Rethinking the Civil Rights and Civil Liberties Revolutions," *Virginia Law Review* 82 (Feb. 1996): 1–67.

On the Court's race rulings during the *Plessy* era, see Owen M. Fiss, *Troubled Beginnings of the Modern State, 1888–1910*, vol. 8 of *History of the Supreme Court of the United States* (New York, 1993), chap. 12; and Charles A. Lofgren, *The* Plessy *Case: A Legal-Historical Interpretation* (New York, 1987). On the Court's race rulings during the Progressive Era, see Alexander M. Bickel and Benno C. Schmidt, Jr., *The Judiciary and Responsible Government 1910–21*, vol. 9 of *History of the Supreme Court of the United States* (New York, 1984), chaps. 18 and 19.

On the early criminal procedure cases, see Dan T. Carter, *Scottsboro: A Tragedy of the American South* (Baton Rouge, La., 1979); Richard C. Cortner, *A "Scottsboro" Case in Mississippi: The Supreme Court and* Brown v. Mississippi (Jackson, Miss., 1986); Richard C. Cortner, *A Mob Intent on Death: The NAACP and the Arkansas Riot Cases* (Middletown, Conn., 1988); and James Goodman, *Stories of*

Scottsboro (New York, 1994). See also Michael J. Klarman, "The Racial Origins of Modern Criminal Procedure," *Michigan Law Review* 99 (Oct. 2000): 48–97.

On the white primary cases, see Darlene Clark Hine, *Black Victory: The Rise and Fall of the White Primary in Texas* (Millwood, N.Y., 1979); and Michael J. Klarman, "The White Primary Cases: A Case Study in the Consequences of Supreme Court Decisionmaking," *Florida State University Law Review* 29 (Fall 2001): 55–107.

On the Mississippi Chinese and *Gong Lum*, see James W. Loewen, *Mississippi Chinese: Between Black and White* (Cambridge, Mass., 1971); and Jeannie Rhee, "In Black and White: Chinese in the Mississippi Delta," *Journal of Supreme Court History* (1994): 117–32.

On *Gaines* and the litigation strategy of the National Association for the Advancement of Colored People (NAACP) generally, see Mark V. Tushnet, *The NAACP's Legal Strategy against Segregated Education, 1925–1950* (Chapel Hill, N.C., 1987). Most of the race cases of this era are usefully discussed in Bernard H. Nelson, *The Fourteenth Amendment and the Negro since 1920* (Washington, D.C., 1946).

On World War II and race generally, see Richard M. Dalfiume, *Desegregation of the U.S. Armed Forces: Fighting on Two Fronts, 1939–53* (Columbia, Mo., 1969); Herbert Garfinkle, *When Negroes March: The March on Washington Movement in the Organizational Politics for FEPC* (Glencoe, Ill., 1959); and Neil A. Wynn, *The Afro-American and the Second World War* (New York, 1976).

On rising black militancy during the war, see Rayford W. Logan, ed., *What the Negro Wants* (Chapel Hill, N.C., 1944; rpt., New York, 1969). See also Kenneth R. Janken, "African-American Intellectuals Confront the 'Silent South': The *What the Negro Wants* Controversy," *North Carolina Historical Review* 70 (Apr. 1993): 153–79; Lee Finkle, "The Conservative Aims of Militant Rhetoric: Black Protest during World War II," *Journal of American History* 60 (Dec. 1973): 692–713; Gary R. Mormino, "G.I. Joe Meets Jim Crow: Racial Violence and Reform in World War II, Florida," *Florida Historical Quarterly* 73 (July 1994): 23–42; and Harvard Sitkoff, "Racial Militancy and Interracial Violence in the Second World War," *Journal of American History* 58 (Dec. 1971): 661–81.

On the Cold War imperative for racial change, see Mary Dudziak, *Cold War Civil Rights: Race and the Image of American Democracy* (Princeton, N.J., 2000); and Brenda Gayle Plummer, *Rising Wind: Black Americans and U.S. Foreign Affairs, 1935–1960* (Chapel Hill, N.C., 1996).

For local histories of the civil rights movement that emphasize the transformative importance of World War II, see John Dittmer, *Local People: The Struggle for Civil Rights in Mississippi* (Urbana, Ill., 1994); Adam Fairclough, *Race and Democracy: The Civil Rights Struggle in*

Louisiana, 1915–1972 (Athens, Ga., 1995); Robert J. Norrell, *Reaping the Whirlwind: The Civil Rights Movement in Tuskegee* (New York, 1985); Charles M. Payne, *I've Got the Light of Freedom: The Organizing Tradition and the Mississippi Freedom Struggle* (Berkeley, Calif., 1995); and J. Mills Thornton, *Dividing Lines: Municipal Politics and the Struggle for Civil Rights in Montgomery, Birmingham, and Selma* (Tuscaloosa, Ala., 2002).

On *Smith* and its consequences, see Hine, *Black Victory*; and Steven F. Lawson, *Black Ballots: Voting Rights in the South 1944–1969* (New York, 1976), chap. 2.

On the higher education cases, see Tushnet, *NAACP's Legal Strategy*, chap. 7; and Jonathan L. Entin, "*Sweatt v. Painter*, the End of Segregation, and the Transformation of Education Law," *Review of Litigation* 5 (Winter 1986): 3–71. On the internal deliberations in the 1950 desegregation cases, see Dennis J. Hutchinson, "Unanimity and Desegregation: Decision Making in the Supreme Court, 1948–1958," *Georgetown Law Journal* 68 (Oct. 1979): 1–87.

On desegregation in transportation, see Catherine A. Barnes, *Journey from Jim Crow: The Desegregation of Southern Transit* (New York, 1983).

On *Shelley* and the restrictive covenant litigation, see Clement V. Vose, *Caucasians Only: The Supreme Court, the NAACP, and the Restrictive Covenant Cases* (Berkeley, Calif., 1959).

On Truman and race, see William C. Berman, *The Politics of Civil Rights in the Truman Administration* (Columbus, Ohio, 1970); and Donald R. McCoy and Richard T. Ruetten, *Quest and Response: Minority Rights and the Truman Administration* (Lawrence, Kans., 1973). On growing black political power at the national level, see Henry Lee Moon, *Balance of Power: The Negro Vote* (Garden City, N.Y., 1948). See also Michael J. Klarman, "The Puzzling Resistance to Political Process Theory," *Virginia Law Review* 77 (May 1991): 747–832.

On the Stone and Vinson courts generally, see C. Herman Pritchett, *The Roosevelt Court: A Study in Judicial Politics and Values 1937–1947* (New York, 1948); C. Herman Pritchett, *Civil Liberties and the Vinson Court* (Chicago, 1954); Frances Howell Rudko, *Truman's Court: A Study in Judicial Restraint* (New York, 1988); Melvin I. Urofsky, *Division and Discord: The Supreme Court under Stone and Vinson, 1941–1953* (Columbia, S.C., 1997); and William M. Wiecek, *The Birth of the Modern Constitution: The United States Supreme Court, 1941–1953* (New York, 2006).

On changing racial practices in the South, see Charles Johnson, *Into the Mainstream: A Survey of Best Practices in Race Relations in the South* (Chapel Hill, N.C., 1947); and Morton Sosna, *In Search of the Silent South: Southern Liberals and the Race Issue* (New York, 1977). See also John T. Kneebone, *Southern Liberal Journalists and the Issue of Race, 1920–1944* (Chapel Hill, N.C., 1985).

There are numerous biographies of the unusually colorful group of justices who decided *Brown*. Among the best are Howard Ball and Phillip J. Cooper, *Of Power and Right: Hugo Black, William O. Douglas, and America's Constitutional Revolution* (New York, 1992); Mary Frances Berry, *Security, Stability, and Continuity: Mr. Justice Burton and Decision-Making in the Supreme Court 1945–1958* (Westport, Conn., 1978); John D. Fassett, *New Deal Justice: The Life of Stanley Reed of Kentucky* (New York, 1994); Linda C. Gugin and James E. St. Clair, *Sherman Minton: New Deal Senator, Cold War Justice* (Indianapolis, Ind., 1997); Bruce Allen Murphy, *Wild Bill: The Legend and Life of William O. Douglas* (New York, 2003); Roger K. Newman, *Hugo Black: A Biography* (New York, 1994); Michael E. Parrish, *Felix Frankfurter and His Times: The Reform Years* (New York, 1982); Bernard Schwartz, *Super Chief: Earl Warren and His Supreme Court: A Judicial Biography* (New York, 1983); James F. Simon, *Independent Journey: The Life of William O. Douglas* (New York, 1980); James E. St. Clair and Linda C. Gugin, *Chief Justice Fred M. Vinson of Kentucky* (Lexington, Ky., 2002); Melvin I. Urofsky, *Felix Frankfurter: Judicial Restraint and Individual Liberties* (Boston, 1991); and G. Edward White, *Earl Warren: A Public Life* (New York, 1982).

On the Court's internal deliberations in *Brown*, see Kluger, *Simple Justice*; Hutchinson, "Unanimity and Desegregation"; and Mark V. Tushnet, "What Really Happened in *Brown v. Board of Education*," *Columbia Law Review* 91 (Dec. 1991): 1867–1930. There are several surviving sets of conference notes from *Brown I*. See Burton conference notes, Segregation Cases, 13 Dec. 1952, Box 244, Burton Papers, Library of Congress; Clark conference notes, *Brown v. Board of Education*, Box A27, Clark Papers, Tarlton Law Library, University of Texas; Douglas conference notes, *Brown v. Board of Education* and *Bolling v. Sharpe*, 13 Dec. 1952, case file: Segregation Cases, Box 1150, Douglas Papers, Library of Congress; and Jackson conference notes, 12 Dec. 1952, Box 184, Jackson Papers, Library of Congress. For an especially fascinating glimpse into Jackson's thinking about *Brown*, see Jackson draft concurrence, School Segregation Cases, 15 Mar. 1954, case file: Segregation Cases, Box 184, Jackson Papers. See also Douglas memorandum for the file, Segregation Cases, 17 May 1954, Box 1149, Douglas Papers. On the internal deliberations in *Brown II*, see Warren conference notes, *Brown II*, case file: Segregation Cases, Box 574, Warren Papers; Burton conference notes, Segregation Cases, 16 Apr. 1955, Box 244, Burton Papers; Douglas conference notes, *Brown II*, 16 Apr. 1955, case file: Segregation Cases, Box 1149, Douglas Papers; and Frankfurter conference notes, *Brown II*, 16 Apr. 1955, File 4044, Box 219, Frankfurter Papers, Library of Congress.

On the post-*Brown* history of school desegregation, see James T. Patterson, Brown v. Board of Education: *A Civil Rights Milestone and Its Troubled Legacy* (New York, 2001); and J. Harvie Wilkinson, *From Brown to Bakke: The Supreme Court and School Integration: 1954–1978* (New York, 1979).

On Little Rock, see Tony Freyer, *The Little Rock Crisis: A Constitutional Interpretation* (Westport, Conn., 1984); Elizabeth Jacoway and C. Fred Williams, eds., *Understanding the Little Rock Crisis: An Exercise in Remembrance and Reconciliation* (Fayetteville, Ark., 1999); and John A. Kirk, *Redefining the Color Line: Black Activism in Little Rock, Arkansas, 1940–1970* (Gainesville, Fla., 2002).

On Eisenhower and race, see Stephen E. Ambrose, *Eisenhower*, vol. 2: *The President* (New York, 1984); and Robert Fredrick Burk, *The Eisenhower Administration and Black Civil Rights* (Knoxville, Tenn., 1984). See also J. W. Anderson, *Eisenhower, Brownell, and the Congress: The Tangled Origins of the Civil Rights Bill of 1956–1957* (University, Ala., 1964). On Kennedy and race, see Carl M. Brauer, *John F. Kennedy and the Second Reconstruction* (New York, 1977); and Mark Stern, *Calculating Visions: Kennedy, Johnson, and Civil Rights* (New Brunswick, N.J., 1992).

The *Southern School News* is vital for following post-*Brown* developments in southern politics and school desegregation. Several books by contemporary journalists are also valuable: Benjamin Muse, *Ten Years of Prelude: The Story of Integration since the Supreme Court's 1954 Decision* (New York, 1964); J. W. Peltason, *Fifty-Eight Lonely Men: Southern Federal Judges and School Desegregation* (New York, 1961); and Don Shoemaker, ed., *With All Deliberate Speed: Segregation-Desegregation in Southern Schools* (New York, 1957). See also Jack Bass, *Unlikely Heroes* (Tuscaloosa, Ala., 1981).

On the anti-NAACP laws, see Walter Murphy, "The South Counterattacks: The Anti-NAACP Laws," *Western Political Quarterly* 12 (June 1959): 371–90. The ferocity of southern white resistance to school desegregation is best captured in the Papers of the National Association for the Advancement of Colored People, microfilm collection, August Meier, ed. (Frederick, Md., 1982). Part 20 of the NAACP Papers—on white resistance and reprisals—is especially useful in this regard.

On massive resistance generally, see Numan V. Bartley, *The Rise of Massive Resistance: Race and Politics in the South during the 1950s* (Baton Rouge, La., 1969); Neil R. McMillen, *The Citizens' Council: Organized Resistance to the Second Reconstruction* (Urbana, Ill., 1971); Benjamin Muse, *Virginia's Massive Resistance* (Bloomington, Ind., 1961); Matthew D. Lassiter and Andrew B. Lewis, eds., *The Moderates' Dilemma: Massive Resistance to School Desegregation in Virginia* (Charlottesville, Va., 1998); Jeff Roche, *Restructured Resistance: The*

Sibley Commission and the Politics of Desegregation in Georgia (Athens, Ga., 1998); Bob Smith, *They Closed Their Schools: Prince Edward County, Virginia, 1951–1964* (Chapel Hill, N.C., 1965); and Clive Webb, ed., *Massive Resistance Reconsidered* (New York, 2005).

On *Brown's* impact on southern politics, see Numan V. Bartley and Hugh D. Graham, *Southern Politics and the Second Reconstruction* (Baltimore, Md., 1975); and Earl Black, *Southern Governors and Civil Rights: Racial Segregation as a Campaign Issue in the Second Reconstruction* (Cambridge, Mass., 1976). See also James W. Ely, Jr., *The Crisis of Conservative Virginia: The Byrd Organization and the Politics of Massive Resistance* (Knoxville, Tenn., 1976); Helen L. Jacobstein, *The Segregation Factor in the Florida Democratic Gubernatorial Election of 1956* (Gainesville, Fla., 1972); Robert Sherrill, *Gothic Politics in the Deep South: Stars of the New Confederacy* (New York, 1968); William C. Havard, ed., *The Changing Politics of the South* (Baton Rouge, La., 1972); and George E. Sims, *The Little Man's Big Friend: James E. Folsom in Alabama Politics, 1946–1958* (University, Ala., 1985). The *Southern School News* also has extensive coverage of southern elections in the post-*Brown* South.

On postwar and post-*Brown* violence in the South, see Michal R. Belknap, *Federal Law and Southern Order: Racial Violence and Constitutional Conflict in the Post-*Brown *South* (Athens, Ga., 1987); and Gail O'Brien, *The Color of Law: Race, Violence and Justice in the Post–World War II South* (Chapel Hill, N.C., 1999). On the most infamous postwar lynchings, see Howard Smead, *Blood Justice: The Lynching of Mack Charles Parker* (New York, 1986); and Stephen J. Whitfield, *A Death in the Delta: The Story of Emmett Till* (Baltimore, Md., 1988).

On the Montgomery bus boycott, see the valuable collection of original documents in Stewart Burns, ed., *Daybreak of Freedom: The Montgomery Bus Boycott* (Chapel Hill, N.C., 1997); and the secondary accounts in David J. Garrow, *Bearing the Cross: Martin Luther King, Jr., and the Southern Christian Leadership Conference* (New York, 1988); and Taylor Branch, *Parting the Waters: America in the King Years 1954–63* (New York, 1988). See also J. Mills Thornton, "Challenge and Response in the Montgomery Bus Boycott of 1955–1956," *Alabama Review* 33 (July 1980): 163–235.

On the conditions necessary for a successful civil rights movement, see Doug McAdam, *Political Process and the Development of Black Insurgency* (Chicago, 1982); Aldon D. Morris, *The Origins of the Civil Rights Movement: Black Communities Organizing for Change* (New York, 1984); Dennis Chong, *Collective Action and the Civil Rights Movement* (New York, 1991); and Donald Von Eschen, Jerome Kirk, and Maurice Pinard, "The Conditions of Direct Action in a Democratic Society," *Western Political Quarterly* 22 (June 1969): 309–25.

There is a vast literature on the civil rights movement itself. Good places to start include Branch, *Parting the Waters*; Taylor Branch, *Pillar of Fire: America in the King Years, 1963–65* (New York, 1998); Taylor Branch, *At Canaan's Edge: America in the King Years, 1965–68* (New York, 2006); and Garrow, *Bearing the Cross*. I have also relied heavily on the following: William H. Chafe, *Civilities and Civil Rights: Greensboro, North Carolina, and the Black Struggle for Freedom* (New York, 1980); James Farmer, *Lay Bare the Heart: An Autobiography of the Civil Rights Movement* (New York, 1985); Louis E. Lomax, *The Negro Revolt* (New York, 1962); Andrew Michael Manis, *A Fire You Can't Put Out: The Civil Rights Life of Birmingham's Reverend Fred Shuttlesworth* (Tuscaloosa, Ala., 1999); and Harvard Sitkoff, *The Struggle for Black Equality 1954–1992*, rev. ed. (New York, 1993).

On the sit-ins specifically, see Martin Oppenheimer, *The Sit-In Movement of 1960* (Brooklyn, N.Y., 1989); and Miles Wolff, *Lunch at the Five and Ten: The Greensboro Sit-Ins: A Contemporary History* (New York, 1970). On the Freedom Rides, see Raymond Arsenault, *Freedom Riders: 1961 and the Struggle for Racial Justice* (New York, 2005). Two books by Martin Luther King, Jr., remain important: *Stride toward Freedom: The Montgomery Story* (New York, 1958) and *Why We Can't Wait*. For reappraisals of the field, see the essays in Armstead L. Robinson and Patricia Sullivan, eds., *New Directions in Civil Rights Studies* (Charlottesville, Va., 1991).

On conflicts between the NAACP and the direct-action movement, see the essays by David Garrow and John Dittmer in Charles W. Eagles, ed., *The Civil Rights Movement in America* (Jackson, Miss., 1986). One can also follow those conflicts as they developed in the NAACP Papers, especially part 21—on the NAACP's relationship with the modern civil rights movement.

On other civil rights organizations, see, for example, Clayborne Carson, *In Struggle: SNCC and the Black Awakening of the 1960s* (Cambridge, Mass., 1981); Adam Fairclough, *To Redeem the Soul of America: The Southern Christian Leadership Conference and Martin Luther King, Jr.* (Athens, Ga., 1987); and August Meier and Elliot Rudwick, *CORE: A Study in the Civil Rights Movement, 1942–1968* (New York, 1973). On the strategy of King and his lieutenants, see David J. Garrow, *Protest at Selma: Martin Luther King, Jr. and the Voting Rights Act of 1965* (New Haven, Conn., 1978).

On the southern politicians who used *Brown* to their advantage, see Dan T. Carter, *The Politics of Rage: George Wallace, the Origins of the New Conservatism, and the Transformation of American Politics* (New York, 1995); Marshall Frady, *Wallace* (New York, 1968); William A. Nunnelley, *Bull Connor* (Tuscaloosa, Ala., 1991); and Roy Reed, *Faubus: The Life and Times of an American Prodigal* (Fayetteville, Ark.,

1997). See also Erle Johnston, *I Rolled with Ross: A Political Portrait* (Baton Rouge, La., 1980).

On particular violent conflicts over school desegregation, see Liva Baker, *The Second Battle of New Orleans: The Hundred-Year Struggle to Integrate the Schools* (New York, 1996); E. Culpepper Clark, *The Schoolhouse Door: Segregation's Last Stand at the University of Alabama* (New York, 1993); William Doyle, *An American Insurrection: The Battle of Oxford, Mississippi, 1962* (New York, 2001); Morton Inger, *Politics and Reality in an American City: The New Orleans School Crisis* (New York, 1969); and Robert Pratt, *We Shall Not Be Moved: The Desegregation of the University of Georgia* (Athens, Ga., 2002).

On Birmingham specifically, see Glenn T. Eskew, *But for Birmingham: The Local and National Movements in the Civil Rights Struggle* (Chapel Hill, N.C., 1997); and David J. Garrow, ed., *Birmingham, Alabama, 1956–1963: The Black Struggle for Civil Rights* (Brooklyn, N.Y., 1989).

On Selma, see Charles E. Fager, *Selma, 1965* (New York, 1974); Garrow, *Protest at Selma*; and Stephen L. Longenecker, *Selma's Peacemaker: Ralph Smeltzer and Civil Rights Mediation* (Philadelphia, 1987).

INDEX

Italicized page numbers refer to illustrations.

and racial violence due to *Brown*,
193, 200, 208–9
in World War II era, 29
Clark, Jim, 197, 209–10
Clark, Tom C.
and *Brown v. Board*, 58, 62–63,
66–67, 73, 76
and *Brown II*, 80, 88, 94–95
in World War II era, 36–37, 44–46
class actions, 79, 82, 119
Clement, Frank, 150, 153, 162
Clemson University, 172
Cold War imperative
in *Brown* era, 56, 65–66, 138
in World War II era, 30, 37, 44, 50
Coleman, James, 96, 167, 180
Coleman, William T., 44, 70
Collins, LeRoy, 98, 160, 166, 182
communism
and Cold War imperative, 30, 44, 65
and McCarthyism, 35, 100, 129,
138, 152
and NAACP, 113, 132, 146
confessions, coerced, 25, 64, 223
Connor, T. Eugene ("Bull"), 171, 197,
199–200, 202, 205–6, 209–10, 229
contract-labor laws, 20–23
contract rights, 3, 6, 38
Cook, Eugene, 171
Cooper v. Aaron, 87, 90, 94–95, 166
CORE (Congress on Racial Equality),
136, 141–42, 145, 148
Corrigan v. Buckley, 26, 46
Courts, Gus, 146–47, 147
Cox, William Harold, 204
cross burnings, 111, 117, 147, 179–80, 197
*Cumming v. Richmond County Board
of Education*, 17–19
Current, Gloster, 191–92

Dabney, Virginius, 28, 52
Dalton, Theodore, 98, 163
Davidson, T. Whitfield, 116
Davis, James C., 196
Davis, Jimmie, 167, 169
Davis, John W., 67, 78
Deane, Charles B., 162
death sentences, 69, 89–90, 129
decolonization, 30, 138–39
DeCuir, Hall v., 51–52

deGraffenried, Ryan, 171
De Laine, J. A., 114, 114
Democrats
in *Brown* era, 91–92, 126–28,
204–5, 208
and *Brown* backlash, 150, 154, 159,
161, 163, 167
in Jim Crow era, 6, 9, 13, 220
in World War II era, 28–29, 31, 37,
39–40, 48
desegregation
and *Brown II*, 76, 79–87, 90–103, 221
and *Brown* backlash/massive resistance, 153–74, 177–87
and *Brown*'s direct effects, 105–24,
222–24
and *Brown*'s indirect effects, 127–31,
134–37, 139–40, 143–45, 148
of military, 29, 31, 44, 76, 126
and racial violence due to *Brown*,
189–212
in World War II era, 31, 34–35, 44,
52, 56
Dewey, Thomas, 29, 31, 151
direct-action protests. *See also names of
protests, e.g.,* Freedom Rides
and *Brown II*, 100–101, 110
and *Brown* backlash/massive resistance, 149, 174, 178
and *Brown*'s indirect effects, 126,
131–46, 148
and racial violence due to *Brown*,
198–200
discretion, administrative
in *Brown* era, 61, 83, 85, 96, 111, 119,
122, 157, 223
in Jim Crow era, 10–12, 14–15, 17–18,
21
discretion, judicial, 79, 83–85, 90
disfranchisement, black. *See also*
voting, black
in *Brown* era, 181, 220
in Jim Crow era, 4–5, 6, 8–14,
19–22, 221
in World War II era, 38–39, 56
District of Columbia segregation,
57–58, 60–61, 63, 66–67, 70–71,
73, 77
Dixiecrats, 29, 31, 35, 150–51, 153
Dormant Commerce Clause, 51–53

Interstate Commerce Act, 49–50
Interstate Commerce Commission
    (ICC), 6, 49

Jackson, Robert H.
    and *Brown v. Board*, 58, 61–63,
        65–78, 216
    and *Brown II*, 80–82, 85, 106, 211
    in World War II era, 36–37, 40–41,
        43–44, 50
Jackson Daily News, 131, 195
Japanese Americans, 218
Javits, Jacob, 194, 201
Jaybird Democratic Association, 40, 69
Jet, 193
Jews, 36, 48, 60, 64, 193
Jim Crow era, 3–26, 64, 217–18, 230.
        See also white supremacy
    disfranchisement in, 4–5, 6, 8–14
    jury discrimination in, 6, 12, 14–16
    segregation in, 5–8
    separate and *unequal*, 16–26
Johnson, Frank, 116–17, 200
Johnson, Jim, 159
Johnson, Leroy, 171
Johnson, Lyndon, 33, 102, 150, 205,
        208, 210
Johnson, Paul, 173–74, 187, 202
Johnston, Olin, 39, 151
Judgment at Nuremberg, 209
judicial activism, 74, 155
judicial discretion, 79, 83–85, 90
judicial enforcement, 46–48
Judiciary Committees (U.S. Congress),
        62, 123
jury discrimination
    in *Brown* era, 111, 153, 155, 164,
        193–94
    in Jim Crow era, 6, 12, 14–16

Kasper, John, 112, 181, 194–95
Katzenbach, Nicholas, 101
Kefauver, Estes, 91, 150, 166
*Kelley v. Board of Education of
        Nashville*, 97–98
Kennedy, John F., 101, 123, 187, 190,
        198, 202–7, 210
Kennedy, Robert, 102, 123, 173, 200
Kilpatrick, James J., 129, 160, 184
King, Martin Luther, Jr., 97, 115, 133,
        135, 140–41, 143, 145, 170

and racial violence due to *Brown*,
        195, 198, 202, 207, 209, 215–16
Knox, Frank, 27
Koinonia Farm (Americus, Ga.), 158–59
Kraemer, Shelley v., 47–48
Ku Klux Klan, 25, 35–37, 64, 91, 113,
        120, 154, 156, 164
    and racial violence due to *Brown*,
        192–93, 199–200, 202, 206, 211

labor unions, 35–36, 38, 127, 138, 152,
        159, 199
Lee, George, 157, 193
Lehman, Herbert H., 130
Lemley, Harry J., 93–94
Life, 92
Lingo, Al, 209
Lippmann, Walter, 91
literacy tests, 3, 9–12, 19–21, 157, 223
Little Rock case. *See Cooper v. Aaron*
Little Rock crisis
    and *Brown II*, 92–94, 93, 98–99, 103
    and *Brown* backlash/massive resist-
        ance, 159–60, 162–68, 180–81,
        184–87
    and *Brown*'s direct effects, 109, 111–12,
        120
    and racial violence due to *Brown*,
        190–92, 191
Little Rose Bowl, 158
local option, 106, 160, 162, 165, 169–70,
        177, 184–86
Lochner v. New York, 35, 51, 74
Long, Earl, 150, 167
Long, Russell, 97
Looby, Z. Alexander, 113
Lowry, Sumter, 160
Lubell, Samuel, 184–85
Lucy, Autherine, 132, 154–55, 161,
        190, 195
lynchings
    in *Brown* era, 127, 180, 190, 193–94,
        196, 198, 208, 222
    in Jim Crow era, 3–4, 23, 220
    in World War II era, 30, 31

malapportionment, 109, 135, 176,
        181–82, 220
Mansfield, Mike, 201
marches on Washington, 28, 205
Marshall, John, 11

and *Brown* backlash, 155, 157, 159,
161, 170, 172
in World War II era, 29, 46
racial attitudes. *See* public opinion
racial classifications, 5, 50, 61, 63, 76,
87, 101
racial differences, inherent, 32–33
racial etiquette, 24, 158
railroad segregation, 3, 5–8, 16, 44,
49–52, 59, 222
Rainach, Willie, 97, 167, 183
Randolph, A. Philip, 28
rape cases, 194
Reconstruction era, 3, 5, 8–9, 14, 31
Brown era compared to, 86, 153, 156,
162, 182–83, 187
"Red Monday," 100
Reed, Stanley F.
and *Brown v. Board*, 58, 59–60, 63,
65–69, 75–78, 217, 219
and *Brown II*, 81–83, 101, 106
in World War II era, 37, 40–41, 43, 50
referendums, 109–10, 118, 158, 161–63,
177, 182, 185
Rehnquist, William H., 74, 76
Republicans, 8, 29
in *Brown* era, 62, 67, 98, 126–27,
187, 193
and *Brown* backlash, 151–52, 163
in Jim Crow era, 4, 8–10, 13, 64
residential segregation
in *Brown* era, 102, 108–9, 199, 204,
226
in World War II era, 35, 46–48
restrictive covenants, 26, 37, 46–48,
226
Reynolds v. Sims, 182
Rice, Elmore v., 39–40
Rice, Gong Lum v., 26
Richmond News Leader, 160, 184
Richmond Times-Dispatch, 52
Rives, Richard, 117
Robinson, Jackie, 158
Robinson, Jo Ann, 131, 133
Roe v. Wade, 129, 226, 228
Rogers, William, 99–100, 194
Roosevelt, Eleanor, 92
Roosevelt, Franklin D., 27–28, 35–39,
48, 60–61, 74, 219
Roosevelt, Theodore, 15

Rosenberg, Ethel, 138
Rosenberg, Julius, 138
Russell, Richard, 128, 187

Sacco, Nicola, 36
Sanders, Carl, 170–71
Scalia, Antonin, 219
scholarships, out-of-state, 26, 41
school boards
and *Brown II*, 83, 93, 95–96, 99
and *Brown* backlash/massive
resistance, 154, 159, 162–63,
165–66, 168–69, 177–78, 185
and *Brown's* direct/indirect effects,
110–12, 117, 119, 122–23, 130,
145, 224
in Jim Crow era, 9, 17–18
school-closing measures
and *Brown II*, 78, 80–81, 86, 98, 101–2
and *Brown* backlash/massive resistance, 154–55, 159, 161, 163–73,
182–86
and *Brown's* direct/indirect effects,
117, 119, 144–45
school prayer, 75, 129, 217–18
school segregation. *See* segregation
SCLC (Southern Christian Leadership
Conference), 135–36, 140–41,
143–44, 148, 199, 202, 209
Scott, Hugh, 193
Scott, W. Kerr, 150, 162
Screws v. United States, 223
Seawell, Malcolm, 98, 120
segregation
and *Brown v. Board/Brown II*, 55–78,
79–104, 109, 218–21
and *Brown* backlash/massive resistance, 150–74, 176–87
and *Brown's* indirect effects, 126–36,
141–42, 144–45, 147
in Jim Crow era, 5–8, 16–17
and racial violence due to *Brown*,
194, 196, 198–99, 201–2, 205–6,
208, 210–12
in World War II era, 27–32, 35, 39,
56–57
in higher education, 26, 29, 32, 37,
41–46, 57, 81
in transportation, 48–53
Selma march, 208–10